OXFORD
UNIVERSITY PRESS

# Complete
# English as a
# Second Language
## for Cambridge IGCSE®

D1615096

Chris Akhurst
Lucy Bowley
Brian Dyer
Dean Roberts

**Oxford excellence for Cambridge IGCSE®**

OXFORD

# OXFORD
## UNIVERSITY PRESS

Great Clarendon Street, Oxford, OX2 6DP, United Kingdom

Oxford University Press is a department of the University of Oxford.
It furthers the University's objective of excellence in research, scholarship, and education by publishing worldwide. Oxford is a registered trade mark of Oxford University Press in the UK and in certain other countries

© Oxford University Press 2014

The moral rights of the authors have been asserted

First published in 2014

British Library Cataloguing in Publication Data
Data available

978-0-19-839288-0

10

Paper used in the production of this book is a natural, recyclable product made from wood grown in sustainable forests. The manufacturing process conforms to the environmental regulations of the country of origin.

Printed by Repro India Ltd.

## Acknowledgements

®IGCSE is the registered trademark of Cambridge International Examinations. The questions, example answers, marks awarded and/or comments that appear in this book and CD were written by the authors. In examination, the way marks would be awarded to questions like these may be different.

The publishers would like to thank the following for permissions to use their photographs:

**Cover image:** Happy person/Shutterstock; **p1**: agsandrew/Shutterstock; **p2**: (a) VLADGRIN/Shutterstock, (b) michaeljung/Shutterstock; **p4**: Danita Delimont/Getty Images; **p5**: (a) Photo Deutsches Museum, (b) Forum/UIG/Getty Images; **p7**: © Axel Heimken/dpa/Corbis; **p8**: REX/c.Col Pics/Everett; **p10**: © Bob Daemmrich / Alamy; **p13**: Michael Rosskothen/Shutterstock; **p16**: Marilyn Volan/Shutterstock; **p18**: Pinkcandy/Shutterstock; **p21**: mironov/Shutterstock; **p23**: Konstanttin/Shutterstock; **p24**: fokusgood/Shutterstock; **p26**: Luiz Rocha/Shutterstock; **p30**: (a) Mr Pics/Shutterstock, (b) Dudarev Mikhail/Shutterstock; **p32**: (a) Africa Studio/Shutterstock, (b) gorillaimages/Shutterstock; **p36**: Marilyn Volan/Shutterstock; **p37**: (a)Tim Barker/Getty Images, (b) Matthew Micah Wright/Getty Images; **p39**: © Bettmann/CORBIS, (b) David Cooper/Toronto Star via Getty Images, (c) REX/Bournemouth News, (d) David Cooper/Toronto Star via Getty Images; **p40**: © Onsite / Alamy; **p41**: (a) Mny-Jhee/Shutterstock, (b) Preto Perola/Shutterstock, (c) B. and E. Dudzinscy/Shutterstock; **p43**: Kwiatek7/Shutterstock; **p47**: © BPI/Matt West/BPI/Corbis; **p48**: Featureflash/Shutterstock; **p51**: cate_89/Shutterstock; **p54**: Nabeel Zytoon/123RF; **p57**: Neale Cousland/Shutterstock; **p58**: Pyty/Shutterstock; **p62**: michaeljung/Shutterstock; **p64**: © Richard T. Nowitz/CORBIS; **p65**: AFP/Getty Images; **p66**: ©Barry D. Kass@ ImagesofAnthropology.com; **p67**: Jonathan Irish/National Geographic Society/Corbis; **p70**: (a) © Maurice Savage / Alamy, (b) © Pictorial Press Ltd / Alamy, (c) © CBW / Alamy; **p72**: (a) LEGO, (b) dboystudio/Shutterstock; **p77**: (a) Dirk Ercken/Shutterstock, (b) Dirk Ercken/Shutterstock; **p78**: (a) DR KEITH WHEELER/SCIENCE PHOTO LIBRARY, (b) REX/NTI Media Ltd, (c) REX/Image Broker; **p79**: David W. Leindecker/Shutterstock; **p81**: (a) RIA NOVOSTI/SCIENCE PHOTO LIBRARY, (b) Image Source/Getty Images; **p84**: Christer Fredriksson/Getty Images; **p86**: Hung Chung Chih / Shutterstock; **p88**: Eduard Kyslynskyy/Shutterstock; **p90**: OUP; **p91**: Martin Woike/Foto Natura/Getty Images; **p93**: Aesop, George Fyler Townsend; **p94**: © Pictorial Press Ltd / Alamy; **p96**: Tupungato/Shutterstock; **p99**: REX/Action Press; **p100**: (a) REX/Food and Drink, (b) hxdbzxy/Shutterstock; **p101**: (a) Annie Griffiths Belt/Getty Images, (b) Ethan Miller/Getty Images for CineVegas, (c) REX/Image Source; **p104**: (a) Hira Punjabi/Getty Images, (b) REX/Image Source, (c) REX/Image Source; **p110**: (a) David Fischer/Getty Images, (b) REX, (c) ROBERTO SCHMIDT/AFP/Getty Images; **p112**: Monirul Bhuiyan/AFP/Getty Images; **p114**: Corina Bona/Corinabona.wordpress.com.; **p116**: Silver Screen Collection/Getty Images; **p119**: Iryna Rasko/Shutterstock; **p120**: (all) OUP; **p121**: Stefano Paterna/Robert Harding; **p123**: (a, b) OUP, (c) Victor Paul Borg/Getty Images; **p124**: Nick Spark; **p127**: (a) OUP, (b) S-F/Shutterstock; **p129**: iStock; **p133**: iStock; **p135**: www.kopalnia.pl; **p136**: OUP; **p137**: David Lazar/Getty Images; **p139**: Redbull Media House; **p141**: OUP; **p143**: suravid/Shutterstock; **p145**: Holger Hage/Warner Classics ; **p146**: © Mirrorpix/Splash News/Corbis; **p149**: © ZUMA Press, Inc. / Alamy; **p152**: (a) © Geraint Lewis / Alamy, (b) © Stuart Kelly / Alamy, (c) © Mim Friday / Alamy; **p153**: Ben A. Pruchnie/Getty Images; **p154**: REX/c. Reliance Big Pictures / Courtesy Everett Collection; **p155**: © Jayne Russell/Demotix/Corbis; **p157**: © Melvyn Longhurst/Corbis; **p158**: Siegfried Modola; **p161**: REX/Geoff Pugh; **p163**: Julien Eichinger/Fotolia; **p164**: © Tim Kiusalaas/Corbis; **p166**: Albert L. Ortega/Getty Images; **p169**: Kuzma/Shutterstock; **p172**: Leenvdb/Shutterstock; **p173**: © Malcolm Fairman / Alamy; **p174**: Cirkle.com; **p175**: (a) magicinfoto/Shutterstock, (b) Bobbiholmes/Dreamstime.com; **p178**: Kuzma Sergeevich Petrov-Vodkin/Getty Images; **p179**: (a) REX/Masatoshi Okauchi, (b) Chris Walter/WireImage/Getty Images; **p182**: (a) Pinkcandy/Shutterstock, (b) Blend Images/Marc Romanelli/Getty Images; **p186**: (a) Michelangelus/Shutterstock, (b) nexus 7/Shutterstock; **p189**: © Dale Spartas/Corbis; **p195**: TungCheung/Shutterstock; **p196**: Syaheir Azizan/Shutterstock; **p197**: © Bobylev Sergei/ITAR-TASS Photo/Corbis; **p198**: NEGOVURA/Shutterstock; **p201**: ZouZou/Shutterstock; **p203**: ex0rzist / Shutterstock; **p206**: (a) Mariya Ermolaeva/Shutterstock, (b) Nuiiko/Shutterstock; **p208**: (a) Travel China/www.travelchinaguide.com, (b) Travel China/www.travelchinaguide.com, (c) Travel China/www.travelchinaguide.com; **p209**: (a) Travel China/www.travelchinaguide.com, (b) Travel China/www.travelchinaguide.com; **p212**: Kerstin Schoene/Shutterstock; **p213**: Jan Zoetekouw/Shutterstock; **p215**: Courtesy of Mark Sloneker www.orijyn.com; **p217**: OUP; **p218**: (a) h4nk/Shutterstock, (b) StockLite/Shutterstock, (c) zentilia/Shutterstock, (d) alexdrim/Shutterstock, (e) Monkey Business Images/Shutterstock; **p219**: (a) Oleksiy Mark/Shutterstock, (b) Umberto Shtanzman/Shutterstock, (c) IM_photo/Shutterstock, (d) Stefan Ataman/Shutterstock; **p220**: (a) elnavegante/Shutterstock, (b) Alexander Lukin/Shutterstock, (c) beboy/Shutterstock, (d) Hywit Dimyadi/Shutterstock, (e) Denphumi/Shutterstock, (f) misima / Shutterstock; **p223**: (a) © Houndstooth Archive / Alamy, (b) © Angelo Hornak/Corbis, (c) Tomas Skopal/Shutterstock; **p225**: (a) Susan Law Cain/Shutterstock, (b) iStock; **p227**: Kean Collection/Archive Photos/Getty Images; **p230**: (a) Alexander Vershinin/Shutterstock, (b)© Morley von Sternberg/Arcaid/Corbis; **p231**: qingqing/Shutterstock; **p232**: qingqing/Shutterstock; **p233**: Algol / Shutterstock; **p236**: (a) iStock, (b) © The Protected Art Archive / Alamy; **p239**: Kritchanut / Shutterstock; **p242**: Roberto Gustavo Fiadone/Wikipedia; **p248**: Boida Anatolii/Shutterstock; **p249**: © Library of Congress - digital ve/Science Faction/Corbis; **p253**: © Kathy deWitt / Alamy; **p259**: AP Photo; **p260**: © Etienne George/Corbis; **p261**: AP Photo/Markus Schreiber; **p267**: Anton Balazh/Shutterstock; **p269**: Ravi S Sahani/The India Today Group/Getty Images; **p270**: Phiseksit/Shutterstock; **p271**: iStock; **p272**: © Earl & Nazima Kowall/CORBIS; **p274-275**: Thomas Nord/Shutterstock; **p276**: Thomas La Mela/Shutterstock; **p277**: OUP; **p278**: newart-graphics/Shutterstock; **p282**: The Meat Free Monday logo is a registered trademark and use of it here is not deemed to indicate any affiliation or endorsement of any third party or their products, services or opinions by the Meat Free Monday campaign; **p284**: Suzanne Tucker/Shutterstock; **p286**: HerrBullermann/Shutterstock; **p287**: Pack-Shot/Shutterstock; **p289**: Sylvie Bouchard/Shutterstock; **p290**: Nucleartist/Shutterstock

Artwork by Six Red Marbles and OUP

The author and publisher are grateful for permission to reprint extracts from the following copyright material:

Shikeb Ali: '25 inventions that changed our way of life', 23 December 2011, from www.list25.com, reprinted by permission of Awesome Motive Inc.

Bat Conservation Trust: excerpts from www.bats.org.uk/pages/echolocation.html and www.bats.org.uk/pages/all_about_bats.html, reprinted by permission.

Jon Blanc: 'A day life of an African Village in Uganda' from www.kabiza.com, reprinted by permission.

Laura Boness: 'Teenage brains in the digital world', 13 September 2012, *Australian Science Illustrated*, reprinted by permission.

Robert Booth: 'Aung San Suu Kyi picks Beatles and Tom Jones on Desert Island Discs', 27 January 2013, guardian.com, copyright Guardian News and Media Ltd 2013, reprinted by permission.

Ray Bradbury: excerpt from *The Martian Chronicles*, published by Simon & Schuster, copyright © 1945 (renewed) by Ray Bradbury, reprinted by permission of Don Congdon Associates, Inc.

The official website of The British Monarchy: 'The Royal Philatelic Collection: History', from www.royal.gov.uk, Crown Copyright, this is public sector information licensed under the Open Government Licence v2.0.

Laura Burgoine: 'Carbon-neutral living', 8 February 2011, *Weekender Life*, www.weekenderlife.co.uk, reprinted by permission.

Catherine Clarke Fox: 'Drinking water: bottled or from the tap?', *National Geographic Kids*, reprinted by permission of National Geographic Creative.

Suzanne Collins: *The Hunger Games*, Scholastic Inc./Scholastic Press, copyright © 2008 by Suzanne Collins, reprinted by permission.

Comic Relief: excerpts and image of Lenny Henry from www.comicrelief.com, reprinted by kind permission.

Common Sense Media: excerpts from www.commonsensemedia.org (Solar System for iPad, Geocaching, SkySafari, Historypin, GarageBand), reprinted by permission.

Richard Danielson and Charles Scudder: 'In a first for the U.S., Bollywood's version of the Oscars coming to Tampa in 2014', 5 July 2013, *Tampa Bay Times*, reprinted by permission.

The Deutsches Museum: excerpts from 'Collections of the Deutsches Museum', from www.deutsches-museum.de, reprinted by permission.

Julia Donaldson: interview with Julia Donaldson from http://clubs-kids.scholastic.co.uk/clubs_content/1472, copyright © 2013 by Julia Donaldson, reprinted and recorded with an actor by permission of Julia Donaldson c/o Caroline Sheldon Literary Agency Ltd.

Kevin Dowling: 'Good boy, Eli. Now pull my socks off and do the washing', 13 January 2013, *The Sunday Times*, reprinted by permission of News Syndication.

Dunstan Baby: 'Is your baby talking to you?' from www.sheknows.com, reprinted by permission of Dunstan Baby (www.dunstanbaby.com).

Michael Durham: excerpt from 'Forty years from now...', guardian.com, copyright Guardian News & Media Ltd, reprinted by permission.

Dyson: excerpts from www.dyson.co.uk, reprinted by permission.

*Continued on back page.*

# Contents

| Language and vocabulary | Range of learning activities | Preparing for assessment |
| --- | --- | --- |
| Specific language focus | Broader skills development | Exam practice |
| Linking words and phrases | Debating the importance of technology | |
| Comparatives and superlatives | Writing a letter to request something | Note-taking (reading) |
| Present simple tense | Delivering a persuasive speech | Multiple choice questions (listening) |
| Avoiding redundant words | Discussing opposing points of view | Developing vocabulary (speaking) |
| Words to attract attention | Carrying out a survey | Using prompts (writing) |
| Specialist science vocabulary | Collaborating on a group presentation | |
| Skimming v Scanning | Writing an advertisement | |
| Context clues | Writing a recipe | Discussing pros and cons (speaking) |
| Collocations | Writing a blog entry | Summaries (writing) |
| Persuasive language | Writing a persuasive letter | Short answer questions (reading) |
| Adjectives | Making a one minute speech | Recognising attitudes (listening) |
| Past simple tense | Researching a biography | |
| | Making a PowerPoint presentation | |
| Collective nouns | Researching books about communities | Range of question types (listening) |
| Active verbs | Writing a story based on a community | Form filling (reading) |
| Comparing and contrasting words | Debating the usefulness of jobs | Informal letters (writing) |
| Suffixes and superlative adjectives | Designing your own community | The Warm Up (speaking) |
| | Collating the results of a survey | |
| | Role playing being given a pet | Note-taking (reading) |
| | Planning for writing | Considering points of view (writing) |
| Simile and metaphor | Establishing point of view | Understanding gist (listening) |
| The future tense | Conveying an anecdote | Responding to a suggestion (speaking) |
| Words to express opinions | Writing a fable | |
| | Writing a resignation letter | |
| | Considering case studies | Form filling (reading) |
| Getting the gist of a piece of writing | Re-creating a counselling session | A talk based on careers (listening) |
| Jargon connected to the workplace | Writing a job application | The flow of a conversation (speaking) |
| | Creating a scene for a play | Describing and informing (writing) |
| | Preparing a display stand about careers | |
| | Sending an email to a friend | |
| Past continuous tense | Writing a travel guide | Specific information in brochures (reading) |
| Analysing questions | Role playing the first ever long-haul flight | Conveying personal views (speaking) |
| Predicting content | Sending a post card home | Selecting relevant details (listening) |
| Relative pronouns | Writing a diary entry | Form filling (writing) |
| | Making a promotional pitch | |

| Language and vocabulary | Range of learning activities | Preparing for assessment |
|---|---|---|
| **Specific language focus** | **Broader skills development** | **Exam practice** |
|  | Interviewing an actor |  |
| Prefixes | Compiling a job description | Introducing a topic (speaking) |
| Varying the use of conjunctions | Writing an outline for a detective novel | Summaries (writing) |
| Adverbs | Sharing first impression writing | Numbers and figures (reading) |
|  | Creating a story board for a film | Follow-up discussions (listening) |
|  | Adapting a book for the stage |  |
|  |  |  |
|  | Miming a hobby |  |
| Persusive writing techniques | Role playing meeting a famous person | Paraphrasing and examples (speaking) |
| Prefixes | Selecting only the required information | Differentiating people's views (listening) |
| Jargon associated with music | Carrying out a survey about reading habits | Paragraphs (writing) |
|  | Responding to a poem | Content for summaries (reading) |
|  | Constructing a short teaching scheme |  |
|  | Writing for a web page |  |
|  | Delivering a short speech | Short and accurate sentences (writing) |
| Synonyms and antonyms | Being interviewed on the radio | Taking control of a conversation (speaking) |
| Punctuation | Writing an article for a wedding magazine | Ensuring a balanced argument (reading) |
|  | Designing a multi-media project | Implication and inference (listening) |
|  | Organising a campaign |  |
|  | Chatting to a guest from the past |  |
|  | Writing a letter to a friend from the past | Discussing abstract matters (speaking) |
|  | Researching a historical event | Identifying redundant material (reading) |
| Homophones | Debating the best period ever to have lived | Using own words in a summary (writing) |
| Past and present tenses | Interviewing someone from the future | Grammatical and contextual accuracy (listening) |
|  | Re-create and act out a scene from the past |  |
|  | Designing an application form |  |
| Anecdotes | Sending a message in the past | Formal essay style (writing) |
| Register and purpose | Giving a talk about graffitti | Accurate structures (speaking) |
| Continuous tense | Contrasting two accounts with same theme | Connected dialogue (listening) |
|  | Asking open questions | Scanning for themes (reading) |
|  | Compiling a secret code |  |
|  | Writing a review of a product |  |
| Concise language | Writing a travelogue | Open questions and prompts (speaking) |
| Conjunct phrases | Attending a public meeting | Recognising attitudes (listening) |
| Comparing and contrasting | Writing a protest song | Diagrams and charts (reading) |
| Reported speech | Role playing a modern job | Note-making (writing) |
|  | Delivering a talk about water preservation |  |
|  | Planning a major festival |  |

# Introduction

## Who is this book for?

This book has been written for students across a range of language levels and contains exercises and activities for students preparing for the Cambridge IGCSE® English as a Second Language series of examinations. The book is ideal for students who are in the earlier stages of learning English, but there is also lots of material which is aimed at refining language skills, helping students to progress towards assessment with confidence. The book contains a large amount of material which is intended to provide practice for the reading, writing, listening and speaking examinations, but also offers material which can used to practise general skills.

## Design of the book

There are 12 chapters in this book and each one is based around a topic or theme. Each chapter covers all four main language learning skills – reading, writing, listening and speaking. We have tried to design the book to allow you to practise related skills. Chapters are structured around 'learning themes' which cover content and skills which flow naturally. For example, a learning theme which begins with a reading article will be extended and developed to incorporate work in the other skills areas. Once you have read about the work of a scientist, it is likely that you will then hear her interviewed. You may then follow this with a letter to a magazine promoting her work, and perhaps a discussion with a group of students about her work. All four skills are interwoven and this is what we have tried to achieve throughout the book. We hope it encourages you to build up all four main skills equally and naturally, so that you feel confident as readers, writers, listeners and speakers.

## Contents

Each chapter contains four 'Study tips' sections - one for each main skill. These have been written to help you practise key examination skills and often use material which looks very similar to the exercises and questions you will see in your examinations. We have also provided guidance on how to achieve your best in the examinations, along with sample answers so that you can look at different levels of performance by other students.

Audio content is a major feature of this book. There are many talks, interviews and discussions which can be found on the accompanying CD. These will help you practise your listening skills in a relevant and focused way. We have also provided lots of opportunities to develop your speaking skills by including a range of situations where speaking is the main means of communication.

## Other features of the book include:

The Big Issue - a chance to engage with a contemporary and lively theme.

Literary Connections - a chance to explore some literature to help develop your language skills.

Reflection - where you will work in small groups on a number of very different interactive projects.

Language Focus - at times it is important to practise key language learning skills.

Building Vocabulary - each chapter introduces new words and phrases and helps you to build up an IGCSE-relevant word base. The new words are introduced using learner-friendly activities.

Video footage – links to short clips of people talking about their lives; their jobs, their hobbies, their experiences and their achievements. We think that *seeing* adds something extra. A glossary of Youtube and alternative links are provided on the CD.

A fresh approach to writing - a range of writing tasks covers almost every occasion when you will have to pick up a pen or type onto a screen. There are texts, blogs, emails, social networking, feedbacks, reviews, autobiographies - a whole range of up to date ways that we all communicate with the written word. There are letters and essays too!

## And finally...

You will find that you are reading and writing about people and places all over the world - we have tried to make the book as international as possible. You will also read about other cultures and listen to many people from different backgrounds doing lots of things with their lives. There is a 'human' feel to the book, so we hope that you will enjoy connecting and engaging with it.

# About the authors

## Dean Roberts

As series editor, Dean Roberts has taught IGCSE English and IELTS for over 20 years, both in the UK and at international schools in South East Asia. He is an examiner and has conducted many training workshops in the past 15 years, travelling to more than 40 countries. Dean also manages professional development programmes for teachers at international schools.

## Chris Akhurst

Chris Akhurst is currently a freelance editor, writer and education consultant based in Cambridge, where he taught in secondary schools and in the university. He has taught and examined and served as an online mentor for tutors. He has also participated in training and support initiatives in Europe and Africa.

## Lucy Bowley

Lucy Bowley has been teaching English to non-native speakers for nearly 20 years. She has taught in Poland and Hungary, teaching students from the ages six to adult. In the UK, she has taught English as an Additional Language, becoming Head of EAL in her most recent post. She has been an examiner for over ten years.

## Brian Dyer

Brian Dyer lives and works in the south-east of England, and is a Director of Business Language Services, a language training organisation specialising in English for students and corporate clients. He has been a teacher of English for the past thirty years. He is an examiner and has conducted teacher training workshops in the UK and a variety of countries around the world.

 **What's on the CD?**

*English as a Second Language for Cambridge IGCSE® Student Book* includes a CD with additional material specifically written to support your learning:

- Audio recordings and transcripts from the Student Book
- Interactive activities to revise and practise your vocabulary and language skills
- A grammar appendix
- A glossary of key vocabulary from the Student Book
- Links to online resources

# 1 Science and technology

## In this chapter you will:

- visit the UK, the USA, and India
- read about a teenage brain, a science museum, and a time traveller
- write to a museum and a teenage boy, and for a local science magazine
- listen to an optician, a writer, and a museum curator
- talk about how science can help us overcome physical difficulties and how technology has developed in recent years.

## Key study skills

- Selecting appropriate notes when *reading* an information text
- Understanding how multiple choice questions work in the *Listening* test
- Developing vocabulary while *speaking*
- Utilizing prompts when *writing* a letter to a friend

# Teenage brains in the digital world

**Thinking out loud**

Who has a "better" brain – an adult or a teenager? Do adults or teenagers have more efficient brains when it comes to technology? Spend a few minutes thinking about how people's brains may be different. Or do you think that all of our brains are the same apart from one feature: size? Think about what it means when we say that someone is "brainy".

1  When it comes to technology, adults won't be able to keep up with their children. It took the radio 38 years to reach 50 million people, but it took only 20 years for the phone to reach the same number, and 13 years for the television. In contrast, it took Facebook 3.6 years and Twitter only needed 88 days.

2  Over the last 15 years, digital communication has brought in more changes than the printing press did in 1570. And those most likely to use them in this world are teenagers, whose brains appear to have an extraordinary capacity to adapt to the world around them, according to Dr Jay Giedd, an adolescent brain expert.

3  We are now discovering that, as a species, our brains during the teenage years are still flexible and capable of adapting. Having a more flexible brain means that certain parts of it, such as

impulse control and the ability to make long-term decisions, haven't developed yet, which may also explain why, unlike some of our ancestors, we spend an extended period living under the protection of our parents rather than leaving home at the age of 12 or 13.

4  This also means that the teenage brain can adapt to new technology, enabling teenagers to keep up with the increasing pace of digital technology and giving them an advantage when it comes to multitasking.

5  In the US, on average teenagers spend 8.5 hours a day using computers, mobiles, and other devices to learn, interact, and play. This increases to 11.5 hours if you include all of the multitasking that goes on, such as talking on the phone while you're watching TV. As they stare at these screens, they're taking in and sorting through an incredible amount of information.

6  There are concerns about how social media is affecting the way in which the brain learns to socialize, as one of the most important skills that we learn as children is how to make friends and interact

with people around us. Geidd says that a lot of what goes on inside our brains is social. Social interactions are now being changed by technology – you could have hundreds of friends, all of whom are real people that you interact with and scientists aren't sure whether we'll be able to develop the same skills using social media.

7  There is an advantage of the growing digital trend: YouTube indicates that teenagers all over the world are watching the same clips and laughing at the same jokes, indicating that they are more global-minded than teenagers in the past.

8  They may be keen on texting their friends and posting updates on social media sites, but teenagers today are probably going to have access to technology and as a result social and educational opportunities that anyone with a less flexible brain may have trouble imagining. However, there is a cut-off point, and by the age of 30, our brains have become more set in their ways, making it harder for us to adapt and cope with new technologies.

**Source: www.scienceillustrated.com**

# Check your understanding

1  How many years did it take for television to reach 50 million people?

2  Why can the teenage brain adapt to new technology easily?

3  Give an example of an important skill we learn as children.

4  What does the trend of sharing ideas on YouTube tell us?

5  Up to what age does the brain remain flexible?

6* Pick out five adjectives from the text which are used to describe brains in a positive way.

## A class debate

You are going to have a class debate. Divide into two teams.

Team one: You are going to give a presentation explaining how important and beneficial it is for teenagers to understand and use modern technology every day.

Team two: You are going to give a presentation explaining that teenagers rely too much on modern technology and that this has its problems.

Each team may ask only five questions of the other team, so please choose your questions carefully.

Your teacher will then decide which team had the strongest argument.

# Reading

## Selecting appropriate notes

When you are making notes about an article, you only need to write down certain key details. In other words, some of the information that you read is not essential and can be ignored. You have to decide what is most important to include. In the examination, much of the text will not be relevant, but it is important that you focus on the key parts.

When you write notes they should always be brief, but make sure you have included all the important information. There is no need to write full sentences; sometimes just one word or two will be enough.

Look at the article on the previous page – "Teenage brains in the digital world". You will see that there are eight paragraphs. Below are some questions and possible answers from the information in paragraph one. Discuss with your partner which answers are right and which are wrong.

**Time taken to attract 50 million people before Facebook or Twitter**

1  radio: 38 years

2  phone: 20 years

3  TV: three years

Next find the relevant paragraph in the text and discuss whether these answers are right or wrong.

**Advantages of a flexible brain for teenagers**

1  ability to make long-term decisions not developed

2  can adapt to new technology

3  able to multi-task

Now by yourself, study the text again and write your own answers under the following heading.

**Advantages of using digital technology for teenagers**

1

2

3

With your partner, check each other's answers and see where you agree. You may not have used the same words to write the correct answers, so discuss which of you has expressed the answer best. If you disagree, why is that?

If you are not sure, look at the correct part of the text again and see if you can agree on the right answers.

## Sample student responses

Let's have a look at how two students attempted this task.

### Student A

1  laugh at same jokes

2  more global-minded

3  access to social and educational opportunities

### Student B

1  teenagers all over the world are laughing at the same jokes

2  teenagers might have trouble imagining

3  our brains become more set in their ways

Discuss with your partner which of the two students showed the best note-taking technique and would have presumably scored the most marks. Give your reasons why.

# History of science
## Science museums

How often do you learn something new about science, and where are the places you are most likely to learn something scientific? When was the last time you went to a museum that had science information in it? Do you seek out scientific things, or do you avoid them?

 **Track 1.1** Listen to **José** giving his talk to an international school.

José is a museum curator in Chile. Part of his job is to go to international schools and tell them about his museum, what they have there, and how the students can get involved.

## Check your understanding

1   How old are the oldest objects in José's collection?

2   Give an example of one thing José has to do in his job.

3   What subject did José study at university?

4   How does José make sure the objects are not damaged? Give two examples.

5   Why does José like his favourite mobile phone?

6*  Which object would you want to find out more information about and why?

## Building your vocabulary

In the following article, the five words below are used:

**exhibits    cell    stock    current    presents**

Sometimes, we may think that we know a word because we have seen it before. However, there are words that have more than one meaning, so although we may think we know a word, we need to read the context carefully so we understand what is being meant by its use.

Each of the words above has at least two meanings; for each, you need to choose from the two choices below the meaning that is being used in the article:

1   Exhibits: pieces of artwork that are displayed for people to see OR puts on display in a museum or art gallery.

2   Cell: a locked room where a prisoner lives OR a small part of the body that, when added to other cells, make organs, skin, and so on.

3   Stock: the number of products stored by a company that have been purchased or gained but have not yet been sold or put on display OR liquid in which meat or vegetables are cooked.

4   Current: the flow of electricity running through a wire OR something that is happening today or at this general time.

5   Presents: shows for display OR gifts given for a birthday or other celebration.

The Deutsches Museum in Munich is a museum that is dedicated to informing visitors about science, as well as entertaining them in the process.

The Deutsches Museum has more than 100,000 objects from the fields of science and technology. The large number of valuable

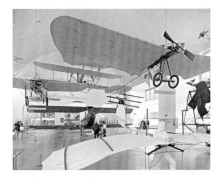

original **exhibits** makes the Deutsches Museum one of the most important museums of science and technology anywhere in the world. The collections are not restricted to any specialized range of topics: They include objects from mining to atomic physics, from a cave to a model of a human **cell**. They extend from the Stone Age to the present time. Collecting historically significant objects is still one of the museum's central tasks, so that the **stock** is constantly growing.

About a quarter of the objects are on exhibition – in the main museum on the island in the river, at the transport museum on the Theresienhöhe, in the hangar at Schleißheim airfield, and in

the Deutsches Museum Bonn. These illustrate important developments in science and technology, right up to **current** research.

Among the particular highlights (besides many others!) are the first motorized aircraft built by the Wright brothers; a submarine; the first program-controlled computer; Diesel's original engine; and the first motorcar by Karl Benz.

A brochure entitled *Masterworks* from the Deutsches Museum **presents** a few of these outstanding inventions. You can find out more about them here under Selected Objects.

**Source: www.deutsches-museum. de/en/collections**

# Check your understanding

1   Which two topics may you be particularly interested in if you went to visit the Deutsches Museum?

2   How old are some of the oldest objects at the museum?

3   What percentage of the objects that the museum has are on display at any one time?

4   Whose aeroplane is on display?

5   Where can you find more information about the Deutsches Museum?

6*   Which object would you be most surprised to see in the Deutsches Museum and why?

 Writing a request letter

You have just visited the Deutsches Museum and your favourite item from the field of science and technology was not there.

Write to the museum explaining what your favourite item is and include reasons why you think they should have it in their museum and on display for all visitors to see.

## Copernicus

People have long been interested in space and the information that the stars can give us. One of the most famous astronomers in history is Nikolas Copernicus. Copernicus studied medicine and law at university before becoming more interested in the stars. He said that Earth travelled around the Sun, which was at the centre of the universe, a new idea at the time. In 2009, Element 112 was named "copernicium" in his honour.

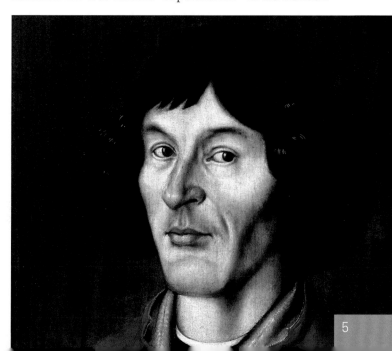

Copernicus has influenced astronomers who have come after him.
In small groups, research some facts about Copernicus. Which of the
following statements are true about him, and which are false?

1   Copernicus was born in 1897.

2   Copernicus thought the world was flat.

3   Copernicus studied Physics at university.

4   Copernicus was Italian.

5   Copernicus was interested in the stars.

6   Copernicus only had one idea that remains well known today.

7   Copper was named after Copernicus.

8   Only scientists interested in the stars have heard of Copernicus.

9   Copernicus never travelled out of his home city.

10   Copernicus enjoyed reading and playing the piano.

 ## A persuasive talk

Once you have decided which facts are true and have learned more about
Copernicus, write a brief speech of two to three minutes' length explaining
why there should be a statue of Copernicus in your town. Explain why he is
a role model and why he has been so important in science and astronomy.

## Key skills

### Linking words

We can use linking words to organize our work and
make it easier for the target reader to read. Group
the following linking words, depending on how
often you use them:

**and      firstly      which      also      but**

**despite     secondly     then     because**

**although     afterwards     since     nevertheless**

Can you label one group "sometimes", another
"often", and another "hardly ever"?

Read the passage below and pick out the linking
words that you find. Which of your groups do they
appear in?

*The most incredible sight I have ever seen are the
Kungur ice caves in Russia. Although they are hard
to reach, they are amazing. Despite having blisters
and frozen hands, I felt instantly fine seeing what
I shall never forget; ice glaciers coloured red, blue*
*green and purple from the natural salts in the ice,
and the sun. It looked like natural stained glass and
was beautiful.*

The use of linking words makes the text easier to
read and allows it to flow better; it is a strategy that
you should use in your longer pieces of writing,
as good links always have a positive effect on the
target reader.

Now link the ideas together in each of the following
paragraphs. You may wish to use one or two linking
words in one or two sentences to do so.

1   The temperature of water rises when it is
    heated. The hotter the water is the faster the
    molecules of water move around. When the
    water approaches 100 degrees, molecules escape
    in the form of steam.

2   The astronomer had a telescope. He used the
    telescope to look at the stars. The telescope made
    the stars seem a lot closer. He could see the stars
    in more detail. He really liked his telescope.

# Inventors and inventions

## Building your vocabulary

engineering   architecture   demonstrate   develop   prototype   manufacturers   patent   perseverance

Fit one of the words above into each gap to complete these sentences:

- He stood on stage in front of the buyers so he could ............................... how his product should be used.

- He was interested in machinery, so he decided to study ............................... .

- It was a good idea but he needed to ............................... it further before he could sell it.

- The ............................... was made of paper and cardboard but the real thing will be made of glass and steel.

- It was the ..............................., while they were making the product, who came up with the name.

- It was important no-one copied his design, so he got a ............................... for it.

- It took many years to get the product right, but it was worth the ............................... in the end.

- He wanted to study ............................... at university because he was interested in the way buildings were put together and the materials they were made of.

## James Dyson

Museums often feature items that were available in the past but are no longer used, but they can also demonstrate ideas that may be used in the future. One man who has made items that could feature in both these areas is the inventor and businessman James Dyson.

Read about James and some of his inventions.

James attended art school painting beautiful objects but he soon found it wasn't enough. He wanted to make and so James studied architecture. He enjoyed creating new things and was able to develop a high-speed landing boat and, with it, his passion for engineering. Pretty soon, he'd also developed a new kind of wheelbarrow – one with a big, fat ball that didn't sink into mud and chunky feet for stability, all the while learning to take risks and use mistakes as a fuel for creativity and solving problems.

Problems like vacuum cleaners that lose suction. Could the technology he'd first spotted on a sawmill work in a vacuum cleaner? He ripped the dusty, clogged bag from his old vacuum and replaced it with a crude prototype. A total of 5,126 prototypes later and along came the first bagless vacuum cleaner.

During the five years it took to develop his first vacuum cleaner, James was trying to make other manufacturers embrace his new technology, as well as to protect his invention when they copied it, so he had to get a patent on some of his designs. It took 15 years of perseverance for James to finally launch the Dyson DC01 vacuum cleaner in 1993 under his own name. Within 22 months it became the bestselling cleaner in the UK and made James famous.

While busy developing his cyclone technology, he'd listed all the other annoying things about ordinary vacuum cleaners, and then fixed them one by one: a stair hose that stretches to the top of stairs; on-board tools; a clear bin (although people thought it would never take off at first); and a carry handle. All quite obvious if you think about it. It's just no other vacuum manufacturer ever had.

James says that when things are hard, you have to look at a problem like a race: "It seems as though you can't carry on, but if you just get through the pain barrier, you'll see the end and be okay. Often, just around the corner is where the solution will happen."

Today, there are not just vacuums that Dyson has invented; there are also fans, washing machines, hand driers and taps with a hand drier built in.

**Source: www.content.dyson.co.uk**

## Check your understanding

1 What job did James want to do when he was younger?

2 How did he become an inventor?

3 When did he set up his own company?

4 For which invention is James most famous?

5 Give one example of another invention James has created.

6* If you could own the patent for one of James' inventions, which one would it be and why?

 Although James Dyson has had several good inventions in recent years, he has also shown that you don't need to be old to be able to invent.

Watch a clip of Ruth Amos, who was 16 when she came up with her idea, describing her invention, available at **www.youtube.com/watch?v = l-Q5Hm6uypE**.

## Check your understanding

1 What is the name of the latest prize Ruth has won?

2 Give one word Ruth uses to describe the prize.

3 What is the name of Ruth's invention?

4 What was the reason Ruth created her invention?

5 What do her employees think is so impressive about Ruth?

6* Who would you recommend Ruth's invention to?

## Q – a fictional inventor

Inventors have different motives for creating new products – profit, need, interest. Q is a fictional inventor who provides the intelligence officer James Bond with cutting-edge products so he can challenge his enemies more effectively.

# Answering multiple-choice questions

At some point in your Listening test you will listen to a scenario – usually an interview – and will demonstrate your understanding of what you have heard by answering some multiple-choice questions. Let's practise this particular examination skill here.

**Track 1.2** Listen to the interview with Q, who works for the British Secret Service as an inventor of ... well, it wouldn't be secret if we told you, would it!

The key skill in being successful with multiple choice is to make sure that the answers you haven't selected are actually incorrect. There will be three options for you and they will all have a similar format or "feel" to them. Some will be worded as questions and others will require you to complete the sentence. Here's what we mean:

1   **Q attended which university and at what age?**

   **a)**  Oxford when he was only 16

   **b)**  Cambridge when he left school at 18

   **c)**  Cambridge when he was a little older at 19

   Have a go at this question by listening to the recording again if you like.

   An example of a sentence completion may be:

2   **Q likes his work because**

   **a)**  he has an active mind

   **b)**  the job keeps him active

   **c)**  it means he is an active member of the service

Here are a couple of questions for you to answer on your own:

3   **When he was at university, Q studied**

   **a)**  engineering

   **b)**  research

   **c)**  English

4   **What do you think Q thinks of Bond?**

   **a)**  That he is very impressed with the work Q and his colleagues do.

   **b)**  That he is just another agent and wastes Q's time.

   **c)**  That he is a team player and shows no signs of arrogance.

(Hint: Q4 is a tricky one as you will have to use your inference skills.)

With a partner, and using other parts of the interview with Q, create two of your own multiple-choice questions – one of each kind. Now present those to another pair of students. You may like to add a few lines of dialogue, and then come up with some more questions.

Discuss what you have learned about the multiple-choice questions you will be asked in the Listening test.

# Operation Jungle!

You are helping a spy who is in the jungle with no access to the Internet or a computer. You can choose one of the following six inventions to send to your spy to help them:

- a knife that can cut through anything, including concrete and steel

- a water bottle that will never run out of fresh water

- a compass that will also send back the spy's location via satellite to your base

- a radio that charges when moved

- tablets that turn water into petrol

- a book explaining which plants and animals in the jungle can or cannot be eaten.

In pairs, decide what to send and why.

What would you change or adapt in your chosen object to make it better?

# Literary connections
## Science fiction

Some inventions are real and can be used. Some, however, have been made up and are only found in fiction or on television, often in science-fiction novels and programmes.

 ## Developing a discussion

What do you think of when you hear the words "science fiction"? Use some of these words, or some of your own, to tell your partner what comes to mind:

| | | |
|---|---|---|
| aliens | time travel | laser technology |
| parallel universe | mind reading | danger |
| chemicals | strange | galaxy |
| Martian | disagreement | stellar |
| lunar | | |

## Michael Moorcock

**Track 1.3** Listen to the interview with the famous science-fiction author Michael Moorcock

# Check your understanding

1 Up to how many words can Michael write in a day?

2 What does Michael say he has to do to write this many words?

3 How old was Michael when his first novel was published?

4 How does Hari describe cities in Michael's novels?

5 As well as science fiction, what else does Michael include in his writing?

6* Give three adjectives to describe what you think Michael likes about being a science-fiction writer.

## Sample responses from students

🎧 **Track 1.4** Listen to the discussion, which is also developing the theme of how agriculture has changed over the last 20 years or so. The college lecturer is conducting a seminar with three students. Listen carefully to how each student responds to him.

- Which of the three students do you think would perform best in the Cambridge IGCSE Speaking test?
- Which would perform the weakest?

Now have a go yourself. With a partner, practise using some new vocabulary, but this time in the specific area of architecture or building. Do some research first and find ten words each that are new to you. Now build those words into a two-three minute discussion. Keep the focus on the main theme.

- Are you starting to use words with precision?
- Was there any evidence in your brief conversation of shades of meaning developing?

This time your teacher will listen in and give you some feedback about how well you deployed your new vocabulary.

In the interview you have just listened to, Michael talked about his contribution to the British television series *Doctor Who*.

## Building your vocabulary

**canals     oak on willow     ship     galaxy     planet     newly mown     arrows     universe**

Which words and phrases here relate to Space? Which other Space words can you think of? Explain to a partner how you would feel if you suddenly found yourself on another planet.

Now write a brief diary entry of your first impressions when you find yourself on a new planet for the first time:

*I felt a thud as the ship landed. It took a few moments for me to be able to stand up but when I did, I looked out of the window and saw …*

Read this extract from Moorcock's *Doctor Who* novel *The Coming of the Terraphiles*.

The planet of Venice had been named well because her golden surface was covered with many waterways. Clouds followed the canals in season and highlighted their character. It was a rich and lively world with more space travellers landing here than on any of the other planets. Cornelius was a lonely figure but was nevertheless in charge of his ship. He was continuing his search for the only person who could help him, and that person was called the Doctor.

Lying back in his chair and tipping his hat just a little lower over his eyes, Urquart decided there was nothing like the noise of oak on willow and the smell of newly mown grass to make one feel all was well in the world. He was enjoying this holiday so far. In front of them, a game was being played and the crowd would murmur and clap occasionally. This was galaxy-class sport.

The men were dressed in green and white, whilst the ladies were in lavender, rose and orange, all wearing straw hats. Hari was lying watching the game.

Amy was enjoying her holiday too. She liked the feel of the straw hat and the floral dress. She and the Doctor had been learning how to dance. It seemed slightly strange to her that people from all over the galaxy were here and also that she herself had only been there for less than a week.

By the time she had joined the Doctor at the Tardis, she had had a coffee and some breakfast. There was something wrong with the normal rules of energy flow. Time and space were increasingly unstable.

Meanwhile, the players in green were still on the field. They were shooting blunt arrows at two others at the other end of the field, who were in full armour and trying to stop these shooters from hitting the round board behind them. Whoever scored 380 first would be the winner.

The players held a game which was known throughout the universe but which only a few were allowed to play as it was held only once every 250 years. The prize was a silver arrow but no-one now knew where it had first come from.

Over in the far corner of the field, Urquart heard someone shout "380!"

# Check your understanding

1 What is the name of the planet the story is set on?

2 Give the names of two people who are watching the game.

3 What have Amy and the Doctor been learning to do?

4 How long has Amy been on the planet?

5 How often is the contest held?

6* Give two adjectives used to describe Venice.

## The language of science fiction

With a partner, discuss why this is science fiction. Come up with a list of reasons, clues, and examples – anything that proves it is about science and that it is fiction. Now compare your list to that of another pair. Is there much similarity? How are they different?

## Language focus

## Comparatives

When we need to describe an event or experience, sometimes we can make a comparison that will emphasize just how good or bad what we are describing is.

● The party we went to was very good.

● The party we went to was better than the one my neighbour had.

Adding the comparative detail adds clarity to the writing, as well as making it more interesting to read.

Look at the next example and decide which sentence is more persuasive in making you buy the new phone.

● The new SV104 smartphone is fast, light, and cheap.

● The new SV104 smartphone is faster, lighter, and cheaper than ever before.

Comparisons themselves can be emphasized. Look at these two sentences, for example, and see how the use of one word can create a very different effect.

● The party we went to last year was better than the one we have just been to.

● The party we went to last year was far better than the one we have just been to.

Now, add a comparative to each of the sentences below. Show these to a friend. This will help you to build up a word base of useful comparatives.

1 The novel is interesting and I enjoyed reading it.

2 The OM102 solar-powered car is new and well designed.

3 I have seen the film *Science Man* and really liked it.

4 The special effects in a film are important.

5 Having read the newly published novel *The Watchmaker*, I can say it is a good science-fiction read.

## Superlatives

When we need to describe an event comparing more than two aspects, we need to use the superlative form. For example:

● It is very warm today. In fact, I think it is **the warmest** day of the year so far

● This book is an extremely interesting book; in fact, it is **the most interesting** book I have ever read

Forming the superlative depends on the adjective which we are using to start with:

1 If we are using a noun with one syllable, we just add "the" before and an "-est" suffix. For example:

> **fast** becomes **the fastest**
> **slow** becomes **the slowest**

Watch out for doubled letters. For example:

> **fat** becomes **the fattest**
> **hot** becomes **the hottest**

2 If we are using a noun of one or two syllables which ends in y, we add "the" before, we remove the y, and add an "iest" suffix. For example:

> **funny** becomes **the funniest**
> **friendly** becomes **the friendliest**

3  If we are using a noun of two syllables (not ending in y) or more, we add "the most" before and keep the adjective unchanged. For example:

**interesting** becomes **the most interesting**
**intelligent** becomes **the most intelligent**

Advertisers trying to sell new products often use the superlative form in their advertising:

- Try the new Tasty Bar – the creamiest, tastiest, most delicious bar you will ever taste

- Why not test-drive the new Bella today – the most comfortable, most high-tech and most affordable car on the road today

Now, add a superlative to each of these sentences:

1  The car is good and is cheap as well

2  My phone is new and light – I like it

3  I have seen Avatar and I thought the special effects were good

4  The objects in the museum were unusual

5  I liked the Martian Chronicles more than other books

Now read another extract from a science-fiction novel: *The Martian Chronicles* by Ray Bradbury and answer the questions that follow.

Tim sat in the back of the boat with Dad. He remembered the night before they left Earth. The rocket that Dad had found somewhere, somehow, and the talk of a vacation on Mars. A long way to go for a vacation and now they had arrived, they were going fishing.

They looked ahead of them excitedly, and saw the city, quiet in the heat of the summer. There were several pink rocks sitting on the sand and nothing else for miles. Just then, a bird flew up. Dad got frightened as he had thought it was a rocket.

Tim looked out into the sky, trying to see the Earth. Then, they felt a pull and saw a silver fish swimming below them. His mother had her hair in a plait and her eyes were blue, almost purple in places. Her thoughts were swimming around as fast as the fish below. She kept looking ahead trying to see what lay ahead. Tim looked too, but all he could see was the line of the canal, becoming purple in the distance as it made its way towards the hills until it reached the horizon.

Dad got out his atomic radio and put it on his wrist. Suddenly, he stopped the boat and listened. Everybody listened. The rocket they had landed in exploded. It was all part of the game.

They continued their journey down the canals. It was getting late and the sun was already setting. Night came quickly and Dad lit a fire. He had brought some papers with him, and now he was adding them to the fire, one by one, burning the old way of life.

Tim looked at the last thing Dad had thrown on the fire – a map of the World, before it wrinkled, creased up and then was gone, like a warm black butterfly.

# Check your understanding

1 What did Tim and his dad do when they first arrived on Mars?

2 Which colours could Tim see?

3 How many people were in the boat?

4 What did Dad put on his wrist?

5 What was the last thing Dad burnt?

6* Why did Dad burn the papers?

## Understanding opposing points of view

**Thinking out loud**    Spend a few minutes looking again at the two pieces of science fiction. Which one appeals more to you, and what are the reasons for this? What is the other piece lacking?

## ⬭ Developing a discussion

Now approach someone in the class who prefers the other extract to the one you chose. Develop a discussion in which you both present your points of view and then respond with an opposing view. You don't need to reach agreement, and you don't need to prove that one is better than the other. You just need to consider and respond to an alternative point of view.

## Language focus

### Present simple tense

The present simple is the first tense you will probably have used when learning English. However, you still need to be careful to use it precisely, as errors in high-frequency words can distract the reader.

We use the present simple for three main reasons:

1 to describe something done regularly

2 to describe something which is always true, or true for a long time

3 to describe a timetable or schedule

When we use the present simple, we are usually using the main verb, and adding "s" in the first person singular (he, she, it). It is easy to forget the "s", especially when writing at speed, so don't forget to check you have added it where necessary.

So, you need to be sure that the noun and verb match; for example:

- *He likes* to go to the football match at the weekend (we use the present simple here to describe something done regularly)

- *They like* to shop at the new shopping centre (we use the present simple here to describe something done regularly)

- *We live* in the town centre (we use the present simple here to describe something which is true for a long time)

- *The Sun sets* in the west each evening (we use the present simple here to describe something which is always true)

- *The train leaves* at 7:49 in the morning (we use the present simple here to describe a timetable)

- *The meeting starts* at 9:10 in the morning and lasts for an hour (we use the present simple here to describe a schedule)

You also need to ensure the verbs have been spelt correctly:

- *He looks* good, but he isn't really

- *They swim* very well and may even win

Choose a verb from the list and add one to each sentence in the present simple:

think     buy     go     walk     listen

1   He _____ all the things he needs from the hypermarket.

2   They _____ to work by train but don't like it.

3   She _____ he is nice but her friends don't like him.

4   We _____ to town every Wednesday.

5   He _____ to the radio every day but does not download music any more.

# The Big Issue – medical science and sight
## Bats and echolocation

## What are bats?

Bats are mammals. Like other mammals, including ourselves and many of our pets, they have hair or fur on their bodies and they are warm-blooded. A baby bat feeds on its mother's milk for at least a few weeks after it is born. Bats are the only mammals that can fly. A bat's wing has very similar bones to the hand and arm of a human, with skin stretched between the very long finger bones and the body to form the wing membrane.

## How big are bats?

The body of the smallest bat found in the UK, the pipistrelle, measures only about four centimetres in length and weighs about five grams – that's less than a £1 coin! In comparison the UK's largest bat, the noctule, is almost twice the size and weighs up to 40 grams. Even the noctule is tiny though compared to the world's largest bat, the Kalong (also known as the Javanese flying fox). It lives in south-east Asia and feeds on fruit. With a wing span of almost two metres, it's the biggest bat in the world!

## How do bats find their way around in the dark?

Many people think bats are blind, but in fact they can see almost as well as humans. However, at night, their ears are more important than their eyes – they use a special sonar system called "echolocation", meaning they find things using echoes.

As bats fly they make shouting sounds, which are too high-pitched for most humans to hear (although sometimes children are able to hear them). The echoes they get back from their shouts give them information about anything that is ahead of them, including the size and shape of an insect and which way it is going. We can hear the sounds bats make using a special instrument called a "bat detector".

**Source: Bat Conservation Trust. Extracts from www.bats.org.uk/pages/echolocation.html and www.bats.org.uk/pages/all_about_bats.html**

---

Hi Jan

I was reading this leaflet all about bats and I wanted to send it to you – it is really interesting.

Did you know that bats are not blind; in fact they can see almost as well as humans. But to fly around and hunt for insects in the dark, they use an amazing high-frequency system called echolocation.

Echolocation works in a similar way to sonar. Bats make calls as they fly and listen to the returning echoes to build up a sonic map of their surroundings. The bat can tell how far away something is by how long it takes the sounds to return to them.

These calls are usually pitched at a frequency too high for adult humans to hear naturally. Human hearing ranges from approximately 20 Hz (cycles per second) to 15 to 20 kHz (1,000 Hz) depending on age. In comparison, some bats can hear sounds up to 110 kHz in frequency. By emitting a series of often quite loud ultrasounds that either sweep from a high to low frequency or vary around a frequency, bats can distinguish objects and their insect prey and therefore avoid the object or catch the insect.

Individual bat species echolocate within specific frequency ranges that suit their environment and prey types. This means that we can identify many bats simply by listening to their calls with bat detectors.

I think it would be really cool to go looking for bats with a bat detector – let's go and do it together – when are you free?

See you soon

Dan

# Surveying your classmates

Conduct an informal survey by speaking to other students in your class. You are keen to know about the animals that your classmates are most interested in and to discover the facts they would most like to know.

Record your results in a format that suits your way of researching.

Now consider your results. Which animal would *you* most like to find out more about? How will you go about doing this? What modern technology would you take with you to help?

Write a short rationale. Your teacher may like to collate all of these for a display or for sharing.

---

## Key skills

# Language devices to attract the reader's attention

If we want to write for people we perhaps do not know, and if we want to keep them coming back to read more, on our blog, for example, then we have to make our writing interesting *all the time*. We need to make sure all the words we have in our writing are important to the story and that we are not wasting words, which is called redundancy. So, we need to be as concise as we can.

With a partner, look at these two blogs:

*Blog one*

Yesterday, I went with my friend, who I have known for more than ten years, to the local bat trust to see if we could find some bats. We took a torch. We bought this torch a few weeks ago on a camping trip – it's a dark green torch and is about 12 centimetres long. We also had a detector with us. We sat for several hours, and while we were there it rained a little and was a little bit windy. Even though we did not see any bats, we heard them using the detector, so we went home happy.

*Blog two*

I just have to tell you what happened to me last night! I went with a friend to the local bat trust which we had read about in a leaflet on bat detection. So, we thought we would give it a go. When we got there, we were kitted out with all the things we needed; we looked really professional as we set off! Well, it was a bit boring for the first few hours, but then we heard something on the detector – a bat! Many bats! It was just the most amazing experience and I'm definitely going again next week – and I'll let all of you know how I got on!

Blog two is the more interesting – can you and your partner work out why?

Here are some possible reasons, but maybe you came up with some more.

- Use of "last night" makes it more up to date than "yesterday"
- Varied use of punctuation and sentence structure
- Use of topic-specific vocabulary
- Use of interesting adjectives

- Use of linking words
- No redundant words

When we are writing we need to make sure the language, as well as the content, is interesting, so the reader comes back for more!

Now have a go yourself. Try to write a blog entry about a visit to a science museum. Write one that utilizes the language devices mentioned, and another that is not so impressive.

## People and echolocation

Watch this clip about Ben Underwood who uses echolocation to move around without bumping into things, available at **www.youtube.com/watch?v = r9mvRRwu5Gw**.

## Check your understanding

1 How old was Ben when he lost his sight?

2 How does Ben move around the house?

3 How does the reporter react when he sees Ben playing video games?

4 How does Ben feel about the way he is?

5 What does Ben feel about the future?

6* Why is Ben a good role model?

## Interview with an optician

**Track 1.5** Listen to the interview with Louise, who is an optician, as she tells us about the eyes and how advances in science have helped opticians and their patients in recent years.

When we go to an optician, it is not just our eyes that are being tested. The optician, when they are looking in our eyes, will also be able to check blood pressure, diabetes risk, and major organ function, which is why it is important to go regularly.

# Check your understanding

1 Why did Louise first become interested in eyes?

2 What percentage of people who are registered blind can actually see nothing?

3 Give one example of how Louise can help people with little vision.

4 Give one example of how we can look after our eye health.

5 Louise uses three words to describe her job; give two of them.

6* Give two examples of why being an optician is a good job to have.

 Writing an article for a science magazine

With a partner, conduct some research into how science has helped improve people's health. There are some very well-known cases of course, such as penicillin and the invention of X-rays. Try to find something more interesting, more recent, and show how science can help save lives.

Collect your information, and then write an article for a science magazine that informs readers of the scientific development and how it has helped people. You may like to look at the science magazine *New Scientist* to give you some ideas!

## Key skills

## Making sound inferences

Sometimes you will need to come to a conclusion about something having been given some, but not all, information relating to it.

Read the passage to see what it was that Isaac Newton *inferred*.

> It was when he was sitting in his garden that Isaac Newton made his famous discovery: gravity. As he was walking past an apple tree, one fell down and that action triggered an idea for Newton that would make him famous.
>
> The falling apple made him realise that objects have a potential force that transfers into a moving force when gravity pulls the objects towards Earth. One of the reasons why we do not float around, and why we return to Earth when we jump in to the air, is because there is the force of gravity pulling us back. Similarly, objects do not just float away, because they too are subject to this force, which keeps them attached to the Earth.
>
> All this was found because on that day, Newton walked past an apple tree.

To infer what gravity is, we may pick out the following three points.

- All objects have a potential force.

- Potential force can become a moving force.

- Gravity pulls objects to Earth.

There are actually a few inferences that Newton made – can you work out what they were?

Now have a go yourself. With a partner, think about something in science or nature *that actually happens*. An example may be that waves get bigger when the wind is stronger. Now test the theory of inference. If something actually happens, shouldn't we able to work how it has happened? Science relies on inference until it has the proof.

Here's a simple case of what we mean:

1 The grass in the garden was very long last week.

2 I saw my father's friend yesterday, and he owns a large petrol lawnmower.

3 Today the garden lawn looks wonderful.

Infer what happened?

Now create some of your own "safe" inferences. Have some fun with them!

# Advances in modern technology

Life has changed over the past few decades, with computers and the Internet making things possible that a couple of generations ago were found only in science-fiction novels.

---

## Building your vocabulary

**cockpit    take off    qualified    safety    features    up to date**

When reading a text with these words in, what do you expect the main theme or subject of the writing to be? Check the definition of these words and phrases in your dictionary.

Using the words, write a paragraph in which all six words feature. Swap paragraphs with a partner. How similar are they?

---

## Technology in the cockpit

 **Track 1.6** Listen to this pilot from India telling us how technology has changed the way we fly.

## Check your understanding

1  For how long has Ajay been a pilot?

2  Give one reason Ajay enjoys being a pilot.

3  Give two favourite places Ajay likes to fly to.

4  Which two subjects did Ajay study at university?

5  What is Ajay's favourite piece of modern technology?

6*  Which aspects of being a pilot appeal to you and why?

## Benefits and drawbacks

All jobs have benefits and drawbacks. What are the benefits and drawbacks of being a pilot? Add to the list below.

| Benefits | Drawbacks |
| --- | --- |
| You get to travel the world. | You are away from your family for long periods. |
|  |  |
|  |  |
|  |  |

# Reflection

Some of the things we are able to do today as a result of science are amazing when you look at how life was 50 years ago. It makes you wonder what humans could achieve in 50 years' time.

Choose an area in which you would like to see a great scientific advance that would help people.

You will need to assign research and presentation roles to each group member. You need to:

- explain the rationale or reason for your advance
- explain what affect it will have on people and on society
- cover and plan for any risks or concerns you have
- show how you will plan to evaluate its progress and its success.

Now make a group presentation. Be sure to include some diagrams, and other visual aids. Each group is trying to persuade the audience that their advance is worth pursuing and funding.

Once you have heard and seen all the developments on offer, have a secret ballot. That is, each of you votes on a piece of paper for the idea you thought was the best. Your teacher will count the votes and if it's a draw, your teacher will have the casting vote! Good luck.

## ☑ My progress

Each chapter includes four study skills. These are skills that will feature in your final examinations. So let's check your progress with these key skills in mind.

| Where am I now? | Very pleased – I think I'm good at this | OK – but I do need more practice | One of my weaker areas – so I need a lot more practice |
|---|---|---|---|
| Selecting appropriate notes from an information text | | | |
| Answering multiple choice questions | | | |
| Using a wider range of vocabulary in a conversation | | | |
| Using prompts to bind together a piece of extended writing | | | |

Now pick out one skill that you would like to prioritize for improvement and produce a short action plan to help you become stronger. Use a template similar to the following, which is filled out for you with an example.

## Action plan

Skill I want to improve using a wider range of vocabulary when speaking.

- **planning** – how I will try to improve this skill:
  listen to some conversations based on a topic and make a list of some of the interesting vocabulary used

- **implementing** – what I will need and what my exact strategy is:
  two or three suitable discussions and a means to pause the recording or video so that I can extract the vocabulary

- **monitoring** – how I will know I am improving and what evidence I may keep:
  try to use some of the words in discussions I have and see how the person I'm talking to responds

# 2 Food and fitness

## In this chapter you will:

- visit China, South America, Nigeria, Australia, and the UK
- read about the Chinese New Year, carnival celebrations, and ways to keep fit
- write your favourite recipe and write about a person you admire
- listen to a chef, a Paralympic athlete, and a marathon runner
- talk about the role that food plays in celebrations and novels.

## Key study skills

- Developing a conversation by *speaking* about broader issues
- Selecting appropriate content when *writing* a summary
- *Listening* to recognize ideas, opinions, and attitudes
- *Reading* to locate specific details in an information article

# Food

**Thinking out loud**

What are your favourite celebrations during the year, and why? Pick your particular favourite and think about why it's your favourite. Is there any particular food connected to it, for example?

## Food and celebrations

There are many celebrations around the world, many of which have food at their centre. See if you can match any of the terms below to a particular celebration:

Turkey  Mooncakes  Fortune cookies  Sheer khurma  Vermicelli  Yule log  Jalebi

## Key skills

### Skimming and scanning

When looking for details in informative texts, two skills that are used are skimming and scanning.

### Skimming a text

We are skimming when we are looking over a piece of writing quickly, to get the general idea of what it is about. This is sometimes called "getting the gist" of the piece, and can equally apply when you are listening to something.

Look for familiar words that will tell you the topic of the reading passage; these may be found in the headings and may be repeated in the text. You are not focusing on every word here or reading whole sentences – you are just looking for the main words that give you an idea of what the piece of writing is about.

### Scanning a text

We are scanning when we are looking for a specific piece of information in the reading passage. You should look at the question first, and then look only for information or details that answer that question. So again, we are not reading whole sentences.

For example, look at Question one that follows the Chinese New Year text – once we have read the question, we know we are looking for two months combined with "Chinese New Year". Scan the text to find the answer to this question. Now have a go at the other questions.

# Chinese New Year celebrations

As the Chinese use the Lunar calendar for their festivals, the date of Chinese New Year changes from year to year. The date corresponds to the new moon (black moon) in either late January or February. Traditionally celebrations last for 15 days, ending on the date of the full moon. In China the public holiday lasts for three days and this is the biggest celebration of the year. Families put lights up outside their homes, rather like our Christmas lights. Doors and windows are often newly painted in red. The colour red is chosen for two reasons. The first is because red is a lucky colour and the second because it is supposed to frighten off the monster Nian who is thought to come on New Year's Eve. The colour gold represents wealth. Families also decorate their homes with lanterns and put stickers on things in their homes. Everyone comes together for dinner, which is a feast. A popular food is "jiaozi" which are dumplings boiled in water. These dumplings are prepared on New Year's Eve and served right after midnight with garlic-soy sauce. A coin is often hidden in one of them. It is thought to be lucky to be the person who finds the coin. The dumplings are shaped like gold and silver bars in the hope that they will bring good luck and good fortune.

**Source: www.topmarks.co.uk**

## Check your understanding

1 In which two months can Chinese New Year take place?

2 For how long does the public festival in China last?

3 The colour red is used on people's doors during Chinese New Year; give two reasons why this is so.

4 What does the colour gold signify?

5 Why do people try to find the coin in the dumpling?

6* What is your favourite part of Chinese New Year and why?

What did you notice about scanning? What did you look for?

 ## Daily blog

Food allows us to come together during a celebration, as well as reinforcing customs that in some cases have continued for centuries.

What are the benefits of joining your family at these times? Imagine you contribute to a daily blog that your friends read. Type a brief entry that tells them about a family celebration that you have been to and why you particularly enjoyed it.

Every January in Harbin, in northern China, there is a month-long ice festival. Tourists flock from far and wide to experience the amazing sights of the ice sculptures, which are impressive by day and lit up spectacularly at night.

 Watch the video and answer the questions that follow:

**www.youtube.com/watch?v = QLLrkWwRemM**

## Check your understanding

1 When did the Harbin International Ice and Snow Festival start?

2 Up to how many sculptors work on the festival?

3 Give two examples of items built at the festival.

4 Up to how much ice is used in each sculpture?

5 Give two ways the ice is lit at night.

6* What would you sculpt if you had the chance to create something at Harbin?

What have you learned about scanning skills? Maybe the most important thing is to look at the questions first – whether it's a reading or listening text – to work out what type of information you are looking for.

# Context clues

**Thinking out loud**

Why do people enter competitions? Have you ever entered a competition? Did you win? Perhaps you received a prize? What was it?

## ✎ Writing a brief advert

You were recently given a golden cup. The person who gave it to you said that you have to use it as the first prize in a competition. It is up to you what kind of competition the cup will be awarded as a prize in.

- Write an advert to appear in a newspaper telling readers what they have to do in the competition, how they should enter, when the deadline for entries is, and what the top prize is.

We are going to use some familiar words in a reading passage to help us understand what some unfamiliar words may mean. We can work out the meaning of the unfamiliar words from the **context** they are in. This is called using "context clues" to help us understand what a word or phrase may mean.

- Read the advert below, and once you have finished you will be using context clues to help you with the meaning of the words in bold:

## Win a trip to the *Let's Cook Festival* in South Africa

Are you aged between 14 and 17? Are you good at cooking? Even better, are you an **outstanding** chef? Can you think of new ways to make delicious food which will have your friends queuing up for seconds? Have you always wanted to go to the *Let's Cook Festival* in South Africa? Then this is the competition for you!

All you have to do is send us a recipe and photo of your dish, including clear preparation and cooking instructions. But it not only has to look great, it also has to be healthy. So, try to include lots of fruit or vegetables; and don't use too much salt or sugar as these are not so healthy. And it has to be all yours – we are only interested in **unique** ideas.

Once you are happy with what you have created, send your entry together with your name, age and address, to **letscookfestival@southafrica.za** by the end of this month. Winners will be **officially** announced by the festival organisers on the website next month, and you could be joining famous chefs at the next *Let's Cook Festival*. Good luck!

1   What are the clues that helped you guess the meaning of each word?
    Match up each word on the left to the correct clue on the right.

| a | outstanding | 1 | announced by the festival organisers |
| b | unique | 2 | ... a good cook. Even better ... |
| c | officially | 3 | all yours |

2   Now look again at the three words in bold in the passage and match
    up the words on the left to their meaning:

| a | outstanding | 1 | the only one of its kind |
| b | unique | 2 | done by the people in charge |
| c | officially | 3 | very, very good |

Context clues allow us to work out what a word may mean and therefore
what the writer is trying to tell us. It's a very useful skill that allows you
to read more fluently and with more confidence.

Here are some words that you will see in the next reading passage about
carnivals in South America:

| prior | congestion | intact |

Remember, it is helpful if we can work out the meaning of a word from
the context it is in.

Look at the following sentences to work out what the words above could
mean:

- The two or three weeks **prior** to Carnival are a great time to visit Rio.

- ... as well as not having to suffer from the sheer **congestion** of people
  in Rio.

- ... and it was left with its spiritual and religious roots **intact**.

Check your understanding by reading these alternative sentences and
seeing if your suggested meanings fit the new sentences:

- I went to the shops **prior** to meeting him in a cafe.

- The traffic had stopped completely because of the **congestion**.

- Although I had dropped the vase on the floor, it remained **intact**.

# South America carnival guide

## The best festivals and celebrations

Carnival season is almost here! Of course the most famous carnival is Rio's, but there are many more. In Brazil alone there are large carnival parties in Salvador, Recife, Paraty and Ouro Preto to name just a few. Traditionally taking place in the lead-up to Easter each country has its own variations on its traditions, dates and purpose.

### Rio Carnival

Rio is the carnival that everyone knows about so let's start with that. The two or three weeks prior to Carnival are, in particular, a great time to visit Rio as you will be able to see many full-dress rehearsals and street parades at a fraction of the cost of Carnival itself, as well as not have to suffer from the sheer congestion of people in Rio. Carnival will continue (unofficially) for the week after as many locals take two weeks off work to party!

### Argentina Carnival

Buenos Aires' carnival manifests itself in the form of murga, a percussion-based rhythm usually performed by a marching band. Performed live on the streets, without amplification, with dancers and political lyrics the form represents both a social commentary and a great excuse to party! There is also a carnival just north of Buenos Aires in Gualegaychu, which again has a pattern of just occurring on the weekends.

### Bolivia Carnival

The Carnival in Oruro is one of the more traditional carnivals in South America, one very much with its spiritual and religious roots intact. In total, there are over 50 different groups and they all represent a different form of traditional Bolivian music or dance. The festival takes place over four days with festivities throughout each day. As well as the street parades there are also plays which explore a number of religious and spiritual tales.

### Montevideo Carnival

The carnival in Montevideo is the longest-running in South America, lasting for well over 40 days. There is drumming in the streets every day and theatre (with mixtures of comedy, song and satire) on temporary street stages, as well as in the sports clubs and major auditoriums.

**Source: www.soundsandcolours.com**

The passage was easier to read because we used context clues to help us. Make sure you try to use context clues the next time you see a word that is new to you.

#  Making a brief oral presentation

You and a friend are in a travel agent's office. You have enough money to go to one of the carnivals described on the opposite page, so you have to decide which one you will go to.

- Discuss with each other which one you will go to. Make sure there are clear reasons for your decision.

- Report briefly back to the whole class, telling them which destination you have chosen, and why.

- Which destination has been the most popular with your classmates?

## Key skills

When we listen to (or watch) something we often listen (or watch out) for specific information. For example, we can see that Question two on the following page asks "What percentage?" – so our response needs to contain a number and the percentage symbol. Making sure you know why you are listening to something is just as important as actually listening to it.

## Study tips
### The Speaking test

When you take your Oral test, you will be given a topic to discuss with your teacher for about six to nine minutes. The aim of this discussion is to develop the topic and there will be five prompts, listed on a topic card, which you and your teacher will need to work through in the exact order that they are given on the card.

Prompt three often deals with general aspects of the topic, aiming to broaden the discussion out to consider its pros and cons, opposing views, and how other people may feel about the topic or issue. Let's practise how you may approach Prompt three for the topic above about festivals and celebrations:

- If there was to be a new national holiday in your country what would be a popular reason to celebrate – what would the holiday represent?

Spend a few minutes thinking about what you will say and how you may develop a conversation about this and then spend two minutes actually discussing this idea with a partner.

### Sample responses from students

Track 2.1 Now listen to these three discussions about the same topic, and with a partner discuss the strengths and weaknesses of each one. This time, there is a teacher and a student involved.

**High achievement:** What do you think makes this a strong discussion?

**Average achievement:** How was this conversation satisfactory?

**Lower achievement:** What was missing from this conversation that would have made it stronger?

## Truffles in France

Some traditional foods are found in nature, and in some cases they have come to represent a community or a region of a country. The harder these foods are to find, the more expensive they tend to be. One example is caviar, which is harvested from a certain type of fish. It is found in many countries, including Russia. Which other unusual or rare foods can you think of? Which of these would you like to taste? Which new food would you find tempting?

Truffles are a type of mushroom that can cost a lot of money. Watch the following video clip on truffles and see how they are found in one area of France.

www.youtube.com/watch?v = L4rg3E_bWeM

## Check your understanding

1 What do the people put in the church collection?

2 What percentage of France's truffle market goes through the town?

3 How much is spent at the market in a single day?

4 To which countries may the truffles be shipped? Give two examples.

5 What exactly do the truffles look like? Give two details.

6* What has caused the decline in the number of truffles?

## Writing a recipe

Now let's look at how to write a recipe. Here are the instructions for how to make a lamb and apricot crumble. Read through it and make note of any key recipe language you can find. Which words are often found in recipes?

# Becoming a chef

 **Thinking out loud** Would you like to be a chef? What would you like about the job, and what would you not like? Is it a "serious career"? Have you heard of any chefs who are well known? What have they done that makes them successful?

## An interview with a chef

For some people, cooking is a career. It can take a long time to achieve success as a chef and many chefs start when they are quite young, working in the kitchens of large restaurants. Training to be a chef is very much about training and learning as you go along.

 **Track 2.2** Listen to the interview with Udobu, a chef from Nigeria, as he tells us about how he built up his career.

## Check your understanding

1 Who influenced Udobu to become a chef?

2 What did his mother cook the sauce with? (Give two items)

3 Why were Udobu and his brother ill once?

4 Where did Udobu train to be a chef?

5 For how long has Udobu had an apprentice?

6* What are the benefits of being a chef?

Listening for *specific* details is a major part of your Listening test, so it's good to get as much practice at it as you can.

# Lamb and apricot crumble

## Ingredients

2 tbsp olive oil

750 g lamb

half a chopped onion

50 ml apple juice

110 g chopped apricots

150 ml stock

90 g plain flour

45 g butter

grated rind of a lemon

a chopped clove of garlic

some chopped rosemary

## Method

Preheat the oven to 180°C. Heat half the oil in a plan and add the lamb to brown. Take out the lamb and then add the onions to the juice in the pan and cook on a low heat until soft. On a higher heat, then add the apple juice and add the browned meat and apricots. Add to an ovenproof pan and cook for about an hour.

To make the crumble, add the flour to a bowl and season. Rub in the butter, and then add the lemon, garlic, and rosemary. Sprinkle over the lamb and return to the oven. Bake until the crumble is golden brown. Allow to rest for a few minutes before you serve.

# Collocations

The recipe uses a variety of spices that will make the final dish very tasty. Any piece of writing will benefit from the same variety, that is, with suitable adjectives, and a range of verbs and adverbs combining to appeal to the reader, and to leave a lasting impression on them.

Some of the nouns used in the recipe have attached to them one or two adjectives, while others seem to have none. In writing, and especially in food writing, some words combine with others to form often-used pairs, for example, "hard-boiled egg" or "long-grain rice". There are several examples in the recipe above – for example, "fresh apple juice"; "freshly ground pepper". Are there any other examples in the recipe of words that seem to fit together?

Words that seem to fit together are called collocations. And many collocations are formed of certain verbs that are associated with particular words. For example, the verb *to take* is often seen in the following collocations: "take a chance", "take a break", "take a look", "take notes", and "take your time".

 # Writing a recipe

Think of a favourite meal and write the recipe for it. You may need to research the ingredients, and you may need to ask someone how to cook the dish. Make a list of the ingredients first, and then follow this with the method, focusing on the same type of language used in the dish here. Remember to use some collocations.

# Life on a farm

## Thinking out loud

What do you think working on a farm is like? You may think that when you have a job you will be working for five days a week, with a few weeks' holiday every year. However, for farmers, the job can often mean working seven days a week, with only rare holidays.

Read the following excerpts from a weekly blog by a young farmer called Guy who grows vegetables.

Instead of being paid a regular amount each month, many farmers have to wait until their crops are harvested to be paid. It is therefore vital for their survival that their crops are as healthy and productive as possible.

## Monday 14th

Got up at 5am as usual today. The sky was just starting to show the dawn. It was an unusual colour this morning, whiter than the usual yellow glow you see in the sky. The weather will be changing in the coming weeks and so I am working hard while the weather stays friendly to my crops. I grow vegetables and they need a lot of water, so we need the rain. But we also need the sunshine!

In the twelve years I have been a farmer, I have really come to understand the colours in the sky and what they tell me about the coming day. I still listen to the radio weather forecast, of course, but nature has a good way of telling me what I need to do. Work hard while the sun shines. And enjoy the rain too when it comes.

## Monday 21st

The last seven days have been tough. The weather changed a lot and it has been very dry. I have had to pump in more water to keep the irrigation system going and the crops moist. The days are longer than normal. The crops are not suffering too much at the moment but I need to make sure there is plenty of water every day.

I may have to hire another worker if the dry period continues, otherwise I could lose some of my crops for this season. It will be more expensive for me but until it starts to rain again, I don't think there is any other option. The next week is going to be decisive.

## Monday 28th

At last! The dry spell has broken and we've had some rain. I can't tell you how glad I am today. Thomas, our new farm worker, has been so useful since he started, I shall definitely be asking him to stay on.

We should now be able to harvest a good crop at the end of the season. And of course, a good crop means a good income, and that makes for a very happy family!

## Writing a blog entry

Imagine you are experiencing a problem at work. Write three blog entries just like Guy's where you talk about the problem in Week one, and then plot how it turns out by Week three. Try to write a couple of paragraphs for each blog entry.

# Fitness

## Having a focused discussion

In groups of five or six, have a discussion about why and how people should keep fit. Be sure to consider pros and cons, and how some fitness regimes may not work for everybody. What has worked for you, for example? Why has it been beneficial? What can you do now that you were unable to do before you started the fitness programme? Include advice such as how much time per week you think people should spend on keeping fit. Try to make your discussion as lively as possible by including lots of opposing views.

## Wildfitness

Our bodies are designed for natural movement patterns e.g. running, fighting, lifting, playing. We evolved in an environment where we needed to do intense short exertion with lots of rest or "active recovery" in between. We might have hunted, fought, run away etc. and then spent the afternoon sitting under a tree or gathering berries....

Wildfitness focuses on several key skills – wild running (or "barefoot running"), boxing, lifting, jumping, balancing, swimming, climbing, throwing and many more which mimic the movements and intensity that our bodies are designed for. This is the key to getting a lean and pain-free wild body.

If you engage in natural movements regularly with varying intensities and eat what your body needs, your body will blossom into its natural potential. At Wildfitness we don't focus on body shape or size as a goal. The act of enjoying moving in itself and enjoying real food results naturally in an athletic and graceful body.

Get pain free: The movements that you do most often: standing, walking, running, or whatever sport you do e.g. biking, are those which will have most effect on your body. Doing certain stretches or isolated exercises may help to alleviate pain but you have to change your movement patterns to change the load to your structure and therefore heal or prevent injuries.

Stay this way for life: In order to change and maintain a change, you have to be motivated by a sense of joy or

engagement in your new activities. They have to feel fun, purposeful and aligned with the amount of energy you have to give them. If you fall in love with movement and your environment you will be climbing trees with your grandchildren.

**Source: www.wildfitness.com**

Which of the activities at Wildfitness appeals to you the most? Have you ever participated in an activity like this that has helped your fitness? Did you like the Wildfitness approach? Share your views with a partner on this approach to fitness.

Wildfitness looks at how we can become fitter by using the same methods used thousands of years ago by early humans. With your partner:

1 Research fitness trends over the last 10 years or so.

2 Now produce a brochure together promoting one of the fitness trends (for example, Zumba). Give clear information about the activity, for example whether it involves any equipment or music, and why it is a good activity to do if you want to keep fit.

3 Then pass your brochures around to the other pairs in the class and compare and contrast the approaches people took. And, of course, learn about a variety of ways to keep fit!

## Study tips

### Writing a summary

A good summary will include key details without repetition and will attempt to use different words and phrases to those used in the original source text. There should also be a logical sequence to the ideas, and the whole piece should read well, ideally without any spelling or grammatical errors.

It is advisable to read the exact requirements of the question and then to read the text with those in mind. You should avoid lifting and copying directly from the text and should make sure that you include only details relevant to the question. This is because summaries are usually "guided", which means that you will be told which areas to focus your summary on.

In this example, let's summarize "the essentials of Wildfitness". Here are three summaries for you to look at. Can you rank them in order of how competent you think they are? What do you think are the strengths and weaknesses of each?

### Sample student responses

#### Student A

Wildfitness focuses on several key skills such as wild runing, jumping, balancing, swimming and many more. The act of enjoying moving in itself results naturaly in an athletic and graceful body. To do isolated exercises may help pain but you have to change your movement patterns to prevent injuries.

#### Student B

Wildfitness is for people who enjoy runing and swiming and hunting. This is for a painfree wild body. Biking is an activity that will have more effect on the body and exercises will help pain. You can fall in love with movment and you will be climbing trees with grandchildren.

#### Student C

The concept of Wildfitness is based on the natural movements that our ancestors used in their daily activities. The aim is for everyone to enjoy moving naturally and freely in order to produce a fit and flexible body. It is much better to concentrate on improving your movement patterns rather than doing isolated exercises because this will prevent injuries in the long term.

##  Writing a persuasive letter

You are trying to persuade a friend to join you on a fitness holiday that you have seen advertised and really want to go on. Write an email to your friend asking them to go with you and include the following points:

- Some of the reasons they should join you on this particular fitness holiday.

- What the plans for the week ahead will be.

- Why they will have benefited from the holiday.

Send this email to a particular friend. It will be interesting to see what response you get!

# Building your vocabulary

Scan the following article on Wild Eating and locate the words or phrases given below.
Use a dictionary to match these words to their correct meanings on the right.

| | | | |
|---|---|---|---|
| **a** | evolutionary | **1** | do well and grow strongly |
| **b** | omnivores | **2** | conditions under which the best results are achieved |
| **c** | optimum | **3** | a gradual change over several generations |
| **d** | thrive | **4** | species that eat food from every food group |
| **e** | selective breeding | **5** | acceptable or pleasant taste |
| **f** | palatable | **6** | an obvious and clear difference |
| **g** | ecosystem | **7** | controlled way that genetics are passed down the generations |
| **h** | pronounced distinction | **8** | the relationship between species and the environment in which they live |

# Wild eating

Our philosophy is based on what we know of our evolutionary origins and what we observe in nature today. We know that we are omnivores and that our ancestors thrived on the foods that they could hunt and gather in their natural environment. We also know that our species has been cooking food for over a million years.

At Wildfitness we serve a mostly "evolutionary diet" because eating this way:

→ Produces the optimum hormonal state in the body to strengthen your body's systems and be naturally lean

→ Prevents cravings and over eating

**How much of each food type would our ancestors have eaten?**

Humans are omnivores – we are one of the most adaptable species in the world. We know of healthy societies living on mostly meat-based diets and other healthy societies living on mostly vegetarian based foods. There is a huge range of foods that we can eat and thrive on, as long as these foods are familiar to our body having been in our diets for evolutionary time scales. We have meat and vegetarian options on offer at Wildfitness.

**Can we find "ancient" food in shops today?**

Pretty much all of the foods we buy today are very different from their ancient ancestors due to selective breeding. Celery and celeriac have a common ancestor only 400 years ago! The main changes to the foods that we grow and rear today are that they are more energy dense, palatable and less fibrous. This, (along with a less active lifestyle) can lead to an excess in the energy we consume. Therefore at Wildfitness we cut down on the most energy-dense foods such as grains and pulses. We cut out wheat altogether as wheat has been most severely bred and changed from its ancient form and many people's bodies find it difficult to digest.

**Where would our ancestors' food have come from?**

Our ancestors would have eaten plants growing within a natural ecosystem. Even when humans started to cultivate plants, they wouldn't have used fertilizers or pesticides or the commercial agricultural methods used today that can change the composition of our foods. With animal produce the distinction between wild animals and farmed animals is even more pronounced. At Wildfitness we source our foods as much as we can from farms that use natural farming methods, or wild foods.

**Source: www.wildfitness.com**

# Developing persuasive language

When writing longer texts, we can develop our writing by using persuasive language. The previous article, "Wild Eating", tries to persuade us to adopt a more traditional approach to eating. We can also use persuasive language when speaking.

- Think of some of the words you may use when persuading a friend to do something. How will you use these words to convey your "argument"? Will you change the way you normally speak, for example?

# A trip to Queenstown, New Zealand

You don't have to take part in a sport that is officially recognized in the Olympics to keep fit; there are many other ways to stay fit. Many people feel able to be more ambitious with their choice of keep-fit activities when they are on holiday. A good place to go where you can find some interesting sporting activities is Queenstown, in New Zealand. Here are three activities you could do if you went to Queenstown on holiday.

## Shotover Canyon Swing

### The world's highest cliff jump!

Shotover Canyon Swing is adrenalinised adventure at its best. Travel 15 minutes from Queenstown in one of our vans, take a three-minute bush walk and arrive at our scenic site. Our cliff-top platform is 109m above the spectacular Shotover River. You freefall 60m past rocky cliff faces into the canyon before the ropes smoothly pendulum you into a 200m giant swing at 150kph.

There are two basic launch methods: jump yourself or be released from our special launch boom. With over 70 different solo and tandem jumpstyles, we can expertly manage the scariness for everyone. We pride ourselves on offering trips with small groups sizes and not rushing the experience and there is often time to have more than one swing and try a different jumpstyle. Total trip is 2.5 hours.

## Brodrick-Landsborough Wilderness Experience

A true backcountry experience, this walk/raft combo is an amazing way to appreciate the unspoiled wilderness of New Zealand. Our adventure crosses the Main Divide on foot, then floats and paddles our way down the remote Landsborough River by raft. A fully guided trip, clients will not need to carry heavy backpacks as all food and other necessary equipment will be provided for.

Far from being a journey "on the beaten track", this trip takes you to high alpine landscapes and country not visited by the average tourist!

## Kawarau Bungy Centre

Your visit to Queenstown just wouldn't be complete without a visit to the World Home of Bungy. Located only 20 minutes drive from Queenstown this is where commercial Bungy started back in 1988, thanks to the Bungy Pioneers Henry Van Ash and AJ Hackett.

Since then this historic site has evolved into a world class visitor destination. So whether you're a hardcore adventure seeker or after something a little more relaxing the Kawarau Bungy Centre – World Home of Bungy – has something to offer people of all ages.

Come view Bungy from our large decks nestled into the rock face over the Kawarau River or shop for gifts and mementos at the Bungy Shop. Sit back, relax and enjoy something to eat or drink from the café or take a turn on the Bungy Trampoline.

If you're interested in learning more about Bungy take our Secrets of Bungy Tour. And of course don't forget the 43m Bungy experience, the world's first and most famous of Bungy jumps.

## Reading comprehension

Here are some questions based on the article about Queenstown that will be very similar to those you will be asked when your reading skills are being tested in your examination. Look at each of the sample responses and decide which you think is the best response.

1   How can participants benefit if there is spare time at the Canyon Swing Experience? Give **two** details.

    **a)** They can have more than one swing and try a different jumpstyle.

    **b)** Not rushing the experience and there is often time to have more than one swing and try a different jumpstyle.

    **c)** 70 different solo and tandem jumpstyles and total trip is 2.5 hours.

2   In what way do the organizers of the Wilderness Experience help their clients to transport items?

    **a)** Clients will not need to carry heavy backpacks as all food and necessary equipment will be provided for.

    **b)** A fully guided trip.

    **c)** Carry their backpacks.

3   Why may you take the Secrets of Bungy Tour?

    **a)** Learn more about Bungy.

    **b)** If you're interested in learning more about Bungy, take our Secrets of Bungy Tour.

    **c)** The 43m Bungy experience, the world's first and most famous of Bungy jumps.

 ## Writing up an interview

Now, with a partner, imagine you are both in Queenstown on holiday. You have each taken part in one of the activities detailed on the previous page. Ask each other questions about what you have been doing while in Queenstown. Be sure to include the following:

- Which activity you did, why you chose it, and whether you enjoyed it.

- What you think of the other activities available to do in Queenstown.

- What you will recommend about Queenstown when you see your friends back home, or what you may warn them about.

Now write a short magazine article focusing on the "holidaymaker" you have just interviewed – what has been said about Queenstown, and the activities it offers.

 ## Making a brief speech

For **one** of the situations below, prepare a 1-minute speech providing a persuasive explanation about why it should be done:

- Eating traditional or ancient food

- Trying an extreme sport while on holiday

- Trying out some new food dishes

- Spending at least an hour a day outside of the home

Write your speech down. Your teacher may ask you to deliver your speech to the class.

# Literary connections

## Starting a conversation

It is a very useful skill to be able to engage someone in a conversation. Most conversations begin in a very informal way, with you and the person you are talking to describing your experiences and your views, and then responding to the views of the other person. With a partner, let's practise these conversational skills by asking each other the following questions:

## About your favourite novel

- When did you first read this novel and how did it make you feel?

- Which character in the novel do you like the most and why?

- Which scene made the biggest impression on you and why?

- Which genre is the most enjoyable for you?

- Is it important to read novels?

When you come to the last question, you will see that you have started a conversation in a very personal way, but that it is developing more depth as you go along and as you begin to swap views, ideas, and opinions.

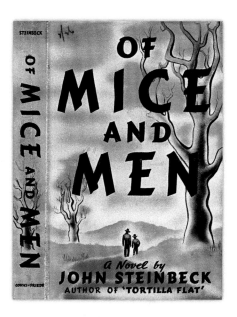

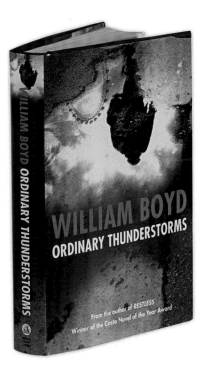

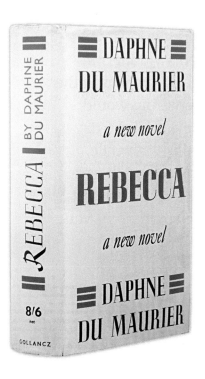

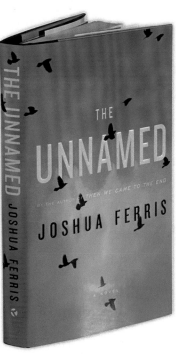

# The Hunger Games

*The Hunger Games*, by Suzanne Collins, tells the compelling story of narrator Katniss Everdeen who has taken her sister's place in the Hunger Games, an event that takes place every year in the fictional country where she lives.

There are twelve zones in the country that the story is set in, and two children are chosen every year from each one to fight to the death with the other participants from the other zones. The whole event is screened on television so that the populations of each district can see the action of the Games, as well as who is doing well. The novel is full of action, as well as maintaining tension throughout. When you are reading it, you are never sure what is going to happen next.

In this extract of *The Hunger Games*, Katniss and her friend Gale Hawthorne are in the woods, before the Hunger Games have started. They are pausing to eat some lunch and to think

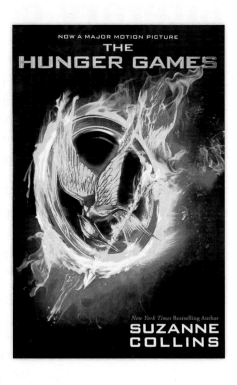

Gale spreads the bread slices with the soft goat's cheese, carefully placing a basil leaf on each while I strip the bushes of their berries. We settle back in a nook in the rocks. From this place, we are invisible, but have a clear view of the valley, which is teeming with summer life, greens to gather, roots to dig, fish iridescent in the sunlight. The day is glorious, with a blue sky and soft breeze. The food's wonderful, with the cheese seeping into the warm bread and the berries bursting in our mouths. Everything would be perfect if this really was a holiday, if all the day off meant was roaming the mountains with Gale, hunting for tonight's supper. But instead we have to be standing in the square at two o'clock waiting for the names to be called out. "We could do it, you know," Gale says quietly.

"What?" I ask.

"Leave the district. Run off. Live in the woods. You and I, we could make it," says Gale.

**Source: *The Hunger Games* by Suzanne Collins. Scholastic. 2009**

So, Katniss and Gale are thinking about whether to run away, or to return and see if they are chosen to take part in the Hunger Games. They don't really have a choice, however. They know that they have to go back, but for a while they are just imagining that they could be free.

# Adjectives

Look again at *The Hunger Games,* extract and find some adjectives. Now substitute each with a different adjective. How has the meaning changed in each case? Is the meaning stronger, weaker, less effective, or perhaps more effective?

## Developing your use of adjectives

Adjectives are words that are used to describe nouns, therefore adding detail and interest to a piece of writing, as well as keeping the readers' attention. You need to use a good range of adjectives in your writing.

For example, if the noun is **book**, you could use any of the following adjectives to describe it: "big", "new", "expensive", or "exciting". For added interest, you could use adjectives such as "dusty", "fragile", "appealing", or "rare".

Look at the three nouns below and add some adjectives that seem to go with these. You can use some of the adjectives you have already found, as well as using your own ideas.

Adjectives are used to develop nouns, giving them depth and interest. Writing can be made more precise and more vivid by the careful use of adjectives. However, they should not be overused, as this can make the writing more difficult to read.

For example, if we said that a book is a new, big, great, heavy, funny, old book, then that would be over-doing it. Have a go yourself at over-doing the use of adjectives by picking three nouns from the extract from *The Hunger Games* and bombarding each word with a list of adjectives. Remember, however, that each adjective you use should be appropriate, and on its own it should be able to describe the noun in question.

**Wood**

**Berries**

**Meal**

# Past simple tense use

When writing about events which have happened to us in the past, we will often use the past simple tense:

- I **wanted** to learn more about the history of the country, so I **decided** to go to the local library where I **borrowed** three books on local history and I **read** them all that night

1 We generally form the past simple by adding "ed" onto the main verb stem. For examaple:

   If I want to use **talk** in the past simple, I add "ed" to make **he talked**

   If I want to use **touch** in the past simple, I add "ed" to make **she touched**

2 There are verbs, however, which are irregular, and these are the ones which need more practice. Here are a few examples of irregular past simples:

   - He felt (feel)

   - I saw (see)

   - We thought (think)

   - She drank (drink)

   - They had (have)

   - You wept (weep)

   - I knelt (kneel)

   - We swam (swim)

It is important to ensure we are using this accurately, as the past simple forms the foundations of all past tense use.

Put the following sentences into the past simple:

1 When I (see) him again, I (run) towards him and (weep) for joy.

2 I (have) a smartphone 1 but last week I (buy) a smartphone 6.

3 My mother (like) her but I (like not) her as much.

4 She (enjoy) putting up the party decorations but (not enjoy) taking them down again.

5 I (start) the book last year and last week I (finish) it.

# Writing a descriptive piece

Choose one of the topics below that you would like to write about:

- the last holiday you went on
- a trip to the local town
- a day in the countryside
- a visit to a zoo

1   Write three paragraphs. Use as many describing words as you can and the simple past tense wherever possible.

2   Once you have finished, underline five describing words you have used. Can you replace each one with a synonym? Has this improved your piece of writing?

You probably know more synonyms than you thought you did, but perhaps you need to remind yourself to use them more often, to add variety to your writing.

# The Big Issue – achieving against the odds

## Alex Zanardi, Paralympian hero

 Watch the video clip about Alex Zanardi.

**www.youtube.com/watch?v = bpT5-rOmzdU**

Alex Zanardi is now a Paralympian, but before this phase in his life, he was a Formula 1 racing car driver for several years – a sport in which he achieved some success. Unfortunately, he was involved in a serious crash that left him fighting for his life. He survived, and he then embarked on a new phase in his life, which would lead him to two gold medals in the London 2012 Paralympics, and on a track he once raced on in his car. Despite what has happened to him, Zanardi has been able to continue achieving in sport, adapting according to how his body has changed.

## Building your vocabulary

Before you listen to Zanardi being interviewed, make sure you know what the following words mean by matching the words to the definitions:

| | | | |
|---|---|---|---|
| **a** | comeback | **1** | person missing at least one limb (arm or leg) |
| **b** | flourish | **2** | person who organizes events (for example, concerts, plays) |
| **c** | accomplishment | **3** | return to form/fame after absence |
| **d** | impresario | **4** | an extravagant gesture made for emphasis |
| **e** | tendencies | **5** | an achievement |
| **f** | amputee | **6** | something that cannot be understood |
| **g** | ecstatic | **7** | extremely happy |
| **h** | unfathomable | **8** | an urge towards something in particular |

## Thinking out loud

Imagine you had the chance to meet Alex Zanardi. What questions would you ask him?

**Track 2.3** Now listen to an interview Zanardi gave shortly after winning his Paralympic gold medal. Alex invited two of his fans to come along to the interview.

The interviewer chose "inspirational" to describe Zanardi. Can you think of some more words that could be used to describe him?

# Writing a fan letter

When people are famous, their fans often start fan clubs, and websites where there is a lot of information about the celebrity. Some people also write "fan letters" to famous people who they admire. You have learnt a lot about Alex Zanardi, so write a fan letter to him, explaining how you felt when watching him and listening to him. Compare your fan letter to one that a friend has written. What similarities are there?

# Angus Macfadyen

## The London Marathon

The London Marathon was started in 1981 by two well-known runners – Chris Brasher and John Disley. It starts every year on Blackheath Common, where every runner has to pass through the black gates before 26 miles 384 yards, and several hours, to the finish line. While some athletes are there to win the race, thousands more participants take part in order to raise money for good causes around the world. Once they have been accepted for the race, runners and participants will have to endure several months, and many, many miles of training.

---

**Thinking out loud**

It is a big commitment to run a marathon and it is a combination of physical and mental achievement for those who cross the finish line.

How do you think people from the general public prepare to run such a long race like the London Marathon? What changes to their lives and diet may they have to make? What other preparations need to be made beforehand? What do you think inspires them to keep going during the race?

---

## London Marathon on Crutches

**Track 2.4** Angus Macfadyen trained for the London Marathon. Listen to the first part of the recording of Angus talking about his experiences while doing the marathon on crutches.

What have you found out about Angus? What impression have you formed about him from listening to him? Make a few notes based on the first part of the interview.

---

## Fabrice Muamba

**Thinking out loud**

Why do some people, and the media, seem to admire athletes more when they have overcome adversity? We are usually fascinated by people who have beaten the odds. Can you think of anyone who has done just this?

## An autobiography

Professional sportsmen and sportswomen are usually very fit and healthy. They can have minor accidents while competing or training. However, it's very rare to have to overcome a life-changing attack on the body.

In March 2012, Fabrice Muamba was playing a professional football match for Bolton Wanderers against Tottenham Hotspur when he suffered a cardiac arrest. His heart stopped for more than an hour but he was lucky that the Bolton Wanderers' team doctor reached him within seconds. On the day, there was also a heart surgeon who had come along to watch the match and who ended up saving Fabrice Muamba's life. Remarkably, Fabrice has since recovered to write his autobiography.

A biography is a book about the life of a person; an autobiography is a biography written by the person it is about. You would therefore write an autobiography about yourself, and you could write a biography about anyone else. You will be writing a short biography at the end of this chapter.

## Discussion

- What do you think makes a good biography?
- What may make a biography not particularly interesting?

Discuss your ideas with a partner.

Read this extract from Muamba's autobiography.

The past few months have changed my life completely. I was a healthy guy who loved playing football every day. I got on really well with my team-mates and did all the things I knew I needed to do to stay fit. I trained in the gym regularly, I ate healthily and I didn't have any bad habits at all.

So it came as a shock to me when I woke up in hospital that day. I had collapsed suddenly on the football pitch and then I remembered nothing. I was told later that a club doctor ran onto the pitch, and then a few minutes later a heart surgeon joined him. He had been in the crowd watching the game.

It was really scary waking up in hospital, surrounded by wires and tubes. I didn't really know what had happened until the doctors came in and explained that my heart had stopped whilst I had been playing football.

Only later did I fully understand what a shock it had been to everyone, particularly to my fiancée and my mother. They had thought they would never see me again. It was far worse for them seeing me lying on the pitch than it was for me, as I was completely oblivious to what had been going on.

I am slowly getting better. And I now have a special machine which the surgeon placed in my body. It will re-start my heart, if it ever stops suddenly like that again. For now though, I have given up playing professional football. I shall definitely miss it as I loved it but I love my life more.

**Source:** *I'm Still Standing* **by Fabrice Muamba.
Trinity Mirror Sports Media. 2012**

## Campaigning for defibrillators

Fabrice Muamba's heart problem is very rare, of course, which is why he made headline news around the world when he collapsed on the football pitch.

**Track 2.6** Listen to the interview with Bill Anderson, who is a heart surgeon. Bill is talking about the importance of defibrillators.

1   Make some notes about what a defibrillator does and why having one available is important.

2   You have been asked to produce a campaign leaflet to supply some defibrillators in your town. You need to explain why a defibrillator is important, as well as saying where they should be positioned in the town.

3   Use your notes and further research. You will need to use persuasive language, to make sure everyone who reads your leaflet will support the cause. Your leaflet should also include some pictures and some striking visual elements to attract readers.

# Reflection

In this chapter we have learnt about Katniss Everdeen, Alex Zanardi, and Angus Macfadyen, and how they have all achieved much against the odds. We have looked at their mental strength as well as what they have done to overcome any physical difficulties they have faced.

##  Writing a biography

1   In small groups, agree upon another person you all admire who has overcome the odds in some way.

2   Research the person, and then work together and write a biography of your person. Each group member should focus on a key part of the person's life, so each group member should contribute a section to the biography.

3   Read one another's biographies and have a whole-class, informal discussion about what makes a good biography, what biographies have in common, and anything else you want to say about biographies!

# ☑ My progress

Each chapter includes four study skills. These are skills that will feature in your final examinations. So let's check your progress with these key skills in mind.

| Where am I now? | Very pleased – I think I'm good at this | OK – but I do need more practice | One of my weaker areas – so I need a lot more practice |
|---|---|---|---|
| Developing conversations by including related ideas and issues | | | |
| Choosing appropriate content when writing a summary | | | |
| Listening to recognize opinions and attitudes people have | | | |
| Locating specific details when reading information articles | | | |

Now pick out one skill that you would like to prioritize for improvement and produce a short action plan to help you become stronger. Use a template similar to the following.

## Action plan

Skill I want to improve <u>developing conversations by including related ideas</u>

- *planning* – how I will try to improve this skill
  <u>have some informal conversations that last about five or six minutes and are based on one topic only</u>

- *implementing* – what I will need and what my exact strategy is
  <u>find three or four adults from different backgrounds and have the conversations – all on the same topic</u>

- *monitoring* – how I will know I am improving and what evidence I may keep
  <u>Compare and contrast the way each conversation developed. What were the related ideas each adult brought in? Record the conversations as evidence for future reference</u>

# 3 Communities

## In this chapter you will:

- visit villages in Uganda and Peru
- read about ants
- listen to a teacher talk about a school community
- write a piece comparing two communities
- talk about your first day at school.

## Key study skills

- *Listening* for information that is being sought in different ways
- *Reading* a text accurately and using it to fill out a form with precision
- *Speaking* in the context of a warm-up
- *Writing* in an informal style

# What makes a community?

**Thinking out loud**

What comes to mind when you hear the word "community"? How many communities are you a part of? Are they important in your life? What do you think the phrase "sense of community" means? Do you think we all live in a global community?

## What ingredients make a community?

In pairs, see how many communities you can name – local, national, and international. What do they have in common? What are the essential ingredients for making a community? Together, work out what the recipe for creating a community may be.

Begin with a list of ingredients:

- Take fifty people of mixed age and background
- Place in families of varying sizes
- Add plenty of food
- Stir in lots of fun

Or you may prefer to make a specialized community:

- Take fifteen sports enthusiasts
- Take ten language learners

See what sort of mix you can come up with. Remember that the object of the exercise is to identify and "pour in" the ingredients to make a good community.

Share your recipe with other pairs.

How has this activity helped you to think about what communities are, or can be?

## Study tips

### Listening – covering a range of question types

The most common format or scenario that is used in the Listening test is the interview. A passive interviewer talks to a person who has a specific interest, job, or lifestyle and seeks to get information from that person. Let's see how this works by looking at an interview with Stanley, who manages a local events group in Hong Kong – it's a community of like-minded people who want to go out and explore their local area, but in more depth.

 **Track 3.1** Listen to what Stanley says about his community group.

There are various ways that your understanding of a listening scenario could be tested. In other words, the examination sets out to test a range of different listening skills. Two of these are:

- to identify and retrieve facts and details
- to understand and select relevant information

Let's see how the examination covers these skills by looking at several types of question. We'll use the interview with Stanley to do this.

Let's take the section where Stanley talks about what he finds particularly interesting about the area near Hong Kong Harbour. Listen to the section where the interviewer asks him about what he likes about the relics.

Here are four ways that you may be asked to locate the same piece of information. With a partner, work out what the common piece of information is.

*Open-ended question (allowing up to three words as a response):*

1 **What does Stanley particularly like to examine at the harbour?**

.......................................................................................

*Gap-filling (allowing only one or two words in a gap):*

2  **Stanley** _____ **bills that are** _____ **near the harbour**.

*Multiple choice:*

3  **Which of these relics is Stanley most interested in:**

   a) Exchange bills

   b) Bills of trade

   C) Bills of sale

*Statements (allowing only one or two words to complete them):*

4  **Stanley is not an expert on** _____ **of sale and he prefers not to collect digests of**

   _____ .

Now with your partner, choose another part of the interview and come up with four different ways, four different types of questions, to test the same piece of information. Give these to another pair to answer. This exercise should help you become familiar with the different approaches to setting a question and how your skills in identifying, understanding, selecting, and retrieving facts and details will be tested.

## A community to learn from

Watch the video "Ants at work marching together, with a twist in the tail" available at **www.youtube.com/watch?v = J6aVYmslPDY**.

How would you describe the way that the ants work together? In pairs compile a list of adjectives that may be used to describe what they do. Compare your list with others and make a note of any adjectives that are new to you.

## Language focus

### Collective nouns

Collective or group nouns can be used to suggest community, too. In fact "community" is itself a collective noun. "Family", "team", and "colony" are collective nouns used in the article on the next page to describe the ants. Identify the collective nouns in the following sentences. For each one say what group they are used for.

1  The whole herd was gathered at the far end of the meadow.

2  There was one big flock on the edge of the forest and a smaller one in the field.

3  The orchestra played to an enthusiastic audience.

4  One of the team was missing. "He's still in the library," his friend explained.

5  He was loyal to his party and served in government for nearly a decade.

Here are some more collective nouns. Choose three from each column to put into sentences. Share your answers with your neighbour and between you work out sentences for the ones not covered.

**Collective nouns**

| People | Animals | Other |
|--------|---------|-------|
| group | herd | bunch |
| crowd | flock | pile |
| team | swarm | set |
| gang | pack | stack |
| board | pride | group |
| jury | nest | series |
| class | gaggle | collection |

Collective nouns usually take singular verbs: Her family **lives** in Russia.

However, if the meaning is plural, they take the plural form of the verb: Her family **live** in several different countries.

In pairs practise using collective nouns. Each of you write down ten collective nouns. Exchange lists with each other. Use your partner's choice to make sentences. Check your sentences with your partner.

# Ants: social insects

# Ants!

Ants are noted for the complex societies in which most of them live. They are often cited as symbols of thrift and industry, because many species seem tireless in their activity and store large quantities of food.

Ants are social insects, living in large colonies. The colony is divided into queens, males, and workers. Although there are great variations in social structure among ant colonies, certain basic features are common to most species.

Ants, termites, many bees, and some wasps have a real family life. They live in communities, and the members of a community depend on one another. They may look a lot like other insects. But as social insects, they lead very different lives.

Ants are social insects because they live and work together in communities. Here, they feed and protect one another. They raise and care for their young. This way of life is very different from that of solitary insects that spend most, and sometimes all, of their lives alone.

An ant community is called a colony. Life in an ant colony is very organized. Each member has a job to do, from laying eggs to gathering food to fighting.

For most ants, colony life centres on the nest. The nest may be underground, in a mound, or even among the treetops. When ants build a nest, the dirt that piles up around the entrance forms an anthill. An ant colony is a very busy place. It can also be very crowded. There may be hundreds, thousands, or even millions of ants in a single colony.

Some colonies have one queen; others have several. The queens are fed and otherwise tended by the workers. The males' only function is to mate with the queens.

The workers carry out such tasks as enlarging and protecting the nest, tending queens and young, and

foraging. There may be only one kind of worker, or there may be several kinds, with body structures specialized for different types of work. The activity of workers is coordinated mostly through body contact.

Depending on the species, queens live about 5 to 30 years, making them the longest-living insects. Workers live about one to three years. Males live only for a mating season.

Like most social insects, ants have three castes, or classes. There are queen ants, worker ants, and male ants. A queen does not rule the colony, but she is an important member. She has one job – to lay eggs. Without her, a colony would die out. The reason is that only the queens in most species of ants can reproduce. Worker ants may be the smallest, but they do the most work. All the workers are females. They care for the queen and her young. Worker ants build and repair the nest. They search for food and fight off enemies. Worker ants usually live one to five years.

Most male ants live only a few weeks or months. They do not work, and they die shortly after mating with young queens.

Ant colonies can grow to be quite large. Some tropical ants build downward to make more room. Their nests may reach 20 feet (6 metres) below the ground. Others, such as European wood ants, build upward. They build huge mound nests that may be 5 feet (1.5 metres) tall. Then the ants connect the mounds with scent trails. The group of nests may cover an area as large as a tennis court. Millions of ants may live in these nests.

The chambers in an ant nest have many different uses. The queen has her own chamber for laying eggs. Some chambers are nurseries for the growing young. Food is stored in other chambers. Still other chambers are resting places for hard-working ants!

The queen tends her first brood of offspring during their larval and pupal stages. This generation consists only of workers, who then take over the duties of tending the queen and her subsequent broods.

Most species of ants start a new colony in the same way. A queen ant is born in one colony, but she usually leaves that colony to start a new one. As young queens grow, they develop wings. A few weeks after becoming adults, young queens fly out of the nest to mate with winged males. The queens then shed their wings and look for nesting places.

When a young queen finds a nesting spot, she builds a chamber and seals herself inside. Then she begins to lay eggs. These develop into small, female worker ants. Some of these workers leave the nest to find food for the colony. Others build onto the nest. The queen lays more eggs. Most develop into female workers. Others develop into males and young queens.

Worker ants work and they work hard. They may have one job or several. They may keep the same job all their lives or change jobs from time to time. Some workers gather food for the colony. They store the food they harvest in special chambers in the nest. Other workers feed and care for the queen and her developing young. Still others build the chambers and tunnels. They use their saliva to make the dirt walls hard.

Some worker ants are soldiers. They defend the colony. In many species, soldier ants are larger than the other workers. The soldiers fight off enemy ants or insects. They may also use their large heads to block the entrances to the nest.

Ants go through four different stages, or steps, of growth. These stages are egg, larva, pupa, and adult. Worker ants care for the young ants through each stage.

# Check your understanding

1  What three categories of ant are there?

2  What do ants share with bees?

3  What are anthills made of?

4  How many ants may there be in a single colony?

5  What is the job of the queen ant?

6*  What examples of teamwork among ants most impress you?

# Extracting information

Ants are good examples of social animals. In other words, they live in communities. Several things are mentioned in the passage about the way they live together. In pairs go through the passage again and note down all the references to community you can find. How many of the ingredients you identified earlier are included?

# ICT project

What other examples of animals that live in communities do you know of? Choose one and do some research with a partner. Your aim is to prepare a presentation of three-four minutes, with about 15 slides, and you will both act as presenters.

## Language focus

## Active verbs

In the passage about ants the community was pictured as the insects worked together, caring for one another, defending the colony, and depending on the contribution of others for survival. This sense of working together can be conveyed by a choice of verbs that mean doing things together.

**cooperate   collaborate   contribute**

**participate   join in   share**

Can you think of any others?

All these verbs are in the active voice. In English there are two voices: active and passive.

In the active voice, someone does something. Look at the following examples of the active voice:

- The ants live in a community.
- They support one another.
- Most people dislike ants.
- They lead interesting lives.

Write down some examples of your own and share them with your neighbour.

In the passive voice, something is done by somebody. Here are some examples of the passive voice:

- The community is built up by the ants.
- They are supported by one another.
- Ants are disliked by most people.
- Interesting lives are led by ants.

See if you can turn your active voice examples into the passive.

Which voice is each of the following sentences in?

1. The community is defended by the soldier ants.
2. The queen is carefully protected by the whole community.
3. She is the one who lays all the eggs.
4. If you are tempted to despise the ant, you should think again.
5. Important lessons can be learned by looking at what ants do.

Now look back through the piece about ants and see what examples of each voice you can find. Write them down and compare your list with your neighbour.

# Life in a commune

One example of a group choosing to live together in modern times is the commune.

## Thinking out loud

There have been many attempts throughout history to create communities. What examples can you think of? How are they similar? How may they differ? Spend a few minutes considering why people form like-minded groups.

## Building your vocabulary

How many of these words do you know? Check the meaning of any you are unsure of and then see if you can use them to complete the sentences that follow.

**wardrobe    graffiti    volunteer    privacy    commodity    aloof**

**camaraderie    allocated    dreaded    hose down    organic    motto**

1  John was the first to ............................... to spend time working in the hospital.

2  Someone had covered the walls in brightly coloured ...............................

3  The ............................... where they kept their clothes was enormous.

4  In the ............................... of their own room they wrote ............................... home.

5  The ............................... helped them to relax and make new friends.

6  Only the most shy remained ...............................

7  Soap, that most basic ..............................., was in short supply, so we made do with a quick ............................... ...............................

8  Her ............................... was "Never give up".

9  We had been ............................... the ............................... 6 a.m. duty.

10  No chemicals were used on the farm so all the food was ...............................

## Show the world a better way

Tom Hudson took a year out after university to backpack round the world. After serving as a waiter in New York he tracked his way south. At every point, he records in his account of his adventures, he was made welcome and received generous help and friendship. A Texan farmer, who employed him as a warehouse odd job man for two weeks, flew him to Lima for the next stage of his journey. As he wanted to follow the Inca Trail, he decided to remain in Peru for a while, but ended up staying rather longer than he had intended...

"It was Matt who introduced me to Finca Commune. I'd failed to find work and was pretty desperate, so thought I would give it a go. "Once you've tried it, you won't want to

leave," he said. And he was right, though I didn't think so at first.

Finca Commune was just south of Lima on a fertile hillside that gave a distant view of the Pacific Ocean. As a volunteer I was shown to the men's quarters where I was allocated a bed, table, chair and wardrobe. The lack of space didn't worry me but the walls were covered in graffiti, there were no coverings at the windows and the paint was peeling.

I soon learned that these rooms were next on the list to be redecorated and very much enjoyed being part of the team that carried out that task. In fact, very little time was spent in our rooms as we only went there to sleep, or for a moment of privacy – a rare commodity in that action-packed community.

My team was truly international and the biggest difficulty was our lack of a common language. At first some remained aloof but were soon won over by the camaraderie of it all. We did everything together. The commune's motto was "Show the world a better way" and we did! Even the dreaded task of cleaning the dishwasher was fun with that group. Every two weeks the ancient machine that served the whole commune had to be taken apart and cleaned. The smell was terrible and water got everywhere, but our team made it one big water play time as we eagerly hosed one another down.

Working on the organic farm was my personal favourite. The sandy soil was not easily cultivated but under the

careful guidance of the resident expert the surrounding land had been turned into a fine example of eco-farming, producing an amazing variety of crops. It was hard work but very rewarding.

Even our free time was spent together as a team. We went swimming most days and played football in the yard. Someone organised a tournament, which, of course, we won.

And I did get to travel the Inca Trail. Four of us from the team pitched in together and made the trip to Machu Picchu...

We still meet up, once a year, in some part of the world. Last time it was London. Next year we'll meet in Tokyo."

# Check your understanding

1   What was Tom Hudson's first impression of the commune?

2   Why did he feel like that initially?

3   How did Tom's team make cleaning the dishwasher fun?

4   What sport did they play in their free time?

5   Where did Tom and his three friends visit?

6*  How did Tom's team demonstrate the commune's motto "Show the world a better way"?

# What was it like?

 **Track 3.2** Listen to the conversation of three past commune volunteers meeting up years later. Supposing you had been there when they met, what questions would you have asked them?

Write them down and swap them with your partner. Then together select the best ones and work out the replies they may have given. Take it in turns to ask or answer the questions.

## ✏ Diary entry

A different volunteer kept a diary of his time in a Finca commune and records his experiences below.

Suppose Tom Hudson had kept a diary of his experiences in the Finca Commune. He probably did. Take one of the occasions mentioned in his article and write the entry he may have made for that day. Try to include some detail about the event and some indication of his thoughts and feelings at the time.

## Monday 10th May

My turn to clear the slops, as Ziggy reminded me by upending my bed a 6 a.m. It's no one's favourite job but one that my team shared round with great delight. It had its compensations. You got to drive the ancient pick-up and were excused other duties till lunchtime. First stop today was the kitchens. Careful not to take any deep breaths, I loaded up the bins. It always amazes me how last night's wonderful meal that had tasted so good managed to stink so abominably the next day. After a quick spin round the compound to collect the rubbish of the week I sped on through the gate. The refuse pit was a few yards outside where our team had dug it just six weeks earlier. That had been a real turning point for me, just six weeks ago! My life had seemed to fall apart as I dropped out of uni and I'd come to Peru to escape.

Someone had suggested Finca commune. It seemed far enough away, so I went. I was so angry when I first arrived – with my uni, with my parents, with everyone, but most of all with myself. I spoke to no one – till Ziggy found me. "Come ... my team," he said, "we mates". He seemed to understand as he took me along. "We dig ... good" and he pushed a spade into my hand. He introduced me to the rest of the team: Fran, Tom, Ko and Abu. Only Tom spoke English but that didn't matter, we had a great time together with lots of laughter as we dug that new pit. It all developed from there ... my team, the best ever.

And there they were again this morning, standing by the refuse pit ready to help me empty the bins. A real team – hard work and such fun!

# Transferring details accurately to a form

In the Reading and Writing test, you will need to complete a form based on a text and write a full sentence or two about particular information in it. When you fill in the details of the form, you must be totally accurate with spelling and capital letters. It will help if your answers are as brief as possible. Don't forget that you may be asked to underline, circle, tick, or delete, so it is a good idea to watch out for that, too.

When you write a full sentence or two in the final section of the task, you must start with a capital letter and end with a full stop. Remember that it must be written in the first person, with inclusion of the possessive adjectives "my" and "our". Do not start with "and or but". Again, you must be totally accurate with spelling and punctuation.

Look at these four pairs of sentences below. Looking at language only, which is correct, **A** or **B**? Each incorrect sentence has two mistakes. Can you find them? What do you need to do to correct them?

**A** – John spend about a year waking in a commune in Peru.

**B** – I spent about a year working in a commune in Peru.

**A** – I worked hard to save up enough money to travel to the commune.

**B** – I worked hard to safe up enugh money to travel to the commune.

**A** – In the winter months i liked to work in doors in the dining room.

**B** – In the winter months I liked to work indoors in the dining room.

**A** – I made friends there and I still see them from time to time in London.

**B** – I made freinds there and I still see them from time, to time in London.

Now create your own pairs of sentences. One of them must be correct and the other must have two mistakes. Swap them with your partner and see if you can spot and correct the mistakes.

Now look at another account of life in a commune. This one is written in the third person, as "he" and not "I". Of course, when you complete the form you have to imagine that you are John and write in the first person.

*John Parry saved up enough money for a year in Peru and spent 12 months in a commune.*

*When he first saw his commune volunteers' room, he thought that he had made a big mistake. There was just a bed with a sheet, a table, chair and a small wardrobe. The walls were covered in graffiti and there were cracks in the uncovered windows. In the weeks that passed, as he began to enjoy himself more, he discovered that he spent very little time in his room anyway.*

*New volunteers did not have a choice of what job they did; people were put where they were most needed and new volunteers usually started in the dining room. John thought it was great in the winter months because you could have lots of hot tea and cakes, and listen to the radio as you worked.*

*In return for working hard everything was free for a volunteer in a commune, including food and accommodation. Volunteers were taken on trips every three or four months, paid for by the commune. Places that John went to included Miraflores and Lima and he was also given time off to travel to Machu Picchu – but he had to pay for that one himself. The worst part was that he had very little pocket money.*

*The social scene was fantastic. There were always barbecues going on, national holidays and weddings when everyone was invited for free food and dancing. For John the best part of being a commune volunteer was the atmosphere at social gatherings when there were around 300 people having a good time.*

*John made friends there that he still keeps in touch with and meets up with even now he is back in London.*

## VOLUNTEER FEEDBACK FORM

Name ...............................................................................................

Male/Female (please delete) .............................................................

Where did you work? ........................................................................

For how long? ..................................................................................

What was the best part of the experience? .......................................

What did you dislike the most? .........................................................

Write one sentence from 12 to 20 words describing how you spent your free time outside the commune.

...............................................................................................

# Sample student responses

Look at the answers from students A and B below. Which one of them has the most correct answers? Where exactly did they go wrong and what would you do to correct them?

**Student A**

Name John Parry

Male/~~Female~~ ...........................................

Where did you work? Peru ...........................

For how long? 12 months .............................

What was the best part of the experience? Social gatherings

What did you dislike the most? Having very little pocket money

Write one sentence from 12 to 20 words describing how you spent your free time outside the commune.

I took a trip to Miraflores and Lima and also travelled to Machu Picchu.

**Student B**

Name John Parry

~~Male~~/Female ....................................................

Where did you work? Peru .................................

For how long? 12 moths ...................................

What was the best part of the experience? the atmosphere at social gatherings where there were around 300 people having a good time

What did you dislike the most? no money

Write one sentence from 12 to 20 words describing how you spent your free time outside the commune.

Tom went to Miraflores and Lima and he was also given time off to travel to Machu Picchu and other places.

# School as community

Track 3.3 Listen to the interview with a headteacher and choose the correct answer to each of the questions below.

## Check your understanding

1 The head thinks that academic success is:

   A  interesting

   B  important

   C  not very important

2 Dr Reese says that the language project is:

   A  expensive

   B  one he is involved in

   C  one he likes

3 The students involved in the project have been helping:

   A  younger students

   B  older students

   C  the headteacher

4 Who is asked to help new students?

   A  The language team

   B  New students help one another

   C  Senior students

5 What word best describes the students, according to the head?

   A  Intelligent

   B  Informal

   C  Integrated

## Other school or college-based communities – creating a flyer

We have heard only an extract from the middle of the interview of the headteacher. What else may show a school working together as a community? In pairs discuss other possible schemes that would show the community spirit in practice in a school or a college. Now choose one and produce a brochure or flyer to promote it, saying what is involved and how it would operate.

# Study tips

## Writing an informal letter

Writing to a friend is different to writing to the principal of your school or college. First, there will be a difference in content, the details that you write about. Most importantly, there will also be a difference in the style that you use to write. Your style will, of course, be informal when you are writing to a friend.

**Remember!** You should always be very clear about who you are writing to because this will help you to focus on the most suitable words and expressions to use.

Which of these two extracts do you think is better if you are writing to a friend or a family member?

**A** – *Good morning. I would like to write to you about a matter that is very important to me and I am seeking your advice.*

**B** – *Hi! Something really interesting has just come up and I'm sure you can help me out with it.*

Now try it yourself. Write three sentences to your principal about something that you would like to change at school. Swap these sentences with your partner and then rewrite them, with the same content, but this time to your best friend in an email. You could swap sentences with other members of your class, too. Keep practising!

Think about what you have changed and discuss this with your partner. Make a list of the most important points you need to remember when you write an informal piece to a friend or member of your family.

You are going to write an email to your best friend who is studying at another school.

1  Write **two** sentences in your introduction.

2  Write a paragraph about a recent event at your school.

3  Write another paragraph giving your opinion about it.

4  Write **two** sentences to finish the email.

## Sample student responses

Here are some words and expressions from emails written by three different students. Which student do you think has chosen the best style and register for an email to a friend? Which one is probably the least appropriate? Now make some bullet point notes with brief comments on the good points and the bad points of each student's response.

**Student A**

*How's it going?*

*To tell you the truth …*

*You won't believe what happened …*

*You should have been there …*

*It was awesome!*

*Write back soon!*

**Student B**

*I send you my greetings.*

*Firstly I want to inform you that …*

*In addition, I would like to state …*

*I was very sorry that you could not attend …*

*In my opinion …*

*I have to finish my email now.*

**Student C**

*How are you?*

*I really believe that …*

*The best part was when …*

*It was a pity that you were not there …*

*It was very interesting …*

*That is all I have to say about my story.*

# Life in an African village

## Building your vocabulary

Do you know these words? Check their meanings and make a note of any that you are unfamiliar with. Then fill in the spaces in the sentences that follow.

**traverse    tilling    creek    protein    kiln-dried    infrastructure    sanitation    sparingly**

1   The queues of patients to be immunized against typhoid ................................ the village square.

2   The sun had so scorched the area they were ................................ that the lush grass had disappeared and the ................................ had almost dried up.

3   The occasional portion of chicken was their only source of ................................ .

4   There were a few ................................ – ................................ brick houses but, with no ................................ and no ................................, they were just an empty shell.

5   The head said that the ban on riding motor cycles had been lifted, provided they were used ................................ .

# A visit to the village of Kitaisa, Uganda

There are not many visitors to Kitaisa, and not much that would bring them there unless they know someone living there. If you blinked, you would be through it. Most of the villagers live a distance from the main road and where they live are paths that are difficult to traverse, especially during the rainy seasons.

There are a few dukas (shops) selling oil, sugar, tea, flour, maize flour, candles, paraffin. There is no petrol station, but one will find a school and a small government hospital. But there are no doctors, just a few nurses and medically trained staff.

It is still early and most people are outside cooking their meals over firewood. Children in uniform and without shoes are going to school, making their way through muddy paths from the night's rain.

You can see some picking beans, or tilling the ground around maize plants. Some children are carrying water from the nearby creek. People are sitting outside having breakfast. Children will have porridge, the family will eat leftover posho, or plantain bananas called matoke. Meat is not often eaten, protein comes mostly from beans.

Here life is tough, there is simply a lack of everything. Some chickens are running around and I am told that they are basically for eggs, though one was caught and given to me for later.

There is a lot of land around, much of it cultivated, since just about everyone grows their own food and vegetables.

Mom Mustala owns her land and her home made of kiln-dried bricks. There are two rooms, one to sleep and one to sit, there is no TV and no radio. A mobile phone is on a small table.

Grandchildren are running in and out of the house, playing with a very worn soccer ball; their clothes are very shabby but clean. One woman is washing clothes.

Many children are not in school, since there is no money for school fees and no government school nearby.

Life here is very simple. There is no library here, no newspapers. There was a little restaurant with some outside chairs, a beauty shop, and about eight places where food and other supplies were sold.

People in villages don't live long for the most part, since there is no infrastructure here. There are no ambulances, and if you do get sick there is no money to pay for treatment. The nearest pharmacy is 15 kilometres away in Busunju, but even that larger town lacks facilities, though a medical clinic is there with a doctor, unlike the small facility in Kitaisa which has few things.

Other obvious problems are with water and sanitation. Water taken from creeks should be boiled and treated. It is not and because it has to be carried from a distance it is used sparingly. Children become ill with diseases that could be prevented through the use of soap and water.

There are no jobs in the village, except cultivating your garden. You can try selling food along the road, but there is no way to make money. You learn to live on little and to make every shilling count. Some support comes from relatives and if you visit someone in the village, you bring those things that they do not have and when you leave you leave them some cash.

Village people in Uganda are friendly and hospitable. They are kind and show their graceful ways to outsiders. Kids hover, adults greet you like they have known you for ever.

An open-air market sold fish, shoes, plastic tubs, and basins. Roasted meat was being cooked. There was music, laughter, shouting, people trying to buy something cheap. Kitaisa was alive and, if you had money, you could buy something just for you.

The people waved goodbye as I headed back to Kampala.

Source: www.kabiza.com/kitaisavillageuganda.htm

# Check your understanding

1 What is the most likely reason for people to visit Kitaisa?

2 What do the village children usually have for breakfast?

3 What is the main reason villagers keep chickens?

4 Where is the nearest doctor to be found?

5 Why is water little used?

6* "Here life is tough" – what evidence can you find in the passage to support this?

## What would you do?

The people of this village are a very deprived community. Imagine it becomes the target of a special international campaign to improve the lives of the inhabitants. Large amounts of money are made available to fund the project. If you were in charge of the project, what would you do? With a partner, discuss what needs to be done. Consider the following needs:

● health

● sanitation

● education

● employment

● entertainment.

The aim is for you to work out a plan. This should include descriptions and drawings, and a short statement saying why what you suggest is needed and what changes it will bring about.

# Village life in Peru

A group of students from the USA had the opportunity to find out about a very different village community when they travelled to Peru. On the following pages is part of their account of what they found.

## Building your vocabulary

Do you know these words? Check those you are unsure of and then complete the crossword.

subsistence    surplus    reputation

designated    timid    adobe

1 Providing the bare essentials for living

2 Fame

3 What is left over

4 Shy

5 Indicated

6 Mud brick

# Village life in the Andes mountains

*by Jerrell Ross Richer*

The Andes mountains are home to tens of thousands of small villages, where families live and work much as they have for centuries, even millennia. Subsistence farming is the common profession. Sometimes people grow enough potatoes, corn or *habas* beans to produce a surplus to sell in the market. But often they simply grow what they eat and eat what they grow. The food is natural and healthy — chemical fertilizers and pesticides are expensive and have not reached the remote areas. Rural electrification projects have connected many of these places to the regional grid. But the expense of electronic gadgetry and the strong sense of community mean that on a given afternoon villagers are more likely to gather in the market or compete on the soccer field than they are to stay home entertaining themselves with television or the internet. Life in these mountains is simple, friendly and bound by tradition.

To get a glimpse of village life in a remote part of the Andes, we travelled eight hours to a place called Colquemarca. The village has a "wild-west" feel to it — people here wear leather boots and felted, broad-brimmed hats. Many small, informal gold mines dot the landscape. The name Colquemarca is Quechua for "money place" and people have been finding gold in these hills since the Spanish arrived in the 16th century. Horses are quickly giving way to motorcycles, but you can still see people riding into town on horseback for Sunday market. This region has a reputation for frontier justice; disputes between rivals are traditionally settled in the fighting ring during specific times of the year — both men and women participate in these refereed, full-contact duels.

We planned a long weekend trip to Colquemarca. We loaded up the bus with enough clothing and water for three days, a dozen over-sized loaves of bread as gifts for our hosts and the kind of excitement that comes whenever one is trying something new — and is not exactly sure what to expect. Our trusted driver, Hugo, started up the engine of his Brazilian-made, 34-passenger Volkswagen bus and we began the slow climb up, down, up again, then down again until we finally reached our destination.

As we approached Colquemarca, students were divided into pairs and we began dropping them off at designated meeting points. Two-by-two, the students greeted their admittedly timid hosts and then followed them back to their homes — small adobe buildings tucked between fields with commanding views of the broad, fertile valley. Most of the students soon realized that they had been given the best room in the house; their host parents or siblings would sleep in another room during their visit. The students also received the biggest portion of potatoes, corn, beans, perhaps even beef, when meal time came. A general observation, which was certainly true in Colquemarca, is that the more humble the family, the more generous they become when guests arrive.

On the Sunday we all met up for a *mesa compartida* (shared meal). The women laid out large mantas (woven blankets) on the ground and one-by-one poured cooked potatoes, *chuño* (dried potatoes) and other foods directly onto the growing pile. Following our meal together, the leader announced it was time for dancing, an indoor activity that is popular during the heat of the day. As special guests, the students found themselves invited to dance over and over again. There were many willing and able participants ... of all ages. As the sun settled into the western sky and the temperature cooled, we said our goodbyes and headed back to the village commons for the final activity of the day: a community soccer game!

Source: www.goshen.edu/peru/
2013/02/06/village-life

# Check your understanding

1 What is the villagers' favourite afternoon entertainment?

2 What is the meaning of the village name Colquemarca?

3 What were the buildings made of?

4 Who were the most generous hosts?

5 Why were the students repeatedly invited to dance?

6* "Life in these mountains is simple, friendly and abound by tradition" says the writer. What examples of these does he mention?

 Writing a letter home

Pretend you are one of the students visiting this remote community. Write a letter home saying how you feel about the experience. Make sure you cover the three areas below:

- the journey there

- the contrast to how and where you live

- how this experience will change your life, and maybe the life of the villagers you visited.

## Key skills

## Comparing and contrasting

Kitaisa and Colquemarca are very different communities. In pairs, see how many points of comparison you can find. For each village compile a list of words and phrases that have been used to convey similarities.

Now do the same, but look for differences, and how these have been conveyed.

When we make comparisons we are in effect placing the things we are comparing side by side so that the similarities and differences can be seen. But the comparison has to be made and that can be done using a variety of expressions, such as:

| on the one hand | on the other hand | alternatively while |
| with regard to | in many ways | whereas |
| by contrast | nevertheless | the reverse is |
| similarly | on the contrary | true |

Look at the following sentences where comparisons and contrasts are made and see if you can supply the missing words or phrases from the list you have just read.

1 While on the one hand the mountain village had good views, .................. / .................. / .................. / ............. the one in the valley was more easily reached.

2 .................. the old city was famous, the new town had better facilities.

3 You may think that the island was warmer but, .................. / .................. / .................. , the mainland had more sunshine.

4 While that place is well served, .................. / .................. / .................. / .................. of the other.

Now go back to the comparisons you were making between Kitaisa and Colquemarca and in pairs swap sentences comparing and contrasting those villages, making use of a variety of expressions of comparison.

## Suffixes and superlative adjectives

The comparative degree is formed by adding the suffix "–er" to shorter words and "more" before longer ones.

> Michael Johnson was fast, but Usain Bolt is *faster*.

> John was *more successful* than Kevin.

This is used for describing the extent of similarity or difference between two things. Where more are being compared, the superlative degree of adjective is used. The superlative is formed by adding the suffix "-est" to shorter words and "most" before longer ones.

> Usain Bolt proved he was the *fastest* by winning the Olympic title.

> John was the *most successful* athlete in his class.

There are a few irregular forms that have to be learned:

|  | Comparative | Superlative |
|---|---|---|
| little | *less* | *least* |
| good | *better* | *best* |
| bad | *worse* | *worst* |

Adverbs can also be used in the comparative or the superlative. These are always formed by the addition of "more" or "most" before the adverb.

> Usain Bolt ran the first fifty metres *more quickly* than his rivals.

> John competed *most successfully* in the sports events.

Negative comparison can also be stated by adding "less" or "least" before the adjective or adverb:

> Usain Bolt ran *less quickly* in Rome than he did in London.

> Alan was the *least successful* in his class.

Rewrite each of the following so that the superlative form of adjective or adverb is used.

1    David was good at art, while his brother was a skilful footballer.

2    The train to Dubrovnik travelled quickly.

3    She tried hard but her results were bad.

4    Oslo is cold in December but warm in the summer.

5    It was a beautiful picture.

# Literary connections
## Community settings

Our literature is full of descriptions and accounts of society and community life.

The community that characters belong to is often the incidental background to the storyline: life at Hogwarts in the Harry Potter books, for example, or the harsh conditions in Katniss Everdeen's District 12, "where you can starve to death in safety", in *The Hunger Games*.

Have you read any of these? What other examples can you think of from your own reading? In small groups, discuss the examples that you come up with.

## *Lord of the Flies*

William Golding's novel *Lord of the Flies* tells of a group of boys who are survivors of a plane crash. The uninhabited island that they land on is full of good things for them to explore and enjoy. The civilized world of grown-ups is a remote memory for them as they try to set up an ordered society. They are going to have fun as they wait to be rescued. But things quickly go wrong. They have good intentions … but communities aren't built on good intentions! In the pre-tech late 1940s their whereabouts are unknown to would-be rescuers and their hopes of survival diminish as all attempts to construct a society break down. Instead of forming a community helping one another, they become savages, hunting and killing and setting fire to the island. The blaze is seen by a passing ship and help finally arrives …

The officer looked at Ralph doubtfully for a moment, then took his hand away from the butt of the revolver.

"Hullo."

Squirming a little, conscious of his filthy appearance, Ralph answered shyly.

"Hullo."

The officer nodded, as if a question had been answered.

"Are there any adults – any grown ups with you?"

Dumbly Ralph shook his head. He turned a half pace on the sand. A semicircle of little boys, their bodies streaked with coloured clay, sharp sticks in their hands, were standing on the beach making no noise at all.

"Fun and games," said the officer.

The fire reached the coconut palms by the beach and swallowed them noisily. A flame, seemingly detached, swung like an acrobat and licked up the palm heads on the platform. The sky was black.

The officer grinned cheerfully at Ralph.

"We saw your smoke. What have you been doing? Having a war or something?"

Ralph nodded.

The officer inspected the little scarecrow in front of him. The kid needed a bath, a hair-cut, a nose wipe and a good deal of ointment.

"Nobody killed, I hope? Any dead bodies?"

"Only two. And they've gone."

The officer leaned down and looked closely at Ralph.

"Two? Killed?"

Ralph nodded again. Behind him, the whole island was shuddering with flame. The officer knew, as a rule, when people were telling the truth. He whistled softly.

**Source: *Lord of the Flies* by William Golding**

# Check your understanding

1  What is the first thing the officer wants to know?

2  What does he think the boys have been doing?

3  Why is the sky black?

4  What do you think the officer means by the question "Having a war or something?"

5  At what point do you think he realizes what has really been going on?

6*  The officer sees Ralph as a little boy. What words and phrases emphasise this?

## What went wrong?

Perhaps you have read the book *Lord of the Flies*, or seen the film. If you have, explain to others who may not have read it what it is about and what you thought of it. Even if you don't know the whole story there is enough in this extract to give some clues. "No grown-ups" should have been an opportunity for the boys (aged from about 6 to 13) to "have fun and games". It wasn't!

Discuss what you think went wrong.

## Research

Choose a book you have read recently and see what you can find out about its social setting and background. What kind of society is being described? Where and when does it take place? What picture is presented of the community? How does it differ from your own?

Make notes as you go along and write up your conclusions for a class/group folder on the subject "Story settings".

## Writing a story of your own

A group of children aged from 8 to 11 are mistakenly left on their own for a day. With a partner, tell the story of what happens. Here are some suggestions for you.

- It doesn't have to be a disaster but think about the effect of there being no adults present.

- How they come to be left on their own may be part of your story but equally you may want to begin at the point where they begin to realize it.

- Try to bring about a successful ending.

# The Big Issue – do the jobs people do create a sense of community?

## Community-based jobs

In pairs, make a list of some of the main jobs required for a community to be fully functional and cooperative. These are jobs that you feel contribute to the sense of community and are therefore useful jobs. So perhaps consider:

- what it involves – what that person does; how it fits into and benefits the community

- the kind of person it would suit – age, experience, temperament

- the kind of person who would probably not be interested in such a job.

# ⬤ Debate

Some jobs are useful. Others are essential. Some may be considered to be self-promoting. Let's have a debate about these ideas.

As a class, share your list of occupations you feel are important to the well-being of a community.

Now spend a few minutes drawing up a list of very different jobs that you feel do not contribute to the well-being of a community.

Your teacher will now split you into two teams and you will have a debate.

## Study tip

## Speaking – the role of the warm-up

As a reminder, this is how the Speaking test will operate:

**Part A** – the teacher will start the recording and explain briefly to you how the test will run. Even if you know all of this, the moderator will need to hear it also. The moderator is the person who checks that the test has been carried out properly and that your speaking skills have been assessed accurately.

**Part B** – there will be a two to three minute warm-up phase (and we will talk about this in a minute).

**Part C** – based on the warm-up, the teacher/ Examiner will select one of the ten topic cards that he/she thinks will work well for you. You will then have two to three minutes to study the topic (and to ask questions about the topic card so that you understand what to do). The recording will be paused while you do this.

**Part D** – the discussion begins, and you will work though all five prompts on the card in sequence with the teacher/Examiner, both adding your own ideas to develop them. You can take six to nine minutes to complete this phase.

The warm-up – Part B – is therefore a very important part of the process. It serves to fulfil two objectives:

1   To place you at ease and to settle you in.

2   To seek out an area of interest you have that may correspond to a similar area on one of the topic cards.

Let's talk here about what your role is in the warm-up and how you could approach it.

Here are some helpful points to remember:

1   Don't talk too much about school, or school subjects, or teachers! This is not likely to settle you down or give an indication about which topic may work well. It is better to talk about the course you would like to take at university or the job or career you would like to follow when leaving school.

2   Don't talk about very specific topics either. Keep it general. Focus on your hobbies and interests. What you do outside of school. What you do at home. Things you like and things you dislike – the latter should help the teacher/Examiner avoid an unsuitable topic.

3   Use the warm-up to relax. Keep it chatty and conversational. Try to smile and take it easy!

The warm-up is *about you*. It's a chance for you to let the person opposite you know who you are, what you like to do in your spare time, and perhaps what your views about certain things are.

With your partner, practise a warm-up. Each of you should take it in turns playing the Examiner. Remember: Focus on hobbies, interests, likes, dislikes, and your views. Time yourselves and make sure you stay within two to three minutes. Short warm-ups and long warm-ups are both counter-productive – that is, they both make Part D (where you are being marked) harder than it should be.

Now for some fun: Conduct a warm-up with your teacher. Select a panel of five students from your class who will speak to your teacher about his or her interests "outside of school". But before you do this, draw up a secret list of five topics that the teacher hasn't seen, and after the warm-up choose the topic that you think will work best if you were to go ahead and conduct a Part D with your teacher.

# Sample student responses

Here are three excerpts from warm-ups. With your partner, decide which topic you would give to each student. You have these three topics available:

1  Human nature

2  Journalism

3  The outdoor life

## Student A

I like swimming, football, and basketball. So I guess I'm quite sporty. I nearly always play some kind of game outside when I can. I'm not really an inside person, like my brother. He plays on his laptop all the time. When I'm not doing sport I like music – playing music that is. I play the guitar in a band. If I'm doing that I'm happy to be indoors though.

## Student B

I read. It's all I do. I read lots of books. I read a book a day. I don't do anything else. I just read. I know all about literature – old and new. But my favourite genre is the gothic novel. I know it's a bit obsessive but I'm addicted to books. I try to watch some TV but I never seem to finish a programme before I pick up another book.

## Student C

I don't really have any hobbies. I just tend to hang out with my friends. I'm happy to spend time at home, or to go out. I know what I don't like though. I don't like reading. I prefer to watch films I guess. I prefer to go to cafes and talk to people. I really like people-watching – you know, observing how people look, what they do, how they interact with other people. I think I might be a junior psychologist.

If there seems to be no area of interest that a student has that relates to any of the topic cards, then a teacher/Examiner will choose a random card, or a topic that is not too specialized. This is fine, as some people don't have particular hobbies or interests. But – the topics should not be chosen at random all of the time.

# Reflections

Working in small groups of four or five, you are going to design your own perfect little community. This chapter should have given you some ideas about what makes a community bind itself together, and also what makes different communities unique.

What kind of community do you want? Discuss this in your group first.

Think about the place where your community will live and decide what you want to use different zones or areas for. Remember, the object is to build the perfect community.

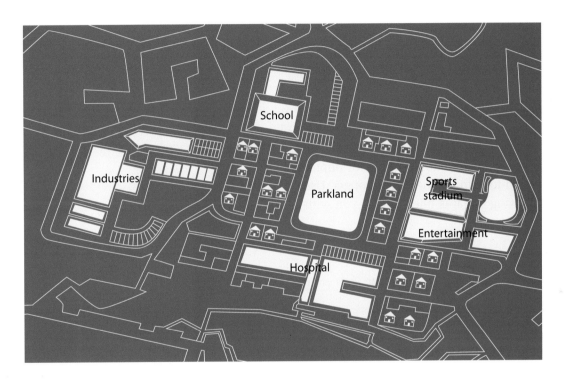

You need to give some thought to where you will place schools, housing, parkland, hospitals, industries, entertainment facilities, a sports stadium and so on.

Give thought, too, to how this is going to function as a community. Your design must create an easy and stress-free place to live!

You can choose to present your perfect community in a variety of ways. You may like to use some computer software, or you may just sketch out your community on a large piece of poster paper. We'll leave that to you and your teacher to decide.

Don't forget to give your community a name. It will be interesting to compare each group's idea of what a perfect community comprises of.

 **My progress**

Each chapter includes four study skills. These are skills that will feature in your final examinations. So let's check your progress with these key skills in mind.

| Where am I now? | Very pleased – I think I'm good at this | OK – but I do need more practice | One of my weaker areas – so I need a lot more practice |
|---|---|---|---|
| Recognizing the different types of question on the Listening test | | | |
| Transferring details into a form with precision | | | |
| Expressing my hobbies, interests, and views about general matters | | | |
| Using informal language and register when writing | | | |

Now pick out one skill that you would like to prioritize for improvement and produce a short action plan to help you become stronger. Use a template similar to the following – that is filled out for you with an example.

## Action plan

Skill I want to improve <u>using informal language and register when writing.</u>

- **planning** – how I will try to improve this skill:
  <u>research letter writing and diary writing</u>

- **implementing** – what I will need and what my exact strategy is:
  <u>access to some letters; maybe in a novel, or maybe some authentic letters during war time etc. Then compare them and note their similarities</u>

- **monitoring** – how I will know I am improving and what evidence I may keep:
  <u>where I find similarities, make notes and try to copy that style in my own writing</u>

# 4 Animals and us

## In this chapter you will:

- visit India, northern and eastern Europe, and the UK
- read about endangered species
- write about some unusual animals and insects
- listen to a discussion about animal welfare
- talk about your pets and other animals.

## Key study skills

- *Reading* a detailed article and taking notes
- *Responding* to the views of others and presenting a balanced view in *writing*
- *Listening* to a conversation in which two people have opposing views and opinions
- *Speaking* in response to a contentious suggestion made by someone

# Pets

## Thinking out loud

Are you an animal lover? Have you ever owned a pet? Perhaps a bird in a cage, or a favourite cat ... or maybe you have been the proud owner of something more unusual? Maybe animals are important to you in other ways. If animals are not part of your life at all, why is that?

## Conducting a survey

Carry out a survey of your class to find out:

- how many of them own a pet animal, bird, or insect
- how they came to have it
- what they call their pet
- who has the most unusual one
- what looking after their pet involves
- what they like and dislike about having the pet
- any interesting stories about their pets.

In groups of three or four, design a questionnaire. Most of the questions will need only one-word answers, or maybe a box to tick. When you are happy with your questionnaire, pass it to another group to fill out. Completed questionnaires should then be returned to the groups that devised them so that the findings can be analysed.

## Writing up the results of the survey

Now in your group write a brief report of the findings of your survey. Your report will:

- say what the survey was about and what its purpose was
- use a few diagrams or charts to show what the results were
- note any interesting, unusual, or unexpected responses
- provide a brief conclusion.

## Unusual pets – stick insects

### Stick insects

The stick insect has been entertaining and educating school-age children in classrooms for years, because of its **unique appearance** and **simple care needs**. Now, more and more people are keeping stick insects as pets at home.

These **intriguing** insects are usually around 7–10 centimetres long and can live for several years in the right conditions.

### Caring for this pet

Stick insects need tall enclosures, at least double the height of the insect, because they like to hang. They are omnivores and **thrive** on a diet of bramble, ivy, or even lettuce. These insects don't like being alone and need other stick insects for **companionship**. Their enclosures should be kept at room temperature and cleaned out weekly. Stick insects **moult** many times

before they reach **maturity** and need enough room to literally climb out of their skin.

### Is this pet right for you?

Stick insects are very **low-maintenance** and generally make good first pets for children, as long as adults are in charge of cleaning and handling duties. Special care should be taken when handling the insects, as their limbs can break easily. The species' **unique** appearance and interesting moulting **process** make them a living science **project** for anyone's home.

Source: www.animalplanet.com/ pets/other-pets/unique-pets.htm

# Check your understanding

1 Where have stick insects long been kept as pets?

2 Give two reasons for their popularity.

3 What do they eat?

4 Why do stick insects need tall enclosures? Give two reasons.

5 What is their "interesting moulting process"?

6* In what ways mentioned in the passage might stick insects "have been educating" children?

## Building your vocabulary

Do you know the words and phrases in the left-hand column? Use a dictionary to check the meaning of any that you are not sure of. See if you can match them to definitions a–j.

| | | | |
|---|---|---|---|
| 1 | unique appearance | a | *seasonal loss of coat or skin* |
| 2 | simple care needs | b | *friendship* |
| 3 | intriguing | c | *topic for study* |
| 4 | thrive | d | *looks like nothing else* |
| 5 | companionship | e | *fascinating* |
| 6 | moult | f | *requires little attention* |
| 7 | maturity | g | *cheap and easy to keep* |
| 8 | low-maintenance | h | *do well* |
| 9 | process | i | *in adult life* |
| 10 | project | j | *action* |

Now read the passage one more time. This time try to substitute a similar word or phrase for each of the words in bold.

## Thinking out loud

Would you be interested in keeping stick insects? Or perhaps you would consider giving some to a younger brother or sister? What may encourage you to consider doing so? What were your reactions to this passage? Did you find it interesting, or did you have a negative reaction?

 ## Taking part in a role play

It is your younger sibling's birthday shortly and you want to give them something interesting and unusual as a present. A friend has suggested you give them some stick insects for them to keep as pets. But your parents don't like the idea.

Some objections to the gift may include:

- Shouldn't pets be cuddly?
- Stick insects don't do anything!
- Aren't they difficult to look after?
- Wouldn't another nicer pet be a better idea?

Act out the conversation between you and one of your parents.

## Writing an advert – Stick insects for sale

Imagine that you have been keeping stick insects as pets. They have proved interesting and unusual. They have thrived and you now have several baby insects to pass to others. Using the information in the "Stick insects" article, and other research you would like to carry out, create an advertisement to go on your classroom noticeboard or in the school magazine, offering your "baby sticks" for sale.

Try to make your advertisement really eye-catching, and be sure to include:

- a drawing or picture
- a brief description of the insect – just a few interesting words scattered around the page, perhaps
- what they should be kept in, what they eat, and how to look after them
- details about the sale.

## Similes and metaphors connected to nature

One way writers try to make their descriptions more interesting and colourful is by using word pictures, or images, to help explain what they mean. It is as if they say, "To understand what I am saying, think of (the example they give). What I am describing is a bit like that."

For example: "He was very angry. His face was like thunder!"

The writer is saying: "How angry do you think he was? Think of a thunderstorm. The sky turns dark, warning us to find shelter. Any moment there will be a loud crash of thunder and the storm will be upon us. That is how angry he was. His face had darkened and any moment he was going to shout at us and we would be in trouble!"

Often these images are drawn from nature, comparing what the writers describe to things we can see around us. In particular, animals are used to make helpful comparisons.

As you read through the following list of animals, try to picture each one in your mind. What do they look like? What do they remind you of? How do you feel about them?

| | | | |
|---|---|---|---|
| ant | bat | cat | chameleon |
| dog | donkey | eagle | fox |
| hen | lion | mole | monkey |
| mouse | owl | peacock | vulture |
| rabbit | scorpion | sheep | tiger |

All these – and many more – are used in English images to add colour and interest to description.

## Similes

For example, to write "Usain Bolt ran like a gazelle" suggests speed, of course, but also gracefulness and ease of movement. The writer is saying: "If you want to know how Usain Bolt ran to win Olympic gold, picture a gazelle. It moves so quickly and elegantly with long graceful strides. He ran just like that!"

The term for this kind of comparison is **simile**. Similes always compare things using the word "like" or "as".

Another example of a simile is to say that someone is "as proud as a peacock" about to describe a person who feels pleased about something they have been successful at. This comparison suggests that a person enjoys showing off how well he or she has done. Just like the peacock displaying his tail, a person may well overdo the celebration.

## Metaphors

If we say, "John Smith was a mole in the enemy headquarters", we are suggesting that John Smith was perfectly adapted to the enemy headquarters, that he was rarely seen, but that he undermined the work he was involved with. This type of imagery is known as **metaphor**.

In a metaphor the comparison is omitted. Instead, the description is made as though the person or thing being described *is* the thing it is being compared to.

"He was a chameleon in his politics. Who he supported depended on who he was with."

Can you see the metaphor? How would you explain it?

## Check your understanding

Here are some more images making use of animals. For each one, decide what word picture the description draws. Is it a simile or a metaphor?

1  The reporters waited like vultures for the man to appear.

2  He was as cunning as a fox in his manner.

3  Tom's grandmother was a fussy old hen as she prepared his meal.

4  The team fought like tigers but eventually lost to their great rivals.

5  "You donkey!" she said. "They left hours ago."

Now try writing some word pictures of your own, making use of the animals listed earlier. Make some similes and others metaphors, labelling each to identify which is which. Share your examples with the person next to you. Which descriptions did you find most vivid?

# Talented animals

 Watch the video of a very clever dog that has been trained to help his disabled owner.

**www.youtube.com/watch?v = 4hy3aMqC0J0**

What did you think of the dog's actions? What impressed you most? Do you think you have what is needed to train an animal?

## Building your vocabulary

Here are some words and definitions that you will find useful as you read about Eli. See if you can match the definitions in the right-hand column to the words or phrases in the left-hand-column.

| | | | |
|---|---|---|---|
| 1 | cerebral palsy | a | *someone, often a nurse, responsible for looking after an invalid on a regular basis* |
| 2 | quadriplegia | b | *a UK charity that trains and provides dogs to help the disabled* |
| 3 | Labrador Retriever | c | *a place where people can stay and take part in a course or period of training* |
| 4 | Canine Partners | d | *a form of brain damage that causes paralysis* |
| 5 | Autism | e | *a breed of dog often trained to help the disabled* |
| 6 | residential centre | f | *a condition affecting a person's ability to relate to others* |
| 7 | carer | g | *paralysis of both arms and legs* |

## Meet Eli, a most talented dog

Eli's owner Lorna Marsh was born with **cerebral palsy** and is **quadriplegic**.

The six-year-old **Labrador Retriever** has mastered 360 tasks that help to give Lorna independence. Jobs done by Eli include posting letters, tucking Lorna up in bed, paying for the shopping, and unloading the washing machine.

Eli was trained by **Canine Partners**, a charity that provides dogs to help disabled people live more independent lives. Andy Cook, a trainer who runs the organization, said of Eli: "He's so full of enthusiasm and ability and he's so keen to learn he even teaches himself."

When he left the charity four years ago, Eli could perform 250 tasks but has since added more than 100 others to his **repertoire**. Some were taught by Lorna; others – including opening a pedal bin to deposit rubbish – were learned by Eli through copying human behaviour.

Other tasks mastered by Eli include helping Lorna, a 34-year-old teacher of **autistic** children, to zip up her jacket and remove her socks.

Lorna met Eli at Canine Partners' **residential centre** in West Sussex where new owners spend a fortnight getting to know their dog. Other tasks performed by the animals include removing money from cash dispensers.

## Collaborating with a partner

The 6-year-old Labrador Retriever has mastered 360 tasks that help to give Lorna independence. Work in pairs. What do you think these "tasks" may include? Make a list and see how many you can come up with. There are ten mentioned in the article to get you started. You don't need to find all 360, but see how many you can come up with in five minutes.

## Developing a conversation

Animals can help some people and can make a huge difference to their owners' lives.

With your partner, have a brief conversation and cover these three points:

- the partnership between Lorna and Eli

- examples of animals helping people you find particularly interesting, and why

- the ways in which an animal can be better, or perhaps worse, than artificial aids.

---

The bond between Lorna and Eli was sealed when – on her first night, while her **carer** was **on a break** – Lorna dropped the **remote control** that allows her to sit up in bed.

"I thought I was stuck and my mind **froze** and I couldn't remember the command to ask him to pick it up," she said.

"But he just got it and placed it into my hand. I burst into tears. For all my life I've needed someone else to help me but suddenly I saw how things would be from now on." Eli helps Lorna with a dance class she runs. He has proved particularly **adept** at giving youngsters confidence, with three children who had never previously spoken **uttering** their first words to him.

"A little boy who had never spoken walked in and said, 'Hello, Eli. How are you?'," Lorna recalled. "His mother was standing behind him and couldn't believe her ears. She just stood there sobbing."

Since it was founded in 1990, Canine Partners has helped about 400 disabled people by providing them with dogs.

However, there are about 700 applications each year. The charity hopes to deliver 70 new dogs this year and will shortly begin building a second centre in Leicestershire.

Source: *The Sunday Times* 13 January 2013

# Animals under threat

**Thinking out loud**

Some of our most interesting animals are under threat. In many parts of the world animals that once roamed freely are now confined to a few specially protected areas. Unless we do something to prevent it, soon some will disappear forever. How do you feel about this? What would you do to protect these animals? Or is it simply inevitable?

## Save the tiger

**Discussing with a partner**

One example of an animal under threat is the tiger. You are going to read about that animal's decline. Before you do that, in small groups, share what you know about tigers with one another.

## Building your vocabulary

For each of the words on the left below choose the word or phrase that most closely matches it in meaning. The first one has been done for you. When you have done this, read the article about saving tigers and you will see the words in context.

| | | | | |
|---|---|---|---|---|
| 1 | decade | a | *broken into pieces* |
| 2 | deploy | b | *illegal hunting* |
| 3 | extinct | c | *plans* |
| 4 | fragmented | d | *sub-division of* |
| 5 | habitat | e | *died out* |
| 6 | integrate | f | *a period of ten years* |
| 7 | legislation | g | *where animals live* |
| 8 | poaching | h | *put to use* |
| 9 | strategies | i | *law* |
| 10 | sub-species | j | *fit together* |

# Save the tiger!

The tiger is the largest of all cat species. It is also one of the most threatened.

There are six living subspecies of tiger: Bengal, Indochinese, Malayan, Amur (or Siberian), Sumatran and South China. The South China tiger is believed by many scientists to be extinct because it has not been seen in the wild for more than 25 years.

There are now estimated to be as few as 3,200 tigers left in the wild, mostly found in isolated groups spread across increasingly fragmented forests stretching from India to north-eastern China and from the Russian Far East to Sumatra. Wild tiger numbers have fallen by about 95 per cent over the past 100 years, and three subspecies – the Bali, Caspian and Javan – are extinct.

Poaching of tigers for skins and body parts used in traditional Asian medicines is the largest immediate threat to the species worldwide. Since the 1970s there has been an ever-increasing demand for these medicines in south-east Asia and east Asia. There are also significant markets among Asian communities in North America and Europe for tiger-based medicines.

Habitat loss due to agriculture, clearing of forests for the timber trade, and rapid development, especially road networks, are forcing tigers into small, scattered areas of remaining habitat. An in-depth analysis carried out in 2006 concluded that there was 40 per cent less tiger habitat than just a decade earlier and that only 7 per cent of the tiger's historical range remains. As a result, the numbers of wild tigers and the availability of their prey have steeply declined. This also means that tigers are increasingly coming into conflict with humans as they stray into areas close to villages, resulting in tigers and people being killed.

## World Wildlife Fund (WWF) in action

The conservation challenge is to ensure that sustained measures are implemented to reverse the tiger's current decline. WWF is working with governments, local communities, and other partners at a global, regional, and national level to deploy effective strategies that will secure and increase wild tiger populations, focusing on three main strategies.

One focus is on habitat availability, security, and quality, ensuring that the tiger will have enough well-protected and well-connected areas in which to live, hunt its prey, and breed.

Tigers are legally protected throughout their range, and any trade in tiger products is prohibited. WWF is working alongside TRAFFIC (the wildlife trade monitoring network) to investigate, expose and crack down on the illegal trade in tiger products, and to reduce markets, so that trade is no longer a significant threat to tiger conservation.

WWF and partners will continue to work with governments to strengthen existing legislation that protects the tiger, and to help integrate tiger conservation into economic development and land-use planning.

The objective is to double the number of tigers in the wild by 2022.

**Source: www.savetigersnow.org**

# Check your understanding

1 Name two regions where tigers are most likely to be found.

2 Why are tigers poached? Give two reasons.

3 What has been the main cause of habitat loss for the tiger?

4 What else is affected by this loss? Name two other, related, effects.

5 WWF is trying to halt the decline of the tiger in three ways. The first of these focuses on habitat and prey. What are the other two?

6* What reasons does the passage give, or imply, as to why this tiger should be saved?

## Language focus

### The future tense

The future tense is formed by the addition of "shall" or "will" between the subject and the verb:

"shall" is used for the first person ("I" or "we")

> I **shall** buy some stick insects tomorrow.
> We **shall** see what they get up to.

"will" is used for the second ("you") and third person ("he", "she", "it", "they")

> You **will** never run as fast as Usain Bolt.
> The tiger **will** disappear if nothing is done.

Change these sentences into the future tense:

1 My father (come) to see us. He (is) our first visitor this week.

2 He (train) guide dogs for a living. They (help) blind people to find their way about.

3 We (give) him our support. I (follow) in his footsteps one day.

If we want to emphasise what we mean we use "will" instead of "shall" for the first person.

> I **will** buy some stick insects tomorrow

means "I am determined to buy them (so don't try and stop me)."

> You **shall** never run as fast as Usain Bolt

means "I am going to do all I can to stop you from running as fast as Usain Bolt."

The emphatic future should be used sparingly.

# Planning an extended piece of writing

Did you notice how easy it was to follow "Save the tiger!"? Some of the vocabulary may have been difficult but what the article said flowed easily from beginning to end. We were told first what the problem was. Then we were told the main causes, before the main part of the article explained what was being done about it. Finally, the writer gave hope for the future that the tiger would be saved.

In other words, the article had been planned carefully. First the information was collected – from WWF records. Then this was organized into an essay plan.

See if you can work out what the writer's plan may have looked like. The beginning has been done for you.

> 1. The problem – decline of tigers worldwide (*quote details*)
>
> 2. Causes – a) poaching
>                      b) ...
>
>    ... ... ...

Or perhaps you think the writer used another means of mapping out the plan? The writer may have preferred something more visual, such as a spidergram. These types of plans are also called "mind maps" and they can be very useful in ensuring that your piece of writing flows smoothly and that you don't miss out anything important!

With a partner, research mind maps. How many different types can you find? Decide on three that you both like and then use them to make a plan for the "Save the tiger!" article.

## Writing an article for a magazine

You are taking part in a sponsored activity to raise funds for WWF's "Save an animal" campaign. Write an article for a magazine explaining:

- why the animal needs saving
- what the sponsored activity is
- how people can support the campaign.

These three topics will probably form the structure of your article, so you will need to begin by giving a brief description of the activity you have selected. Try to engage the interest of your readers by choosing an activity that will be popular and one that they will believe you can do. If it is also something that reminds people of animals then that would be a bonus.

You will want to be persuasive, so make good use of facts and figures. Statistics to show how threatened or endangered the animal is will help, and you may like to add a picture to remind your readers of what the animal looks like. End by saying clearly how people can help.

And remember to make a plan! Why not use your favourite mind map?

## Giving a short talk

You are going to give a talk on tigers based on the "Save the tiger!" article. Choose one of the following themes and make some brief notes to help with your talk.

- Tigers
- Tiger poaching
- World Wildlife Fund (WWF)

Jot down some notes, making sure that your points are relevant to your topic. When you have finished, compare notes with your partner. Discuss any differences in how you have both gone about doing this.

# Note-taking

As part of your Reading test, you will be asked to complete a note-taking exercise. This also involves some writing skill, of course, but the main skill being tested is to locate relevant notes from a long passage and to produce notes in two or three specific areas. You will be told what these areas are.

Here are some useful techniques for making notes:

- Be aware of the specific areas you are taking notes for *before* you read the article – this focuses your reading so that you scan for only relevant details in the text.

- Scan and highlight the text for relevant details. Ignore all irrelevant detail.

- Transfer relevant details in note form – full sentences are not required and are usually counter-productive.

- Make your notes as brief as possible.

- Only include one note (so one detail) on each line. You will never be required to provide two notes on one line.

- Make sure that each note refers to a different detail – so try to avoid repeating the same facts or details in separate notes.

Now let's practise making some notes based on the *"Save the tiger!"* article. The two specific areas that you will be taking notes for are given for you. Now scan the article for some notes – remember the advice and the useful techniques.

Now let's have a look at how three students completed this task to different levels of accuracy. Let's take the first specific area – threats to surviving tigers – and evaluate some responses.

## Sample student responses

**Student A**

- poaching for body parts for use in medicines
- losing their habitat
- conflict with humans

**Student B**

- poaching for skins and body parts used in traditional Asian medicines is the largest immediate threat to the species worldwide
- habitat loss due to agriculture clearing of forests for the timber trade and rapid development
- they stray into areas close to villages

**Student C**

- stealing bits of the body and skin to make people in Asia improve health
- chopping down trees doesn't help them as it's where they like to live
- people like to kill them – people need kill them to protect their families

Which of the three students do you think followed the useful techniques advice most closely? In which ways did the other two students not follow this advice? Which of the notes while not ideal were just about acceptable?

| Threats to surviving tigers | Different aspects of the work of the World Wildlife Fund |
| --- | --- |
| 1. | 1. |
| 2. | 2. |
| 3. | 3. |

# Animals being exploited

The story of Lorna and her dog is an example of human relationships with animals at their very best. Unfortunately, some people are not so kind in the way they treat animals in their care. Some of the cruellest treatment is of animals that are exploited for money. Have you come across any examples of the mistreatment of animals? How did you feel about it?

## About dancing bears

**Young bears are captured in the wild, separated from their mothers, and taught by a trainer to become dancing bears in conditions of unimaginable cruelty.**

The young animals are forced on to sheets of glowing hot metal and, in order to escape the pain, the bears alternate lifting up one paw and then another while music is played. The process is repeated again and again until the animals automatically begin to raise their paws – to "dance" – in fear of the pain, even when there are no metal sheets.

As the bears get older the trainers keep them under control by inflicting pain. They do this by putting rings through the bears' highly sensitive noses and jaws. No **anaesthetic** is used for this painful process. Chains are attached to the rings so that the trainers can control the animals, which weigh up to 350 kilograms, with only a slight tug on the chains.

The bears' claws are trimmed several times a year and their teeth broken or removed so they can't injure their trainer. The bears also suffer with an inadequate diet that usually consists of white bread, sugar and cheap fruit juices. All these cause serious physical health problems for the bears. Many also display **strange behaviour** such as swaying and pacing and **harming themselves** as they can't follow natural behavioural patterns and instincts.

Source: www.four-paws.org.uk

## Check your understanding

1  Where do the young bears come from?

2  Why are the sheets of metal painful for the bears?

3  What makes the bears "dance" even when the metal is not hot?

4  How are the bears controlled and why is this cruel?

5  What renders the bears harmless?

6*  How does the writer try to gain the reader's sympathy for the bears?

# Writing some feedback

You have just read about this cruel treatment of bears and want to express your immediate opinion about it. Respond to the article with a web page comment. You can write anything you like, but you are only allowed a maximum of 60 words to get your point across.

**Post your comment**

[                    ]

Post

## Language focus

# Words and phrases used to express attitudes and opinions

In conversation, we express our opinions in several different ways. The vocabulary we choose is one obvious way. We select words that convey not just what the thing we are describing is like but also what we think about it. For example, the same action, the training of animals perhaps, could be described as

**firm**      **cruel**      **determined**

**harsh**      **cowardly**      **disciplined**

by different speakers. Each word tells us the attitude of the speaker to what is being done.

Another way we express our opinions in conversation is **how** we speak. We may raise our voice if we are angry, while speaking quickly at a higher pitch often conveys our excitement about what we are saying. If we are not sure about something, we speak slowly and with hesitation.

There are other ways of making our opinions known, too. Try to come up with a few other ways of how we are able through our speech to express our attitudes, views, and feelings. Discuss your ideas with a partner.

Listening carefully to a speaker's choice of words helps us to understand their attitudes and opinions. One person's "revolting meal" is another's "delicious treat". As we hear them starting to shout, hesitate, interrupt, or as we notice the sudden drop in voice, we are picking up clues as to what the speaker is actually saying

and thinking that help us understand and respond appropriately.

Now, you try. For each of these five statements, what attitude or opinion do you think is being expressed? Take turns with your partner in reading them out. Try using different tones and experiment with emphasizing different words.

"This is appalling!"

"That's wonderful!"

"I'm not sure ... let me think ..."

"Is there some way of stopping this?"

"I was so upset to read ..."

And have a go at writing some of your own. Complete the following sentences to convey the five emotions:

1  *anger*      Those people should ... _____

2  *dismay*      I can't believe that ... _____

3  *surprise*      I never realized ... _____

4  *caution*      I'll try but ... _____

5  *curiosity*      I wonder if he would ... _____

Read your completed sentences out to each other and, again, experiment with how you can convey an attitude or opinion by the words you choose and how you speak

# Establishing speakers' different points of view

🎵 **Track 4.1.** Listen to a bear trainer and an animal rights objector being interviewed and answer the questions, some of which will help you detect the attitudes of both people.

## Check your understanding

1 Where is the interview taking place?

   **A** in a forest clearing

   **B** in a city street

   **C** in a television studio

2 Why is Gregor there?

   **A** to protest against cruelty to bears

   **B** to discuss the bears' diet

   **C** to be entertained by the bear

3 The bear is

   **A** holding a plastic pail

   **B** swaying to the music

   **C** eating soft food

4 How does Gregor say the bear has been trained to dance?

   **A** by being burned

   **B** by having its teeth removed

   **C** by gentle persuasion

5 Do you think Gregor wants to

   **A** congratulate Radu on his training of the bear?

   **B** suggest ways in which the training may be improved?

   **C** put an end to it?

6 Which word do you think best describes Gregor?

   **A** angry

   **B** sad

   **C** relaxed

7 How do you think Radu feels about the bear?

   **A** he loves it

   **B** he sees it as just a way of making money

   **C** he is sorry for it

8 Which word do you think best describes Radu?

   **A** frightened

   **B** defensive

   **C** apologetic

For questions five to eight, discuss with your partner why you made the choices that you did.

# The Big Issue – preservation or progress?

## Preparing for a debate

### The problem

A wild area not far from you is the last remaining example of its kind in the country. It is a haven for wildlife, supporting an impressive range of animals, birds, and insects, many of which cannot be found elsewhere. A species of water spider is a particularly rare inhabitant and the reserve is the refuge of a rare breed of warbler. But the area has been included in a major development plan for a new airport. This will relieve pressure on the overloaded city airport, provide jobs for many local people, and attract overseas investors and visitors to your country.

The Aquatic Warbler is not often seen and is under threat internationally. It is easily frightened and will fly off at the slightest disturbance. The destruction of this area will almost certainly mean that the bird will disappear from your country altogether.

The proposed new airport could be built a little further to the north of the region. But the countryside there is much more broken and unstable, including some marshland. To build the airport on this alternative site would involve much more expense. In any case, an airport on this second site would be less conveniently placed.

### The choice

The choice is between saving rare species and a wild habitat – striking a blow for international conservation – or sacrificing the endangered species for the sake of economic development.

Which side are you on? Will you be attacking the airport proposal? Or are you going to defend the proposed development?

An important life skill is to be able to understand and empathize with another person's point of view, even if it is completely opposite to your own. In a debate, you argue as strongly as you can for a particular point of view, but you do

this by understanding as much as you can about the opposing view – so that you can provide a strong counter-argument.

## Presenting your view orally

Your teacher will organize a class debate about this theme of preservation versus progress. You may not be on the side you'd prefer, that is, the side that matches your views. But, remember, it's a useful skill to be able to argue successfully for both sides of an argument, whatever your particular viewpoint.

---

### Study tips

#### Presenting your view in a piece of extended writing

In the written part of your examination, you will be asked to write an essay that takes into account the views of several people on a particular issue. Have a look at the following advice, which offers some useful techniques for you to consider when completing this type of writing task:

- Include a brief introduction and a brief conclusion.
- Use paragraphs to separate your ideas and give balance to your essay.

- You can argue totally *for* the proposal or totally *against* the proposal.

- You can also write a balanced piece if you prefer, giving both sides of the argument.

- You should use connecting phrases and linking words, such as "on the other hand", "in my opinion", and "from a different point of view".

- Try to use persuasive language to convince the reader of your opinions.

We're going to use the theme of your recent debate – but we will change the audience and the register. This time it's a piece of formal writing and it's going to be sent to someone official.

### Essay question

*The government of your country is proposing to build a new airport in a conservation area for wildlife. Write a letter to the government giving your views on the proposal.*

## Sample student responses

### Student 1

"It has come to my attention that our government is proposing to build a new airport in a beautiful conservation area. I would like to express my views on this issue.

Firstly, there is a strong argument for the construction of a new airport. The present one in the city is very busy and there are often delays at peak times. A second airport would certainly help to reduce the traffic problems. Furthermore, the proposed site is in a region where there is high unemployment. Hundreds of people would be needed to build the airport and many more would have permanent jobs working there.

However, there is a major problem because the proposed site is in a conservation area and a new airport would seriously affect the wildlife there. Some of the animals and insects would disappear and never return.

There is a possible alternative site further to the north of the country. It would be more expensive to build because the area there is very wet and unstable. However, in conclusion, I strongly believe that we must seriously

consider this option because we cannot keep destroying the wildlife on our planet."

### Student B

"I would like to write about the proposal to build a new airport.

We need a new airport because the one we have in the city is very bussy and there is a lot of trafic and too many cars. Many people could have a job there and this would help people to have more money to spend.

There is a problem with the animals and birds and insects who live there. The new airport would mean that they do not have a home and some of them would die. A speces of water spider is a rare inhabitant.

I think we could build the new airport in a different place. There is an area in the northern part of the country and we could please all the people. The people who want the airport would be happy and also the people who want to save the wildlife.

In my opinion, it would be the best idea to build the airport in the north and I hope you accept my idea."

### Student C

"Their is a very big problem in our country and that is the airport. People want to bild a new one but there is a very big problem. We have to move all the aminals out of the region. They can not live at the new airport. The water spider is an aminal that can not live at the new airport. Their will be jobs for people and they will get money. Then they will have money to buy nice things like cloths and big cars. This is a good thing for familys. The goverment will build the new airport in the place far away from the city and there will be less cars and less trafic. This is a good idea. Thank you and I hope you like my suggest."

With a partner, discuss what you feel are the strengths and weaknesses of these three pieces of writing.

Now have a go at marking each piece of writing, basing this on your own marking scheme. A marking scheme is just a way of awarding marks for positive aspects, but also recognizing areas that students cannot do fully or properly. Design a mark scheme out of 20 marks – you can split the marks in any way you like by including your own criteria. Now mark each essay. It will be interesting for you to share your mark scheme with other students.

# Animals in literature

Perhaps you have recently come across a book in which a particular animal appeared. In many stories, animals play an important role and are even the main characters of some stories. One early example that you may have come across is *Aesop's Fables*. These were simple tales in which the animals and the setting for the story became an extended metaphor for people's lives, usually to teach a simple lesson, or "moral".

**Track 4.2.** Listen to two of Aesop's fables being read out and discuss with a partner which you preferred and why. Why were animals used in this way in these stories? Can you think of situations that you could be in where these fables would be useful lessons?

## War Horse

In Michael Morpurgo's novel *War Horse* the horse is not only the principal character, he is the narrator of his own story.

Set in England and France 100 years ago *War Horse* tells the story of Joey, a handsome young horse who strikes up a close relationship with Albert, the teenage son of Joey's owner. But war breaks out and they are separated and plunged into the horrors of trench warfare in France. Both survive and are finally reunited after a remarkable series of events seen through the eyes of the splendid war horse, Joey.

The following extract comes from near the beginning of the book after Albert, much to his father's surprise, has succeeded in training Joey to pull the plough.

It was some months later, on the way back from cutting the hay in Great Meadow along the sunken leafy lane that led into the farmyard that Albert first talked to us about the war. His whistling stopped in mid-tune. "Mother says there's likely to be a war," he said softly. "I don't know what it's about–something about some old duke that's been shot at somewhere. Can't think why that should matter to anyone, but she says we'll be in it all the same. But it won't affect us, not down here. We'll go on just the same. At fifteen I'm too young to go, anyway – well, that's what she said. But I tell you, Joey, if there is a war I'd want to go. I think I'd make a good soldier, don't you? Look fine in a uniform, wouldn't I? And I've always wanted to march to the beat of a band. Can you imagine that, Joey? Come to that, you'd make a good war horse yourself, wouldn't you, if you ride as well as you pull, and I know you will. God help the Germans if they ever have to fight the two of us."

One hot summer evening, after a long and dusty day in the fields, I was deep into my mash and oats, with Albert still rubbing me down with straw and talking on about the abundance of good straw they'd have for the winter months, and about how good the wheat straw would be for the thatching they would be doing, when I heard his father's heavy steps coming across the yard towards us. "Mother," he shouted. "Mother, come out, Mother. It's war, Mother. I've just heard it in the village. Postman came in this afternoon with the news."

**Source: *War Horse* by Michael Morpurgo. 2007. Egmont**

## Check your understanding

1  How old is Albert?

2  What does Albert want to be?

3  What does he think Joey could be?

4  What is the news that breaks at this point?

5  How do you think Albert, his mother, and his father each feel about that news?

6*  Why does Albert want to be a soldier?

*War Horse* is unusual in that the events are all seen through the eyes of an animal. What the human beings think and feel is reported only indirectly. Joey doesn't have enemies in the way the people in the story do. As he is captured and eventually reclaimed, he responds to kindness from friend and foe alike. Yet he is caught up in the horror and cruelty of the fighting and proves a remarkable survivor.

## Conveying an anecdote

Animals would have interesting tales to tell if they could. A day seen through their eyes could be very revealing! Choose an animal and write a brief anecdote about something interesting that happened to them one day. Write in the first person, that is, as if you are the animal. And keep it brief – you'll see why soon.

Most anecdotes, however, are spoken – they are little stories that people tell that are intended to be humorous. Reread your anecdote and try to memorize it so that you can convey it orally.

Now tell your anecdotes to one another.

# Animals in the service of humans

**Thinking out loud** We have already seen how dogs like Eli have been trained to help their owners. Can you think of other animals that help us in various ways? The fact is that we rely on animals for a number of services. If you were to train an animal to help humans, which one would you choose?

How many different animals can you match to the services in this list? Can you add another row, covering another area where animals assist humans?

| Area where animals can help humans | Animals involved |
| --- | --- |
| security and defence | |
| delivering messages | |
| helping with hearing/sight difficulties | |
| helping the police | |
| farming | |
| providing food | |
| | |
| | |

## A very unusual little helper

## Building your vocabulary

Scan the article on the next page to check for any unfamiliar words. Use a dictionary to check their meaning, and also see if you can pair up the words 1–10 with the definitions a–j in the lists below.

| | | | |
| --- | --- | --- | --- |
| 1 | rodents | a | *strips (of ground)* |
| 2 | probing | b | *first to do something* |
| 3 | pioneering | c | *recognize difference* |
| 4 | swathes | d | *a group of animals* |
| 5 | acute | e | *an explosive* |
| 6 | TNT | f | *pests* |
| 7 | detection | g | *examining carefully* |
| 8 | distinguish | h | *keen (sense of something)* |
| 9 | deployed | i | *discovering something* |
| 10 | vermin | j | *put to use* |

A baby rat in a tiny red and black harness twitches its pointed nose incessantly, **probing** a grassy field where it is being trained by a **pioneering** Dutch organization to smell out deadly landmines.

Other rats trained under the same scheme have already helped clear large **swathes** of land in neighbouring mine-infested Mozambique.

Babette, the two-month-old baby, walks unsteadily across the weedy patch followed by two trainers rolling a bar that teaches her to go back and forth across the patch in straight lines. Light, with an **acute** sense of smell and easily motivated by food rewards, giant African pouched rats have been found to be highly effective in mine detection by APOPO, the Dutch non-governmental organization that launched the training project – the first of its kind – in this Tanzanian town.

The **rodents** are trained to detect the **TNT** in landmines through learning to respond to a click sound to signal a food reward whenever they make the correct detection. Training begins at four weeks old when the baby rats are exposed to humans to rid them of their fear of people and new surroundings, after which they are taught to associate a click sound with food.

Once that is achieved, they are then trained to distinguish TNT scent from other smells. When they successfully **distinguish** it, the click is sounded and they are given a bit of banana, thus reinforcing the link between positive TNT identification and food.

In all, it takes nine months of painstaking on- and off-field training for a rat to be **deployed** for mine detection.

"This work is not easy," says trainer Abdullah Mchomvu, holding a rat cage under his left arm. "You have to be patient. Sometimes I get frustrated, but then again I tell myself these are animals."

But "This work saves lives," he added.

It takes two de-miners a day to clear a 200 square-metre (2,150 square-feet) minefield, but if they work with two rats they can sweep it in two hours.

"**Detection** is the most difficult, dangerous and expensive part of mine action. Since rats are much easier to train than dogs, rats in this environment are much more appropriate," said Bart Weetjens, the founder of APOPO.

"They are very effective. We have very high success rates. So far they have helped re-open almost two million square metres (21.5 million square feet) of land" in Mozambique. Despite their contribution, rats are more often seen as **vermin** that spread disease and destroy harvests.

"Rats have an image problem. People don't like them and that is one of our biggest struggles," said Weetjens. "We are trying to change that perception. Rats are very sociable, very intelligent, highly likeable creatures."

APOPO calls its sniffers "hero rats" in recognition of the work they perform. The organization's website pictures rats that could be straight out of a children's story-book: all pink noses and quivering whiskers.

APOPO has even launched an Adopt-a-Rat scheme where individuals and corporations can contribute to the upkeep and the training of a sniffer rat, receiving in exchange an adoption certificate and email updates on the animal's training or career.

Weetjens said the next frontier would be to use the "hero rats" to sniff out narcotics or to search for survivors of disasters such as earthquakes or collapsed buildings.

Source: www.news.discovery.com

# Check your understanding

1 What are the pouch rats trained to do?

2 How long does it take to train the rats?

3 How quickly can they clear a minefield?

4 What is their "image problem"?

5 What measures has APOPO taken to change that?

6* Why are the rats so good at this work?

# Speaking test – Prompt four

When you take part in the discussion for your Speaking test, you will be guided by your teacher, who is acting as an examiner, through the various stages of a focused conversation. A topic will have been chosen for you and you will have had two to three minutes to think about what you may say. There are five prompts on the topic card – you can regard these as separate areas for you to talk about, all of which link together with the overall topic or theme.

Prompt four is usually a suggestion, or an idea, that you and your teacher/examiner will discuss in some depth. The aim of Prompt four is to provide an idea or suggestion that has two opposing views or opinions. You can, of course, agree with the suggestion, but you can oppose it. Whichever your view is, you need to consider both sides of the issue and talk about them objectively, and then reflect on where you stand.

Prompt four therefore tries to dig a little deeper into an issue that has perhaps been touched on in the conversation so far. It requires deeper thinking, and tests your ability to consider both sides of an argument.

Here's an example of what we mean, connected to the theme of animals and humans:

*The suggestion that some animals are better off in zoos.*

With a partner, see if you can come up with some opposing points of view for the prompt above.

| On one side … | One the other side … |
|---|---|
| • zoos can help preserve endangered species | • wild animals need to be free and in their natural habitats |
| • | • |
| • | • |
| • | • |
| • | • |

## Sample students responses

**Track 4.4** Listen to the three short samples of conversations from a typical Speaking test. With your partner, place the three responses in rank order, from the best one to the weakest one.

As you do this, discuss why you are placing them in this order.

# Reflection

In small groups, discuss some themes raised by the material in this chapter:

- animals as pets and helpers
- endangered species and how to protect animals
- the way we sometimes abuse and misuse animals
- unusual and remarkable animals.

## Writing your very own fable

Your discussion should have featured lots of examples of particular animals. Now decide on one animal – it's going to play the leading role in a fable that you will all work on together. Remember, a fable needs to convey a moral or a message. Be sure to assign particular roles to each member of the group. Some of these may be:

- the Mind Mapper – someone good at mapping out a writing plan
- the Researcher – someone tasked to find some other fables from the library or from the Internet maybe
- the Illustrator – someone good at sketching, so that the animal can be brought to life in art form
- the Moral Maker – someone who is tasked to come up with the message you want to convey
- the Action Planner – someone who designs the plot, its sequence, where the conflict is, and how it's resolved.

These are just ideas, however, and you will need to assign your own unique roles also. And, remember, a fable does not need to be very long to get its message across, so aim for something short and sweet!

 **My progress**

Each chapter includes four study skills. These are skills that will feature in your final examinations. So let's check your progress with these key skills in mind.

| Where am I now? | Very pleased – I think I'm good at this | OK – but I do need more practice | One of my weaker areas – so I need a lot more practice |
|---|---|---|---|
| Taking notes based on an article I read | | | |
| Presenting my own view in writing based on the views of others | | | |
| Listening to people with different views and working out what the differences are | | | |
| Responding orally to a strong point of view | | | |

Now pick out one skill that you would like to prioritize for improvement and produce a short action plan to help you become stronger. Use a template similar to the following – that is filled out for you with an example.

Skill I want to improve: listening to people with different views.

- **planning** – how I will try to improve this skill
  Watch some TV news reports where a panel of guests are present.

- **implementing** – what I will need and what my exact strategy is
  some DVDs to record appropriate programmes so I can watch them in my own time.

- **monitoring** – how I will know I am improving and what evidence I may keep
  keep a record of the different views I hear so I can build up a list of opinions about a range of topics.

# 5 Working life

## In this chapter you will:

- visit Uganda, Australia, and Europe
- read about some very unusual jobs and jobs related to travel
- write a letter of resignation and respond to people applying for jobs
- listen to a flying doctor, two people on work experience, and a footballer
- talk about a dream job and act out a work-based scenario.

## Key study skills

- *Reading* forms to provide useful and concise feedback
- *Listening* to a talk based on a job or career
- Improving the flow of a conversation when *speaking*
- *Writing* a descriptive letter in an informal style

# The best job in the world?

## Thinking out loud

What are your plans for the future? Do you have a career in mind? What do you think your dream job would be? Or perhaps you would like to sample a number of possibilities – what kinds of jobs appeal? What sort of things do you think you would be good at or would like to have a chance to try?

## Building your vocabulary

ultimate    craving    liaise
brand    tasting    clients
certified    budget    stint
exotic    loan shark
simultaneously    limb
don    pyjamas

All of these words appear in the passages you are about to read. Check any you are unsure of and keep a record of them. Then try using them to replace the words highlighted in the following sentences.

1   The child's **nightclothes** were an unusual **make** but well within her parents' **planned expenditure**.

2   You must **put on** your thickest rainwear and risk life and **arm or leg** to go out in this **most extreme** weather; it really is severe.

3   In spite of being a **qualified** accountant the **man who lent money at extremely high rates** misled his **customer**.

4   The **strange** food she was **sampling** left her with a **strong desire** for home cooking.

5   His **turn** at being headmaster left him to **work together** with parents and pupils **at the same time**.

## Chocolate consultant

This could well be the ultimate job for anyone with even the smallest craving for chocolate – and yes, jobs like these really do exist. There are lots of different types of chocolate consultant, too, from people who work with high-street brands and liaise directly with their outlets to people who work with more specialized brands.

Louise Thomas has worked in the chocolate industry for two years and has been passionate about chocolate for more than six years. She became frustrated by the lack of education and awareness regarding fine chocolate, so started her own company to share her love of the cocoa bean. She now runs events and tastings as well as doing consultancy for hospitality and retail, to find a particular chocolate for a client or to extend their range.

If you don't yet have what it takes to be a chocolate consultant you can still work with chocolate as a pastry chef.

## LEGO sculptor

Who hasn't at some point in their life sat down in front of a box of Lego and set about building (or helping someone else to build) a fantastic creation in multi-coloured blocks? For some people this becomes more than just something you did as a kid.

Lego has a number of certified professionals who work with the company to create sets and build models for them.

They work against fairly tight budgets and thematic constraints, and are based in Legoland Discovery Centres around the world. However, competition for the jobs is fierce, with estimates varying as to exactly how many there are in the world – from 9 to 30. The latest one to get a job was 23-year-old Andrew Johnson who submitted a clever video, and then competed in a tough three-round build-off, allegedly beating 45 other competitors.

If you love childhood toys but don't fancy building them, why not consider joining the retail sector and working in a toy shop?

## Island caretaker

OK, everyone lists this but what a job! It was advertised as "officially the best job in the world" in 2009 and involved working for the Queensland Tourism Board. The role was a newly created position designed to help promote the islands of the Great Barrier Reef to the world.

Briton Ben Southall won the job, earning £73,400 to live on an island in the Great Barrier Reef for six months, swimming, exploring, and generally enjoying himself while filming and blogging about all the fun he was having. And it didn't end there; after his six-month stint on the island, Ben went on to become Global Tourism Ambassador at Tourism Queensland.

If you're not lucky enough to land a job caretaking an exotic island, the travel and tourism industry can still take you to some pretty interesting places.

## Shark tank cleaner

Window cleaning is probably not the most fun of professions. However, add in the requirement to share your job with a bunch of sharks while simultaneously being watched by a crowd of people, all of whom are no doubt secretly hoping at least one of the sharks is feeling a little hungry, and suddenly the interest levels rise up a level or two.

However, if you don't fancy risking the odd limb, but still want to work with fish, then perhaps a career as a fishmonger would be a better choice.

## Professional sleeper

If you're addicted to the snooze button on your alarm or spend all day at your desk yawning and drinking cups of coffee to stay awake, then maybe you should consider turning your vice into a profitable career. Believe it or not, you can actually get paid to don your pyjamas and catch some Zs.

Typically, professional sleepers participate in university studies on sleep or dreams, but others make sure that beds are comfortable. In 2009 during an art show at The New Museum of Contemporary Art in New York, women were paid to sleep as part of a "living art" exhibition, so you never know where you could be asked to rest your head next.

If you enjoy your sleep, you probably want to avoid jobs that typically lead to sleep deprivation.

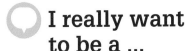

## I really want to be a ...

In small groups each member of the group should write on a piece of paper the name of the job that would complete the sentence "I really want to be ... " for them. Fold these in half and mix together in a container. Each member of the group should then pick one out. You each have five minutes to prepare to lead a short discussion on the subject on your piece of paper.

This should include:

- a brief description of the job
- why it may be interesting
- what additional information someone really wanting to be in this job may need
- places to look for that information

The person whose job suggestion this originally was should act as note-taker and then present a brief summary of the discussion.

## Developing a discussion

In pairs, look at each of the "dream jobs" described on pages 100–1 in turn and discuss:

- what you actually have to do
- what is attractive about the job
- what hidden problems there may be.

## Writing a resignation letter

Suppose you are employed in one of these dream jobs. But things are not going well! The job has not lived up to its promise and on top of that you have already received a warning from your boss. In response, send him an email. Focus on three areas:

1 Say what you had expected from the job and what problems there were in reality.

2 Make a few points about the warning you received and your feelings about it.

3 Conclude by saying why you have decided that enough is enough and you are resigning.

## Key skills – getting the gist

A quick scan of a passage can help us gain a general understanding of what we are reading (or listening to). "Getting the gist" is what we sometimes call it. But to be sure of the meaning we need to look closely at the whole passage. We need to ask ourselves what main point or points the writer is making. In particular, we need to read the final sentences carefully. Often there will be a summary of what has been said. Sometimes there may be a surprise that we could easily have missed.

For example, look at the following description of chocolate eating.

> Many people's idea of a perfect treat is to be given a bar of super-smooth, rich chocolate, preferably laced with their favourite sort of flavouring: mint, butterscotch, mocha coffee, orange, fruit and nut, or whatever. They take it carefully from the packet, break off a tasty morsel, and place it lovingly upon their tongue. Slowly they savour the moment … aah! Wonderful! But not for me. Chocolate – I can't stand the stuff.

On a quick scan we see "perfect treat", "favourite", "tasty", "lovingly", "savour", and "wonderful" and may think that the writer loves chocolate. But a close look at the last two sentences of the paragraph shows that not to be the case. With those final words, the paragraph takes on a different meaning. As we read it again, we can begin to see shades of meaning – "many people", "their favourite" – and even a hint of sarcasm. Could the writer be making fun of chocaholics?

In pairs, take it in turns to read the five job descriptions to each other. As you do so, pay particular attention to the final sentences of each one. Does that change your understanding of the meaning? Some careers advice for teenagers is being given. But what exactly is being said? With your partner, work out what the advice really is in each case. Then think about the whole passage. What are the writers really trying to convey?

## Situation vacant

The web page from which these five jobs were taken described more "dream jobs" to introduce other sorts of employment for teenagers to consider. For each one, an amazingly exciting "too-good-to-be-true" dream job was used to get readers thinking. Now it's your turn. In small groups, make up a "dream job" and produce an advert for it. Give the job a catchy title. Add pictures and a brief description. Include details of the salary and working conditions.

# The Big Issue – what job will you choose?

## Work experience

One of the best ways of finding out if a job or profession is the one for you is to try it out first. Shadowing someone in a job for a day – or longer – is a good way of doing that. Or you may be able to take part in a work experience scheme. On the following page, three young women write about their work experience weeks. Their examples give us a clear idea of some of the benefits of job shadowing and work experience, although the opportunities they had were rather special.

## Building your vocabulary

First, scan the following three case studies for any unfamiliar words. Check their meaning in a dictionary or on the Internet and then see if you can match the following words 1–10 with their definitions (a–j).

| | | | |
|---|---|---|---|
| 1 | placement | a | *checking accounts* |
| 2 | passion | b | *well known* |
| 3 | colleagues | c | *setting* |
| 4 | spreadsheet | d | *afternoon rest* |
| 5 | auditing | e | *beneficial* |
| 6 | familiar | f | *strong feeling for* |
| 7 | environment | g | *where you are put* |
| 8 | efficient | h | *people you work with* |
| 9 | rewarding | i | *working well* |
| 10 | siesta | j | *information set out in a table* |

# Case study 1

I undertook my work shadowing **placement** abroad at a music shop in Segovia, Spain.

I massively enjoyed my time there, not only because I was allowed to play whatever instrument I wanted, which satisfied my **passion** for music, and because my improvement in Spanish totally exceeded my expectations, but also because my **colleagues** were lovely and made sure I was never bored and always enjoying myself. Moreover, the experience as a whole was unforgettable because of my amazing work placement, the fabulous city I was in and also because of the friends I have made. So I would definitely recommend this trip to anyone who wants to improve their language skills, make foreign connections, truly experience a different culture, and never fail to enjoy themselves.

—Helena

Source: Halsbury Work Experience Abroad www. workexperienceabroad.co.uk

# Case study 2

During my work experience I feel like I have learned valuable information on how to work effectively in an office. Before my work experience I did not know how to use a **spreadsheet** or know what **auditing** was, but now I'm much more confident with doing these tasks. I also feel that from my work experience, I have become more **familiar** and confident with learning new skills, being **punctual**, and dressing according to the dress code. All of these factors have helped me gain an insight into the work **environment** and have given me preparation at being punctual and **efficient** at learning new skills that will be invaluable for future jobs.

I thoroughly enjoyed my experience and I am very grateful to all the staff for giving me the opportunity to work at their office and for making me feel welcome and a part of the team. Thank you.

In conclusion, I would highly recommend anybody to undertake work experience – it is an excellent way to acquire skills and experience of a work environment and will make you feel more confident for future careers.

—Naomi

Source: www.mysignppost.org

# Case study 3

For my work experience I worked in a nursery in Ravenna, Italy, for a week. Throughout the day I played games with the children, helped with mealtimes, and general tidying up tasks. Working in the nursery was so **rewarding**, at first I found it difficult to understand them, but as time went on I found myself making up games and playing them with the children. Everyone was so friendly and the children by the end were saying my name and asking to play with me! When I wasn't working there was loads to do. We went shopping, to the cinema, out to some amazing restaurants for dinner, and occasionally a **siesta** after the long day at work! Going on this trip has been one of the best experiences of my life and I am so glad I did it. I made so many new friends who will be friends for life and I am so much more confident in my ability to speak Italian and have realized I can do it and people do understand!

—Rachel

Source: Halsbury Work Experience Abroad www. workexperienceabroad.co.uk

## Study tips

## Form filling

You may already have been asked to complete some *application* forms for your school, or when you have joined clubs and societies. As you go through life you will probably join organizations, order products or services on the Internet, and fill out *feedback* forms, about your experience in a restaurant, for example. It is very important that you complete these forms in a direct way, providing only the information that has been requested and using concise sentences.

Let's have a closer look at this skill by focusing on the feedback section of a form that has been generated to gather information from the three people involved in the case studies.

But before you look at these, discuss with a partner which types of questions in general you could ask to gather feedback. Ideally, you would restrict responses to single words or to short sentences as you will need to collate the responses you get and turn them into data.

Now reread the case studies, and draw up a list of ways that you could obtain feedback if you were to design a form.

## Sample responses from students

Here are three forms that have already been filled out based on the case studies. Which do you think provides the most useful and appropriate feedback? How would you improve the feedback given in the other two forms?

**WORK EXPERIENCE FEEDBACK FORM – Student A**

Name     Helena

Where did you work?     In a shop

Please list two issues, concerns, or problems.
There weren't any – it was fab.

Write a sentence about the benefits that you gained from your work experience.
I really loved it. I made friends, and I felt really comfortable out there.

Explain why you would or would not recommend your placement to others.
I would definitely recommend this experience to others.

**WORK EXPERIENCE FEEDBACK FORM – Student B**

Name     Naomi

Where did you work?     In an office

Please list two issues, concerns, or problems.     1. I lacked
confidence   2. I wasn't always punctual   3. I didn't know what to wear.

Write a sentence about the benefits that you gained from your work experience.     I learned how to use a spreadsheet

Explain why you would or would not recommend your placement to others.     People can learn how to use spreadsheets
and they can also gain confidence.

**WORK EXPERIENCE FEEDBACK FORM – Student C**

Name     Rachel

Where did you work?     In a nursery in Italy

Please list two issues, concerns, or problems.     1. At first,
communicating with the children  2. A lack of confidence initially in
my use of Italian

Write a sentence about the benefits that you gained from your work experience.     I developed my skills in using game playing as a
teaching tool and I got lots of experience of engaging with young children.

Explain why you would or would not recommend your placement to others.     A placement in another country can help
boost your confidence as well as help you broaden your base of friends
and colleagues.

# Check your understanding

**1** Who had a good time on his work experience placement?

A Pete

B Jon

C Remi

**2** Jon's guide for the week was

A Remi

B Lecto

C he didn't have one

**3** Lecto's are best known for

A producing parts for Formula One

B their repair workshop

C their designs

**4** What best describes Jon's experience?

A disappointing

B quite interesting

C memorable

**5** What do you think Pete's experience was like?

A disappointing

B quite interesting

C memorable

## Pete's work experience – role playing

We never hear about Pete's work experience but we are given clues as to what it was like. Listen again to the conversation and in pairs identify as many clues as you can as to what it was like and discuss what may have led him to feel as he did.

Now have a go at continuing the conversation. One of you will need to be Pete and the other, Jon.

## Language focus

### The language of work

The language of work is sometimes very difficult to understand without careful explanation of the *idioms* used. For example, to say that someone has "started on the wrong foot because they are under the weather" is a way of saying that they have not begun something properly because they are not feeling very well.

Sometimes the meaning can be worked out from the literal meaning in the original context in which it is being used. So "starting on the wrong foot" sounds like a mistake in dancing – begin with the wrong foot and you feel very awkward and may have to start again. In the context of work the phrase is particularly used to indicate an awkward beginning. Being late for your first day in a new job is one way of starting on the wrong foot.

What do you think "under the weather" means? Can you work it out?

Each of the sentences below contains an idiomatic phrase. See if you can identify the phrases and work out what they mean.

1 As it was getting late and they were tired, they decided to call it a day and go home.

2 You must learn to think outside the box if you are going to have the sort of unusual ideas our company is wanting.

3 After a series of bad reports and failures, he was given his marching orders. It was the second time he had lost his job.

4 Our manager wears many hats: she is chair of the social committee, designer of the firm's website, and our representative on the local council as well as being the director's wife.

5 You made the mistake. You must face the music!

How many more of these types of idioms, connected to working life, can you think of? Ask a friend to help you and aim to find at least five more.

# A day in the life of...

## Thinking out loud

What might a typical day at work be like? How might it differ from your current daily routine? If you have a job already, reflect on a typical day at work. Are you happy with your work? What would you change about it to make it more rewarding?

## Building your vocabulary

For each of the words below choose the word or phrase that most closely matches it in meaning. The first one has been done for you. When you have done this, read the following accounts of two very special working lives and you will see the words in context.

| 1 | domestic work | a | household cleaning and maintenance |
| 2 | outreach | b | things offered |
| 3 | counselling | c | place |

| 4 | reviewing | d | friendly and welcoming |
| 5 | dedicated | e | providing services |
| 6 | location | f | encouragement |
| 7 | facilities | g | committed |
| 8 | Aboriginal | h | giving advice |
| 9 | hospitable | i | checking through |
| 10 | promotion | j | suitable position |
| 11 | niche | k | of native Australians |

## A social worker

Rose is a social worker in Patongo, Northern Uganda. Like many women across Africa, she wakes at 5:30 am to fetch water for her family, she makes breakfast, and gets her two daughters ready for school. She then does an hour of **domestic work** and puts the food for the day on the fire to cook slowly while she is out at work. At 7:30 she leaves for Patongo Counselling Community Outreach (PCCO), a five-kilometre walk. Once there, she spends half an hour talking to other social workers about the day ahead. Then she's off to her first **outreach** group. Rose spends about three hours with each group every day (except market day), offering **counselling** and **reviewing** their savings associations' progress. She says the community understands the benefits of counselling and people tell her they are grateful for her efforts. Rose says that her job makes her "happy from my heart. Being a counsellor is like a doctor doing an operation on clients that always has a good outcome." The PCCO office is supposed to close at 5 p.m., but Rose and the other **dedicated** social workers often see clients in the evening. To them, this is more than a job. As Rose says, it is an opportunity to "work on people's hearts to make change".

**Source: www.network4africa.org**

## Check your understanding

1 What organization does Rose work for?

2 How long does each counselling session take?

3 What does she help people with?

4 Why does she work some evenings?

5 What does Rose like about her job?

6* What might the timetable for a typical day for Rose look like?

## A counselling session

With a partner, talk about Rose's day. Discuss what a counselling session with her may be like. Recreate a session she may have with one of the clients she sees in the evening. Act this out.

## A flying doctor

**Track 5.2.** Listen to Ceinwen Rataj, a health training officer with the Royal Australian Flying Doctor Service, as he tells us about his work.

## Study tips

### Listening to a talk based on a job

Your Listening test will feature people giving talks. A talk can be given by someone for the purpose of providing specific information about a subject, or it can be to inform a listener or an audience about what the person does or is interested in. Let's practise the latter. The previous talk given by Ceinwen was about his life including his previous jobs, but mostly it is about the work he is currently doing.

In the Listening test, you will be asked to complete some sentences by adding one or two words – and no more than two words. We'll use Cienwen's talk to practise this particular skill. Listen to him again and fill in the missing words. You can use the exact words he uses, or you can use your own words if you feel they have a similar meaning. But remember that after you have added your words, the sentence must make sense.

1   Before working with the Flying Doctor Service, Ceinwen was a .............. and he also ...............

2   With the project officer, Ceinwen provides free .............., first aid training, and ...............

3   Recently, their services have been offered at two .............. and three exploration ...............

4   Two aspects of the job that Ceinwen does not like are the .............. and the ...............

5   By working in health ............... in particular, Ceinwen feels that he has found the ideal ...............

### Sample responses from students

Let's have a look at three responses to Question 1:

**Student A**

A   Before working with the Flying Doctor Service Ceinwen was a   an overseas worker   and he also   Australian .

**Student B**

B   Before working with the Flying Doctor Service Ceinwen was a   educator   and he also   worked in the building industry .

**Student C**

C   Before working with the Flying Doctor Service Ceinwen was a   house builder   and he also taught.

Discuss these three responses with a partner. Which is the best response? Would you mark any of them as being wrong? Why?

Now have a go at the same task but with three answers to Question 4.

**Student A**

A   Two aspects of the job that Ceinwen does not like are the   long distances   and the   flying

**Student B**

B   Two aspects of the job that Ceinwen does not like are the   long hours   and the   heat and flies

**Student C**

c)   Two aspects of the job that Ceinwen does not like are the   high temperatues   and the   insects

Now have a go at providing some responses to the other three questions that you think are interesting – that is, that you think are close attempts that may be correct. Pass these to your partner to mark them. This should provide a useful discussion for you both about acceptable and unacceptable responses.

## A special guest

Ceinwen is on a holiday trip to your country and your school has invited him to come and talk about his work with the Royal Flying Doctor Service of Australia. Your class has been selected to act as hosts for the occasion and one of you will have the task of interviewing him.

1   *Prepare* to meet this special visitor – invitations will need to be designed.

2   Discuss what the *programme* for the afternoon should be – should it be formal or informal? What else might you include?

3   Agree on a *set of questions* to be put to the guest.

4   Prepare a talk *welcoming* the special guest.

# Jobs involving travel

## Thinking out loud

Some careers appeal because they offer the chance to travel and see the world. Would you like a job that gives you the chance to go to other countries? Or are you a person who prefers to stay at home perhaps? Think about some of the advantages and challenges of working in another country. How well do you think you would cope?

## Building your vocabulary

Do you know the meaning of these words from the passage you are about to read? Check any you are unsure of and then see if you can fit the words below into the crossword spaces.

globe          capable          tend to          permanent

relate          emergencies          struggling

relief convoys          gratification

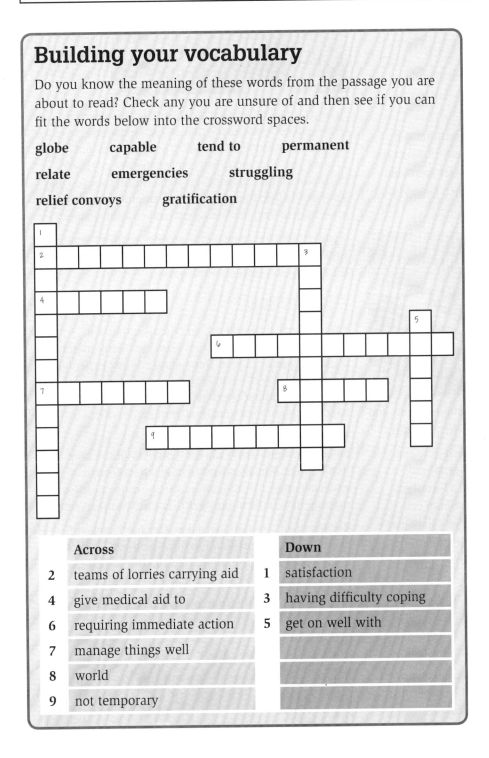

| | Across | | Down |
|---|---|---|---|
| 2 | teams of lorries carrying aid | 1 | satisfaction |
| 4 | give medical aid to | 3 | having difficulty coping |
| 6 | requiring immediate action | 5 | get on well with |
| 7 | manage things well | | |
| 8 | world | | |
| 9 | not temporary | | |

# Careers for travellers

When you think about travel jobs, the travel industry (pilot, flight attendant) probably jumps to mind, but there are also many not-so-obvious career options for people who like to get around. We've searched the **globe** and found some of the best careers for people who love to travel.

## Nurse

These days, good nurses are in high demand and short supply. That nursing shortage can work to your advantage if you're trained and **capable**.

You could always get a job at your local hospital, but then you'd be dealing with the same responsibilities and working with the same people every day. Or you could travel around from one hospital to another, caring for people in many different cities.

Travel nurses temporarily fill open positions wherever they're needed. You may **tend to** a jellyfish sting in Hawaii one day and nurse a broken leg in Aspen the next.  Labour and delivery nurses, emergency room nurses, and operating room nurses are just a few of the positions that are in constant high demand.

As a travel nurse you work for a company that will provide you with accommodation (often a furnished home), a travel allowance to help you get from one hospital to another, and a very competitive salary that is usually higher than what **permanent** nurses earn.

## Tour guide

One of the most obvious career choices if you love to travel is to become a tour guide. In what other job can you spend your days exploring cities like Athens, Rome, or London – and get paid for it?

Every city that attracts tourists needs tour guides. Some guides work for a particular museum, while others lead themed tours (like ghost tours or historical bus tours). If you're particularly good at your job, you can eventually work your way up to become a director or even owner of a tour company.

To be a tour guide, you not only need to know your city inside and out – its history, culture, and hidden secrets – but you also need to **relate** well to people. You've got to make your tour group feel comfortable in a city that's unfamiliar to them. Depending on the type of tour, you may also need to help them handle small **emergencies** that arise, from getting medical care to finding lost luggage.

If you're planning to be a tour guide abroad, it helps to speak another language and to have a solid education in the history and culture of the area.

## Aid worker

International aid workers help countries that are **struggling** or recovering from economic crises, natural disasters, war, or famine. Depending on their experience, aid workers may teach in Afghanistan, organize **relief convoys** to combat areas in Somalia, or introduce new heat-resistant crops to nations throughout Africa.

The desire to help others is important if you want to be an international aid worker – but it's not the only requirement. You also need to have a background in a relevant area, like agriculture, engineering, business management, education, health, or crisis management.

Becoming an international aid worker has its rewards – and not just the **gratification** of helping people in other countries. Some international aid workers earn a lot of money.

Source: www.howstuffworks.com

## Check your understanding

1 Why are these not "obvious" careers for those who love to travel?

2 How does being a travel nurse differ from a regular hospital nursing job?

3 Why does a tour guide need some basic medical skill?

4 What is the first thing that someone wanting to be an aid worker needs to have?

5 What are the rewards of being an international aid worker?

6* Apart from opportunities to travel what else do these careers have in common?

## ✏ Writing in response to job applications

In small groups, read through the emails from applicants asking for more details and discuss the career in travel that is likely to suit each candidate. Discuss the strengths and weaknesses of each one and the extent to which they fit the requirements of the job.

Now choose one applicant and compose a reply making a recommendation. This could be saying that they are suitable for a particular job, or perhaps suggesting that a travel career is not for them. Write only a single paragraph – and keep your message concise and direct. You will probably need to write in a formal style.

## Skills, experience, and personal qualities

Now read through the article again and complete the table comparing and contrasting the three jobs. Use the headings below:

|  | Key skills | Personal qualities required | Experience needed |
|---|---|---|---|
| **Nurse** |  |  |  |
| **Tour guide** |  |  |  |
| **Aid worker** |  |  |  |

A   I was very interested in your "Careers for travellers" and would like further information. After training as a nurse I decided that nursing was not for me and became instead a teacher of history in an international school. While my great interest is local history, I have always wanted to travel.

B   I qualified as a National Registered Nurse in 2003, specializing in antenatal care and midwifery. For the past ten years I have been working as a trained midwife in my local hospital. I love my job but recently went part-time so that I could spend some time as a volunteer with Towards World Peace, an organization close to my heart. I have travelled a little but would love to do more.

C   Thank you for your interesting article "Careers for travellers". It really made me think. I speak two languages fluently and am studying English as a mature student part-time. I have worked as a museum education officer for the past five years and would now like to extend that to work overseas. I am a trained Home Visit Nurse.

D   Free travel, or better still, being paid to travel is my idea of a perfect job! Please send me further details of your career opportunities. I began training as a social worker but didn't complete the course as I'm not really a people person. I have tried several careers – builder, store manager, chef – but none of them were quite right for me. Next time will be the right one, I'm sure.

E   As a keen observer of the international scene I was interested in your article "Careers for travellers". I am a fully qualified engineer working for the National Clean Water Company, helping to improve the supply of good drinking water. For the past eighteen months I have been acting supervisor for my unit and am ready to take on more responsibility.

F   My mother passed to me your article "Careers for travellers" and suggested that I may like to apply. I have done some nursing as a volunteer at my local hospital, where I have been an outpatient for the past year. I am interested in visiting other countries and hope that my allergy to milk and wheat and my fear of heights will not be a problem. I would like to be an aid worker, or possibly a travel nurse or even a tour guide.

# A career in sport or leisure

## Thinking out loud

What do you do in your spare time? Are you a keen sports player? Do you play a musical instrument or make models? Have you ever thought that a hobby or interest of yours could be turned into a career?

🎵 **Track 5.3.** Listen to the interview with a famous sports personality. He is talking about his career as a football player.

## Check your understanding

1  Which team did Kim play for?

2  What were the highlights of his playing career?

3  What did Kim have to do as a football apprentice?

4  What went wrong?

5  What job did Kim take up after his accident?

6* In the light of what Kim says, how would you advise a friend who is keen to be a professional sports player?

## Study tips

### Improving the flow of a conversation

In Part D of the Speaking test, you will engage in a 6 to 9 minute discussion based on a topic. The topic will have been chosen for you and it is then up to you to develop the topic. You will be given some prompts that will help you do this, but if you want to do well in the test you will need to make sure that the whole discussion flows well from beginning to end. It's worth bearing this in mind, therefore, when you are given the two or three minutes to look at the Topic Card and think about what you will say.

Have a look at a typical Topic Card about famous people:

### Famous people

*Use the five prompts to guide you through a discussion about famous people with your teacher:*

1  *A famous person you really admire*

2  *Whether you would like to be famous; why or why not?*

3  *Some positive and some negative aspects of fame*

4  *The suggestion that famous people should always be good role models for younger children*

5  *The idea that becoming very famous is only about one thing – getting more money*

You can see how the prompts get more challenging as they progress. You will always be asked to talk about yourself or your views for a while to get things going, but then you will be asked about more sophisticated ideas. This is so that there is a good flow and development to the conversation. In fact, one of the assessment criteria tests your skill in this area – development and fluency.

Let's practise this skill. Think of a famous person you admire. Tell your partner about him or her. Now work through the other four prompts with your partner and time yourselves – aim to talk for five to six minutes, and aim to cover all four remaining prompts. Now swap roles and listen to your partner tell you about their favourite famous person.

Did you feel that the discussions flowed well? What was good and what was lacking?

## Sample student responses

Here are some comments from a teacher relating to three discussions that she had with students based on the famous people Topic Card. Which of the three students do you think managed the flow of the discussion best? Which discussion seemed to lack any sense of development in a logical manner? And which was satisfactory, that it, it was just about on the right track?

### Student A

Talked for too long about the famous person. Didn't talk very much about whether they would like to be famous. Could only provide positive aspects for prompt three – struggled to come forward with negatives. Recognized that famous people are role models but didn't have a view on the impact on younger children. Agreed completely that fame = the desire for money, but could not explore the depth of this or provide examples.

### Student B

Went straight to the problems of fame, even though I asked about who their favourite famous person was. Then talked for two minutes about how certain famous people have set very bad examples to others with their poor behaviour. Understood the connection to money, but brought in another idea instead which was that fame = the desire for power. When asked about prompt two, replied with "not sure" and didn't return to this.

### Student C

Spoke about a local hero, a woman who works for a local sports facility. Was clearly very impressed with her and her work. Went on to say that if fame could help others, then yes, would like to be famous. But did not seek fame for itself. Gave a balanced account of good things and bad things about fame for people in general and used this to lead into prompt four by commenting on how younger people look up to famous people as heroes. Accepted that prompt five seems to be true in many cases, but was able to come up with some notable exceptions.

## Working with puppets

 Watch the video of Corina Bona and her home-made puppets.

www.vimeo.com/44307918

## Check your understanding

Read the article on the following page, and then answer these questions:

1 What nationality is Corina?

2 Where did she find Treelo?

3 What does she use Treelo for?

4 As a child she travelled the world. Why?

5 How old do you think she is?

6* From the evidence in the passage, what do you think makes a good puppet?

##  Creating a puppet show

Let's assemble a small cast of puppets, and put on a production! First, choose your setting and come up with a basic plot. You can modify an existing story or you can write a new one. Now put together a script. A narrator should tell some of the story while the puppets mime the action. But try to include as much dialogue as you can.

It would be great if you could make the puppets and put on the show for real – perhaps to a younger audience?

# A career with puppets

Corina Bona is retraining me to count to ten, writes Graham Snowden. With my right hand **buried** inside the head of Treelo – a fluffy green and blue **lemur** – I **snap** its mouth open and shut as we go through the numbers. We get as far as three before she interrupts.

"Look at your puppet so you can see what he's really doing," she instructs me, "so that the mouth is really opening when you say the numbers."

Treelo's head, I realize, is **bobbing** helplessly all over the place. "It's important to understand that the top of your hand is where the eyes are and your focus is," she goes on, "so it's really **vital** to make your thumb do the work. Otherwise, you flap the head up and the eyes lose the **focus**."

Prior to being **salvaged** from a charity shop by Bona and converted into a puppet, Treelo was once little more than a **discarded** old stuffed toy. But Treelo earns his keep, accompanying his new owner on the puppetry workshops she holds with autistic schoolchildren. "They recognize him and feel more comfortable with him," she says, fondly. "He's quite a friendly little chap."

Puppeteer Corina Bona with one of the puppets in her Bristol studio

Bona has lived and worked in Bristol for 11 years, the last five as a puppet maker, **puppeteer** and puppetry teacher. She speaks in a dislocated transatlantic accent acquired from a childhood spent following her Argentinian mother and Venezuelan father – a travelling Gillette executive – around the world. "I grew up in Colombia, Mexico, the US, the UK ... I went back to Argentina when I was 15, I left when I was 18, and I've been here ever since," she says, looking weary at the thought of it all.

**Source: www.guardian.co.uk**

# Study tips
## Descriptive writing

You will often want to write an email or a letter to a friend or family member about something that really interests you. Imagine that you are receiving that type of letter. What would make it more enjoyable *for you*? Obviously, there needs to be a good story and plenty of interesting detail. It also needs to be written in a friendly way with words and expressions that express enthusiasm for the subject.

Here's a task that you may be asked to do in your reading and writing examination.

Imagine that you have found a new hobby. Write a letter to a friend about it.

Remember to include as much detail as you can and think about using language that will really get your friend interested in this new hobby.

In your letter you should:

- explain how you heard about the new hobby

- describe the new hobby

- say why you think it would be a good idea for your friend to try it.

# Sample student responses

Here are three letters responding to the task. Which one do you think has the best content and style? Discuss with a partner why you made your decision.

Then decide which letters you think are the second and third best, and find reasons why you think they are not as good.

## Student A

How are you at the moment? I hope that your exams went well. I am a bit tired after the activities at the weekend.

I was reading a magazine two weeks ago and it was all about archery, where you have a bow and arrow and you have to hit the target with your shot. I saw a bit of it at the Olympic Games in London.

The magazine had an advertisement about a new archery club which is opening at the sports centre near my house. I phoned them and they invited me along to the first sesion to see if I like it. There were loads of young people there but there also plenty of bows and arrows so we had a chance to try. I got better during the sesion. I won the competition at the end of the sesion.

I think that you should try archery because you are always looking for something to do. It would be more active than to sit at your computer all the day.

I hope you like my letter. See you soon.

## Student B

Hi! I am really looking forward to your visit in two weeks. We have just started the holidays here and I have found a great new activity that we can do.

You know that recently they opened a new arts centre in our town … I told you about it in my latest email. Well, they put a poster on the school wall advertising all their activities. Guess what? I have started guitar lessons there and I have been to three now. They are fantastic! The teacher is really patient and helpful and I have made good progress, although I have blisters on my fingers! We are using the guitars that the centre has loaned us at the moment and we have formed a small group. The aim is to play together at the end of the year in front an audience. It sounds exciting and scary at the same time!

I am sure that this is just what you have been looking for as a new hobby. You are very musical, you have a great voice and, if you learn, you could sing and play guitar at the same time. Why not come along with me when you visit. … I promise you will love it!

Say hello to your family from me … and see you soon!

## Student C

I worked with the computer and I found a program that is on there. I found it when I was finding information for my homeworks in biology. It is very interesting program and make me want to spend all my time there. It is a program about nature and tells about animals and fishes and leaving things. I did not know many facts that the program tells me so now I look this all the time on my computer and it is my new hobby. It is good to teach child from early age to use computer. They are more new and uptodate than books and we can get more in touch with the latest technology.

If you have a computer then you can have this new hobby too. I think it will enjoy you very much because you like animals. I hoped you like reading about my new hobby.

Now let's think more precisely about what we mean by content:

"**Content** covers relevance (whether the piece fulfils the task and has an awareness of purpose/audience/register), and the development of ideas (the detail/explanation provided and how enjoyable it is to read)."

With your partner, mark the three letters out of ten marks for content. Think about these four areas:

1  How well did the letter fulfil the task – that is, how well did it do what it was supposed to do?

2  Was the writer always aware of the person it was being written to?

3  How well were the various ideas developed?

4  How enjoyable was it to read?

When you agree on your mark out of ten, compare this to marks that other students have awarded. It is hoped that you will all have given similar marks to each of the three letters.

# Literary connections –
# *To Kill a Mockingbird*

## Thinking out loud

Work and the workplace often feature in literature. Sometimes it is the setting for the story that is being told – the office, the factory, or even the school where the action is based. Are there any other work-based settings that you have come across in your reading? Can you think of some good ones? Or perhaps you've read stories where the main characters have particular jobs? What jobs would make for an exciting story?

*To Kill a Mockingbird* by Harper Lee is the gripping story of the work of a lawyer and one family's stand against prejudice, as seen through the eyes of a nine-year-old child.

Scout and her older brother, Jem, watch their father defend a man against false accusations in the central event of the novel. In the process, they – and we – learn a lot about the work of a lawyer. We see the lawyer in the courtroom defending his client. We learn what it means for a lawyer to uphold the law.

When the children first hear that their father has taken on a difficult case, he says to them:

" ... sometimes we have to make the best of things, and the way we conduct ourselves when the chips are down – well, all I can say is, when you and Jem are grown, maybe you'll look back on this with some compassion and some feeling that I didn't let you down. This case, Tom Robinson's case, is something that goes to the essence of a man's conscience ... "

"Atticus, you must be wrong ... "

"How's that?"

"Well, most folks seem to think they're right and you're wrong ... "

"They're certainly entitled to think that, and they're entitled to full respect for their opinions," said Atticus, "but before I can live with other folks I've got to live with myself. The one thing that doesn't abide by majority rule is a person's conscience."

**Source: *To Kill a Mockingbird* by Harper Lee**

## Check your understanding

1　Who is Atticus?

2　Who does he not want to let down?

3　Who does Atticus defend?

4　Do the majority think Tom Robinson guilty or not guilty?

5　Why won't Atticus accept the majority verdict?

6*　From the evidence of the extract what adjectives would you use to describe Atticus?

 ## Creating a scene for a play

The book shows the work of being a lawyer, and being presented with a difficult situation or scenario that needs to be resolved. How many other careers can you think of that involve similar scenarios? In small groups see how many you can come up with in 5 minutes. Then choose one of the work-based scenarios and put together a short scene from a play that acts out the scenario.

Here's a plan you could utilize:

1 Decide on a work-based context that clearly has a challenging situation to deal with.

2 Set out clearly what the problem is and what the choices are.

3 Establish a group of characters – three or four.

4 Develop the dialogue.

5 Act out the scene.

# Reflection

In small groups you are going to prepare a display stand for a careers convention. The aim is to introduce your fellow students to a wide range of careers, especially ones that they may not have considered.

Your display stand will feature a number of different jobs and you can make use of a variety of ways of informing visitors to your stand about these jobs. You will need to do some research – for example, you may be able to visit a careers stand somewhere else and see how they have done it.

You could include:

- brochures

- short video clips about particular jobs

- jobs that match certain qualifications and/or experience

- some unusual or adventurous, or even dangerous jobs

- advice for job hunters

- what employers are looking for.

But whatever you decide to include, each group member should be responsible for a particular section of the stand.

When you are ready, open up your stand for others to peruse!

# ☑ My progress

Each chapter includes four study skills. These are skills that will feature in your final examinations. So let's check your progress with these key skills in mind.

| Where am I now? | Very pleased – I think I'm good at this | OK – but I do need more practice | One of my weaker areas – so I need a lot more practice |
|---|---|---|---|
| Filling out forms where longer sentences are needed and where quality feedback is the aim | | | |
| Listening to talks based on jobs and careers | | | |
| Improving the flow of the conversation when I'm speaking | | | |
| Writing in a descriptive style and using interesting and entertaining content | | | |

Now pick out one skill that you would like to prioritize for improvement and produce a short action plan to help you to become stronger in this area. Use a template similar to the following – that is filled out for you with an example.

## Action plan

Skill I want to improve writing in a descriptive style and using interesting and entertaining content

- *planning* – how I will try to improve this skill look at the writing of other people in a similar style

- *implementing* – what I will need and what my exact strategy is get hold of some magazines that have letters sections, or perhaps a book containing letters – particularly informal letters

- *monitoring* – how I will know I am improving and what evidence I may keep keep a list of the language used by writers of these types of letters and start using it myself

# 6 Travel and transport

## In this chapter you will:

- visit Uruguay, Poland, Mauritius, Costa Rica, Australia, the USA, and Space

- read about Felix Baumgartner and about how travel guides offer insider information, and all about holidays

- write an email to an employer asking for a job, volunteer for some work abroad, and write a postcard to send home

- listen to Jessica Cox, a ski instructor working in Dubai, two students working with Operation Raleigh, and a man who enjoys holidaying in caves

- talk about being on the first ever commercial flight from London to New York, and talk about what living in Space would be like.

## Key study skills

- *Reading* an information text to locate specific details

- *Speaking* to convey your experience and your views on a particular topic

- *Listening* to a talk and distinguishing between relevant and irrelevant information

- *Writing* an application form

# Travelling around
## Modes of transport

**Thinking out loud**

What was the most exciting journey you were ever on?
Where did you go and how did you get there?

## Building your vocabulary

Which of the following forms of transport have you travelled on, and where did you go? Copy the chart and complete it, and see if you can add another row or two – that is, another form of transport.

| Form of transport | When I travelled on it | Where I was going |
|---|---|---|
| Train | | |
| Tram | | |
| Bus | | |
| Ferry | | |
| Taxi | | |
| Car | | |
| Aeroplane | | |

Now with a partner see how many words associated with travel or transport you can come up with in two minutes. Compare your list to other people's lists in your class.

How do you prefer to travel around your favourite city? Train, bus, cycling, or by foot? List some advantages and disadvantages for each of these forms of transport.

| | Advantages | Disadvantages |
|---|---|---|
| Train | | can be late |
| Bus | always packed | |
| Cycling | healthy | |
| By foot | | takes too long |

# Transport available in and around Montevideo

## Bus

Montevideo's modern bus terminal is about three kilometres east of downtown. Its facilities include a tourist information booth, decent restaurants, a luggage service ($83 per 24 hours for up to three bags), public telephones, and a shopping mall upstairs.

A taxi from the bus terminal to downtown costs about $100. A much cheaper alternative is to take a city bus – numbers 21, 64, 187, or 330 all go from the terminal to Plaza Independencia via Avenue 18 de Julio for $13.50 (15 minutes' journey time).

Other destinations you can reach by bus include Corrientes and Mendoza, which have at least two departures a week, and Santa Fe and Rosario with four. There are two weekly departures to Santiago, in Chile.

## Boat

**Tres Cruces** terminal runs daily high-speed ferries direct from Montevideo to Buenos Aires (2¾ hours). Fares are $1,560.

Tickets for less expensive bus–boat combinations to Buenos Aires ($1,005) can be purchased at the **Ferry Tourist Office** (tel: 900-6617) on Plaza del Entrevero. These journeys take four hours.

**Trans Uruguay** (tel: 401-9350; website: www.transuruguay.com) operate a twice-daily scenic combined bus and river boat service to Buenos Aires via the riverside town of Carmelo and the Argentine Delta suburb of Tigre. The eight-hour trip costs $599 one way.

## Air

Montevideo's **Carrasco international airport** (tel: 604-0272 from 8 am to 5 pm) is served by far fewer airlines than the international airport in Buenos Aires. Three local airlines do fly frequently and directly between Carrasco and Buenos Aires, however.

There are services from Montevideo to international destinations provided by these airlines: American Airlines fly direct and daily to Miami, Iberia fly via Havana to Madrid, TACA fly with one stop (in Bolivia) to Lima, and TAM fly non-stop to Rio de Janeiro.

Five more airlines maintain offices in Montevideo but have no current flights to/from Uruguay.

Source: www.lonelyplanet.com

# Check your understanding

Let's practise locating numbers, dates, times, and amounts.

1   The bus terminal is ................. east of downtown and it charges ................. for left luggage.

2   There are ................. weekly bus departures to Santiago, Chile and ................. to Santa Fe.

3   The scenic boat trip to Buenos Aires costs ................. and takes ...................

4   If you need to call Carrasco International Airport then the number is ................. and it's not advisable to call before ...................

5   There are ................. different airlines that fly between Carrasco and Buenos Aires, and ................. airlines that are not currently operating in Uruguay.

#  Writing an email

Now, you are going to email a friend. Pretend you have just relocated to a new town and as it's a very pretty town, you have been out exploring. Tell your friend how you have been getting around. Make sure you include:

● how the house move went

● what you most like about the new town

● the transport you have been using and its good and bad points.

It's probably best to use three separate paragraphs, one for each of these areas, in your email.

# Locating specific detail in an information text

In the early part of your Reading test, you will be asked to scan a brochure or a similar information text to locate some very specific details. Quite often, this will involve looking for numerical information, but will also require you to convey other details in as few words as possible.

## Sample student responses

Let's have a look at some sample responses from three students to these questions:

1 What does the bus terminal in Montevideo offer travellers? Give *two* details only.

2 What is the cheapest means of transport by bus and boat to Buenos Aires?

3 Where can international passengers fly direct to from Montevideo?

**Student A**

1   public telephones and shopping mall

2   Trans Uruguay scenic combined service

3   Miami and Rio de Janeiro

**Student B**

1   tourist office, decent restaurants, shopping mall upstairs, public telephones

2   the $599 one

3   Buenos Aires

**Student C**

1   $83 discount for luggage service

2   the less expensive bus-boat combination

3   There are no direct flights to Uruguay

Try to mark these answers based on what you think the correct answers should be. See if you can pick out the best responses and analyse the problematic responses. Then have a look at the advice below for completing this type of task and fill in the gaps with the following words:

**clues    skim    first    changing    sentences**

- Read the questions ..................... so you know what type of information you are looking for.

- Scan the text for some ..................... about its purpose – for example, pictures and sub-headings will all help you make a quick judgment about the gist of the text.

- ..................... read the text quickly and note relevant detail.

- Copy the words from the text without ............. them – there is no need to use your own words.

- Answers should be brief – they do not have to be full ......................

# Travel guides

Before we leave for a new place we have not been to before we may decide to look it up on the Internet. In the past, people would have bought a travel guide, and in some cases they still do.

One hundred and fifty years ago George Bradshaw lived and worked in England, as a mapmaker and printer. He decided to travel the country, and wrote about the best way to see the sights in a book. He later travelled around Europe and wrote a similar book on how to travel and what to see. Both books were very popular at the time.

Look at the extract on the right in which Bradshaw is describing Hampton Court Palace in London, where Henry VIII once lived with some of his six wives during the 16th century.

Hampton Court Palace began to be built when Henry VIII was King, and continued to be added to by the kings who came after him, changing it from being a house, to being a palace. It was completed in 1604, having been designed by Sir Christopher Wren, who, before designing Hampton Court, had designed St Paul's Cathedral in London.

There are several plaques and original notices which are displayed around the Palace which relate to the several stages of the architecture. On closer inspection, the various stages of building works can be spotted to the keen eye.

If you visit, you will see large staircases and famous old paintings. You should make sure you see the interesting clock over the gateway in the second court. One feature of the garden is the large vine in the glass hothouse. It can have up to 3,000 bunches of grapes on it, although if you wish to see it, you will have to tip the gardener.

**Source: www.amazon.co.uk**

How do you know that Bradshaw has actually been to Hampton Court? Make a few short notes – the first one is done for you:

*Bradshaw at the palace*

1. He wrote a guide about it
2.
3.
4.

Another example is in Malta, where there is a famous Blue Grotto; insider knowledge will tell you that the best time to visit is in the morning, before 11 a.m., as that is when the sun will be shining on it.

Do you think it matters whether the person who is writing a travel guide has actually been to the place he or she is describing? Discuss this idea with a partner.

## Insider knowledge

When we are reading a travel guide, what makes it special and worth reading is the "insider knowledge" the writer adds to the guide. This can be knowledge about a place that not everyone knows about – and that makes it into an attractive place for tourists to visit.

For example, you may have heard that the traffic in London is bad, but have you seen the traffic light tree? Knowing about it is *insider knowledge*.

 **Writing travel guides**

You are going to describe a place you know that may be attractive to tourists. You need to include some "insider knowledge", which only locals would know about.

Do some research on your location. Perhaps you can visit it again. Maybe you can ask some of your relatives or friends about what unusual or particular interests the place holds. You are trying to find details that will help you give some insider knowledge!

Now, write an entry in a travel brochure for the tourist attraction you have chosen.

Share your travel guides with others – can you spot the insider information?

# Working in the travel industry

## Jessica Cox

 You may think that some jobs are not available if you have no arms. Driving a car or becoming a pilot may seem impossible if you had only legs to rely on. However, Jessica Cox, with the use of her legs and feet, has not only learned to drive a car but also become a pilot, and more. Watch the clip of Jessica in action.

**www.youtube.com/watch?v = f3Wp6NLuRWI&list = UUs5jagVlHxa2Lmqo5u8qx-g&index = 5**

What is your immediate reaction to what Jessica has achieved? Share your thoughts with the people around you.

**Track 6.1.** Listen to the interview with Jessica and complete the gap-filling task. Insert the following words into the spaces to complete the text.

| 120 | future | without arms | pilot | schools |
|---|---|---|---|---|

Jessica was born ..................... but this does not mean that she has been unable to do things other people have done. Indeed, it has meant she has achieved far more than many fully able-bodied people have

achieved. She has become a driver, a water-skier, a Tai Kwando black belt and, most recently, a ..................... She spent ..................... hours gaining her licence and now can fly alone. As well as achieving so much herself, Jessica spends time going to ..................... to encourage students to achieve as much as they can. It is especially important to Jessica to meet people who are like her, so she can show them what is possible in the ..................... and seeing that a life without arms does not mean a less full life.

##  Writing a formal email

Jessica has achieved so much; she inspires people around the world, whatever their physical abilities. As such, she would be a desirable celebrity for commercial brands to use in their advertising to sell products.

Imagine you are the chief executive officer (CEO) of a global brand. Send Jessica an email telling her about your company and why your brand would benefit from having her as a global ambassador. Tell her also how she would benefit if she agrees to promote your company.

## Creating a scene for a play

Travel allows us to go to places that we may otherwise never see, in our own countries and overseas. Have you been anywhere, for example, that you may never had seen had you lived 100 years ago?

Let's create a short dramatic scene based on how much transport has changed in the last 50 years. It doesn't need to be a long scene – maybe about ten minutes.

Form small groups. One of you will be the pilot on the first ever long-distance flight from the UK to the USA – London to New York. Now write the dialogue and include parts for the co-pilot, the flight attendants, and some passengers. The action of the scene is up to you – be creative!

# Prompt two of the Speaking test

In the early stages of your Speaking test, you will be asked to present your own experiences and views to get the conversation going. The Speaking test is structured so that it starts with you talking about personal **experiences** you have had that relate to the topic or theme. You may also be asked about your personal **views** about something to do with the topic – and this is likely to occur with Prompt two. Remember, there are five prompts, and they are written to move from the personal, to a discussion of general matters (related to the topic), and to finish up with some more sophisticated and advanced themes.

Here's an example of a typical Prompt two connected to travel and transport:

- The way you think people travelled around in the past, and how you think it may change in the future

Remember that the Speaking test is not a test of your knowledge of a topic, but a test of how you develop your ideas in a fluent and logical way.

Before the prompt above, you will probably have been telling the Examiner how you travel around, the types of transport you like and don't like, and places you have been – your personal experiences. This will then be developed into some ideas that you may have in terms of older transport systems and possible future systems. In both cases, you can't be wrong. So with Prompt two, it's best to get your ideas across and to be creative and this will also help you settle into the rhythm of the test as a semi-formal discussion. Lots of ideas usually lead to an interesting discussion; and an interesting discussion will often mean a quality discussion.

## Sample student responses

Have a look at the three approaches given by three different students. Which do you think is the strongest? Why? Which approach would keep the conversation going in a satisfactory way, staying on task? And which approach may lead the conversation elsewhere and may result in areas of the prompt not being covered?

**Student A**

> For the second prompt, I think I'll talk about how people used to travel around on horses. That's it. Horses. And now we have cars, and trains ... and planes. Things have changed a lot in 100 years. I think I'll focus on that. How much things have changed...

**Student B**

> For the second prompt, I'll talk about space travel. I really like that. I'll talk about space stations and how people can live on them. In 200 years, humans might be travelling to Mars. I know a couple of films about space I could mention – like *Star Wars* ...

**Student C**

> For the second prompt, I'll talk about how humans developed their skills in engineering and how humans have always planned for better transport, whatever the historical period. I may even mention Leonard de Vinci and his 13th-century drawing of a helicopter. I'll definitely mention the railways, and then the effect of the motor car in the 20th century. There's no real point mentioning horses – how can I develop that? No, focus on early modern transport and the way that computers have made transport so different ...

How would you prepare for the prompt? What would you include and what would you avoid? Spend two to three minutes thinking about this but don't make any notes. Remember – you cannot make any notes during the Speaking test. Now share your approach with a partner.

## Past continuous tense use

Once we can use the past simple, especially the irregular past simple, accurately, we can add range to the past tenses we use in our work by adding other past tenses, for example the past continuous.

We use the past continuous by choosing either **was** (for singular nouns) or **were** (for plural nouns) and adding the verb with the "ing" suffix. For example:

If I want to use **go** in the past continuous, I pick my noun, for example he, and therefore choose was, as he is a singular noun. I then add "ing" to the verb to make **he was going**. In context, this might read *He was going to the cinema with his friends to see the latest Spiderman movie.*

If I want to use **look** in the past continuous, I pick my noun, for example we, and therefore choose were, as we is a plural noun. I then add "ing" to the verb to make **we were looking**. In context, this might read *We were looking at several flats and decided to buy the one overlooking the river.*

This tense can be used to set the scene for some action:

- As I **was walking** along the road, I saw a man on a motorbike.

- When I **was reading** my book, Dan came in to surprise me.

Add the past continuous to these sentences:

1   As I (sit) on the sofa, I suddenly heard a crash from outside

2   When James (walk) along the road, he noticed a shiny coin on the pathway

3   They (watching) their favourite television show when the telephone rang

4   The meal (cook) on the stove but then he forgot all about it and it boiled over

5   He (think) about the solution to the problem when his friend rushed in and said "I have solved it!"

# Holidays
## Postcard from Mauritius

Grand Bay was the first area of the island to fully experience the tourist boom. A shopping and leisure paradise, Grand Bay also happens to be the area that Mauritians head for when they want a fun-filled night out (restaurants, bars, and discos).

The wonderful Pereybere public beach is popular because of its shopping facilities, restaurants, and pubs.

A few metres away from Baie aux Tortues, which 17th-century sailors named after the many tortoises in the area, can be found the ruins of the old Balaclava estate. Visitors will be able to see the sea walls, whose initial foundations were laid down by Mahé de Labourdonnais.

The longest village on the island, Triolet, offers an opportunity to visit the biggest Hindu temple, the Maheswarnath, first built in 1819 in honour of the Gods Shiva, Krishna, Vishnu, Muruga, Brahma, and Ganesha.

Discover a large variety of tropical fruit trees as well as colourful and perfumed exotic flowers. Trips on mountain bikes or hiking are possible.

**Source: www.mauritius.net**

## ✏ Writing a postcard

Imagine you have been to one of the places described in the postcard above. Send a postcard to someone close to you. Write about what you have seen and done, and include how you felt about the day. Did anything unusual happen?

Now read someone else's postcard. How is it similar to yours? How does it differ? Have a brief chat to various people about their postcards.

## Skiing in the Middle East

If we want to go to a beautiful island, we may pick Mauritius or Fiji. If we want to go skiing, we may pick Austria or Switzerland. Or maybe even Dubai? Ski Dubai is another example of overcoming apparent limitations to gain what we want. In the middle of a desert, it is now possible to go skiing at below zero temperatures.

# Listening to a talk and selecting relevant information

In your listening test, you will be asked to listen to a talk, usually given by a specialist or by someone who has an interest in something specialized. The main skill that will be tested is to understand and select relevant information from the talk. One way that you may be asked to provide this information is filling gaps in partial notes to make them full and clear.

Let's practise this by listening to an interview with a ski instructor who works at Ski Dubai, an indoor ski resort in the Middle East.

**Track 6.2**. Listen to Franz, who has been working at Ski Dubai since it opened several years ago. Some of the information he gives will not be needed to complete your task – remember, you are listening only for relevant information. You can perhaps work out what this information is likely to be from the incomplete notes – it's always good advice to look at any questions for a listening test before you listen, as you will usually find some clues in the questions as to what type of content (details and information) is required.

When you complete the notes you should use only one or two words. You should never need to use more than two words.

Have a go at inserting some words that you think complete the notes. Remember, only one or two words is allowed in each space (so a maximum of four words where there are two spaces), and whatever you put in must make sense when you read the note back to yourself. You can use the words straight from the recording or you can use your own words if they have the same meaning.

## Sample student responses

Now have a look at how three students approached two of these sentences. Which do you think are the most accurate? Which do you think may be acceptable? Which do you think is not acceptable? Try to see how *reasonable* responses, which may not use the exact word from the recording, can still make sense.

### Ski Dubai – indoor ski centre

1. Ski Centre Dubai has been open for business since ..................... and Franz is a ..................... there.

2. Just before he worked at Ski Dubai, Franz was a ....................., but he was missing .....................

3. Ski Dubai also has a place that provides a natural habitat for ..................... and this is very popular, but it's not as popular as .....................

4. There are ..................... ski runs and we even have a ................. run.

5. Specialist equipment can be ..................... from Snow Pro, where you can also book .....................

**Student A**

1  Ski Centre Dubai has been open for business since ....*2006*........ and Franz is a ...*ski instructor*... there.

4  There are ......*five*......... ski runs and we even have a ...*extremely difficult*... run.

**Student B**

1  Ski Centre Dubai has been open for business since ......*for ages*..... and Franz is a .......*manager*.... there.

4  There are ...*five or six*.... ski runs and we even have a .......*black*........ run.

**Student C**

1  Ski Centre Dubai has been open for business since ........*2006*........ and Franz is a ...*area manager*.. there.

4  There are ........*five*......... ski runs and we even have a .....*blacker*....... run.

# Operation Raleigh

**Thinking out loud**

If you could go on a charity working holiday for a month, where would you go and why? What charity would you like to support? What do you think you would learn from going on such a holiday?

There may be a reason why we are travelling to a particular place on holiday – we may wish to relax on a beach in the Indian Ocean, meet new people while working on a project in South America, admire an oil painting in a French art gallery, or see an iconic building in India. Some people go on holiday to relax, while others like to try something new.

However, some people go on holiday to work. They may do this to help others who are less fortunate than they are, but they will also gain a lot themselves: some new skills and some new friends, for example.

 **Track 6.3** Listen to the interview with two university students who joined Operation Raleigh and travelled to Costa Rica one summer.

## Key skills

### Analysing questions to predict the types of responses needed

It is always a good idea to read the questions being asked before you listen to a recording. This is so you can try to work out in advance what type of response or information is needed.

When reading the questions, underline the main word in the question that is crucial in terms of knowing the response required. For example, if the question is:

- How many times has Jake been there?

You may wish to underline "many" as this will prompt you to write a number in response.

Alternatively, you may wish to write "number" next to the question, which will also prompt you to give a number.

In other questions, this may seem harder to do, but with plenty of practice, you will gain confidence. Look at the next example below:

- What project did Martha help with?

So, here we may underline "project" or write "name of project" next to the question.

We will be answering this second question in the next listening passage.

Another example of this is:

- Which country did Jake and Martha go to?

We know when we read this that the answer will be the name of a country.

Sometimes, the question will need a longer response, requiring a few more words – but not usually complete sentences, so these should be avoided. Such questions often begin with "How" or "Why":

- How did Jake get involved with the community project?

- Why did Martha feel she could carry on with the trek even after she had fallen?

Using the questions to help us find the information we need in order to respond well is an important skill that we will practise in the next listening exercise.

# Check your understanding

1 What made Jake first get involved with Operation Raleigh?

2 How long did Jake go on Operation Raleigh for?

3 What project did Martha help with?

4 What happened to Martha on the trek back?

5 What does Jake say he has learnt from his experience?

 **Writing a diary entry**

In small groups, research some more about Operation Raleigh, or a similar working holiday programme. Why do people join and what have they gained from doing so?

Now, write a personal diary entry for your final day on Operation Raleigh. Include:

- what you have done
- how you feel about leaving
- the skills and memories you will take home with you.

---

## Study tip

## Completing a form

Sometimes in the examination you will be tested on your skill in combining reading and writing – and one of these occasions is when you are asked to fill out a form based on information you have been given beforehand to read. This information relates to a particular person – and your task is to pretend to be that person and fill out the form as if you were him or her.

Here's how it works – here is some information about Elizabeth Jones, who like Jake and Martha is keen to be involved with the work of Operation Raleigh. Read this carefully and start to form an idea of what she is like. It's a little like being an actor and learning a part.

*Elizabeth Jones will be 18 years old in four months' time. She already has a place at university to study geography but wants to take a gap year before starting her further studies.*

*She has researched many organizations for ideas on how she can best spend her gap year. First, she plans to work at a local restaurant for eight months to earn enough money to pay for her expenses as a volunteer abroad. She has looked at the possibilities of volunteering for different organizations. Some of them offer opportunities for volunteering in Asia, Africa, and Europe, and, although she loves Spain, Elizabeth particularly wants to work in Central or South America.*

*She has found the brochure of an organization called Operation Raleigh in the school library, and has decided to apply to them. Operation Raleigh offers young people the chance to work in Central America, either in Costa Rica or in the Republic of Nicaragua. In both countries the work would be in remote areas. This excites Elizabeth because she lives in a very big city at 4, Bushy Avenue, Birmingham B32 7YA. She would love to have the experience of a completely different lifestyle.*

*She has read the brochures carefully and has made some important decisions. She has decided to apply for Costa Rica and she has decided that she would definitely like to volunteer for six months, the longest period possible. There are two possible starting dates. She would like to begin on 15 October 2015 so that she could be in Costa Rica during the cold British winter. However, she knows that she would not have earned enough money for her travels by that time, so the only possible date to start is 15 March 2016. She would be very interested in working on projects that involve the environment. She has already taken part in conservation work at school and is the secretary of the school environment group.*

*Elizabeth realizes that it would be very helpful if she had a basic knowledge of the Spanish language in order to integrate better with the local people in Costa Rica. She has the opportunity to join a class at school but it is too advanced for her, so it is better if she joins a group organized by Operation Raleigh.*

*She has her own email address lizjo@bestmail.co.uk and can be contacted there or on her mobile phone 074896311.*

Here is what a typical form may look like:

OPERATION RALEIGH

VOLUNTEER APPLICATION FORM

<u>Personal details</u>

1. Full name ..................................................................
2. Address ..................................................................
3. Age ..................................................................
4. Gender (please delete) MALE/FEMALE ..................................
5. Email ..................................................................

<u>Volunteer details</u>

6. Which location would you prefer to work in? ...........................
7. Which project would you prefer? (please circle)

   constructing schools          office work          researching forests and animals

8. How long would you want to volunteer for? ...........................
9. Which starting date would you prefer? ...........................
10. Which language would you like to learn? ...........................
11. Where did you find out about our organization? ...........................
12. <u>Write one sentence</u> about why you want to volunteer for our **organization**.

   ..................................................................

# Sample student responses

Here are some interesting responses from students who filled out this form – covering all the required information, and a range of levels from PA: precise/accurate, to CA: close attempt but not good enough, to NA: not accurate and/or not acceptable.

With a partner, decide whether each of these is PA, CA, or NA.

1 Full name: **a)** Elisabeth Jones  **b)** Liz Jones
  **c)** Elizabeth jones

2 Address: **a)** 4 Bushy Avenue  **b)** Birmingham
  **c)** 4, Bushy Avenue, Birmingham B34 7YA

3 Age: **a)** nearly 19  **b)** 18  **c)** 17 and a half

4 Gender: **a)** FEMALE  **b)** Female (written above)
  **c)** FEMALE

5 Email: **a)** elizabethjones@bestmail.co.uk
  **b)** Liz Jo at bestmail uk  **c)** lizjo@bestmale.co.uk

6 Which location would you prefer to work in?
  **a)** Costa Rica  **b)** Central United States  **c)** Spain

7 Which project would you prefer? (please circle)  **a)** constructing schools
  **b)** researching forests and animals
  **c)** anything environmental (written above)

8 How long would you want to volunteer for?
  **a)** eight months  **b)** six weeks  **c)** some months

9 Which starting date would you prefer?
  **a)** 15/03/2017  **b)** October 15th  **c)** March 2016

10 Which language would you like to learn?
  **a)** Spain  **b)** Costa Rican  **c)** South American

11 Where did you find out about our organization?
  **a)** a brochure  **b)** Operation Raleigh
  **c)** the school resources room

12 Write one sentence about why you want to volunteer for our organization.

  **a)** she wants to work in South America

  **b)** I want to work on projects

  **c)** I want to learn Spanish

# Eco-friendly holidays

Some holidays are just for pleasure, but we still have to take care of the environment when we are there. Modern tourists are, more than ever, aware of the need to leave beaches and parks tidy, as well as being aware of the need to make more ecologically friendly choices about the holidays they decide to go on.

---

## Building your vocabulary

Here are eight words that you will see in the next reading passage.

**marine**    **pristine**    **wetland**    **curious**

**appeal**    **aware**    **impact**    **swampy**

Put the correct word into each gap in the sentences below:

1    She tidied her bedroom completely so it looked ..................

2    Alex liked water and sea animals; in fact, Alex liked all .................. life.

3    Thomas was .................. to know what the answer was.

4    The land was muddy and .................., so she got her boots stuck.

5    The ecosystem that interested her most was ..................

6    It was popular because of its great .................. to everyone.

7    It had a huge .................. on him and made him decide what he would do in the future.

8    We all need to be .................. of the dangers of smoking.

---

## Giving a presentation

Work in small groups and prepare a promotional presentation about a place that could be a great place to have a holiday that involves more than just lying on a beach. Be sure to include the following:

● where the destination is

● what you can do there

● why it is such a great and unique place to visit

Try to insert a "voice over" in your presentation in order to add another dimension. You will need to write the commentary of course.

Ecotours are unique adventures that incorporate nature and sightseeing all into one exciting package. Learning about the environment and the world around us is the **appeal** of an ecotour because you get to experience the natural world firsthand. A great way for students studying biology and environmental sciences to experience **marine** life and nature is to take your own ecotour! Orlando airboat rides can give you an experience to remember and can be a fun and exciting way to learn more about the Florida environment.

Eco-tours involve travelling to a natural environment where you are guided by a naturalist who helps you learn about the surrounding environment and further your environmental education. This can include learning how the plants and animals on your Orlando airboat rides benefit from each other, or it can be simply becoming more **aware** of conservation and Everglades preservation efforts.

Orlando airboat rides can help you learn about Florida history, observe alligators and other wildlife, and experience the **pristine** nature of the swampy wilderness. Taking an ecotour can help you become more aware of your environment and further educate you on the **impact** we have on the environment. Our goal is to help you understand the Everglades and how important it is to preserve the largest **wetland** in North America.

Wild Florida airboats provides the perfect opportunity for a school trip that caters to those interested in learning more about environmental sciences, or to those just **curious** about the Everglades. Hands-on and active learning on an airboat ride is often a more exciting and adventurous alternative to sitting in a classroom, so why not plan your ecotrip with Wild Florida?

Wild Florida specializes in creating a breathtaking and unique ecotour that's fun for everyone in your family! You will be gliding through the **swampy** Everglades in our airboat rides while observing and learning about alligators, bald eagles, the history of the Everglades, and so much more. Book your Orlando airboat rides today by calling us at 407-901-2563 to experience a one-of-a-kind ecotour that you won't soon forget.

Source: www.wildfloridairboats.com

# Holidays with health benefits

## Building your vocabulary

Look at the following words. They will appear in the next article:

**unique**     **stable**     **manner**     **chamber**

**responds**     **hike**     **mine**     **impressions**

Place one of the above words into each space on the speech bubbles:

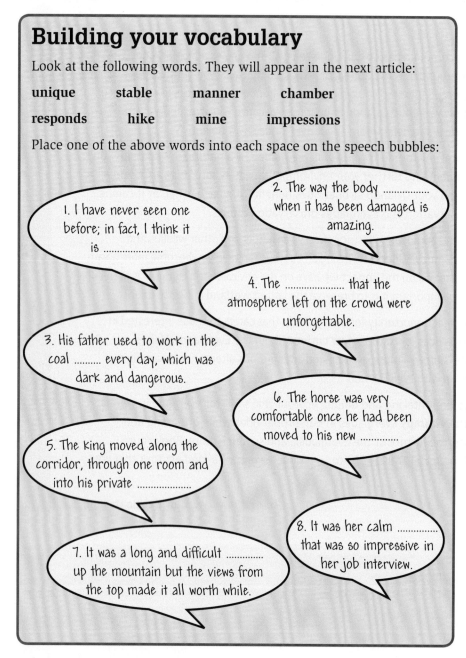

1. I have never seen one before; in fact, I think it is ....................

2. The way the body ................ when it has been damaged is amazing.

3. His father used to work in the coal .......... every day, which was dark and dangerous.

4. The .................... that the atmosphere left on the crowd were unforgettable.

5. The king moved along the corridor, through one room and into his private ...................

6. The horse was very comfortable once he had been moved to his new .............

7. It was a long and difficult ............. up the mountain but the views from the top made it all worth while.

8. It was her calm ................ that was so impressive in her job interview.

## A salt-mine holiday

Health is also an important reason for people to choose their holiday destination; some places offer cures for illnesses as well as a range of relaxation remedies. Salt has long been considered a healthy solution to bathe in and people have been doing so, as well as drinking the waters at spas, for centuries.

One of the most famous salt mines in Poland is the Wieliczka Salt Mine, just south of the historic city of Krakow. People travel there to admire the salt carvings, but recently a new style of holidaying has been started there.

Stays are offered to those who are looking for interesting places and **unique** experiences and who would like to spend their time in an unusual **manner** or see how their body **responds** to the underground environment. Overnight stays in the **mine** underground are a combination of relaxation, mental and physical rest, and unforgettable **impressions**.

Here, there is no pollution that the environment on the surface has today. Stays are organized in the Eastern Mountains' Stable Chamber, which used to be a real **stable**, in which horses were still kept in the early twentieth century, working in salt mine excavations. At present, it

1 What two things do people do with the water at the Wieliczka Salt Mine?

2 Why do people stay overnight at the mine?

3 Name two things that people must bring with them for their stay.

4 What is the lowest temperature in the treatment part?

5 Where else can you visit at the same time?

6* How would you enjoy a night in the salt mine? Give three adjectives to describe it.

## Developing a conversation

Discuss with a partner where you would **both** go on a holiday that offered health benefits:

● Would you ever consider going on a treatment holiday? If so, where would you like to go and what treatments would you have? How would they be beneficial to you?

● Are there any treatments you have heard of that you would like to try? Explain why they appeal to you.

---

performs the role of a modern treatment **chamber** – a "natural inhaler" with underground brine graduation towers, a reading room, and comfortable beds.

## Worth knowing

● The offer is available for individual tourists.

● Maximum number of participants: 36 persons; minimum number of persons: 10 persons.

● The adventure starts at 8 p.m. and lasts overall for approximately 11 h.

● Bring warm, comfortable sports clothes and walking shoes for the **hike** and a change of light sports shoes for the Eastern Mountains' Stable Chamber.

● Bring your own sleeping bag. You can rent bed linen.

● The temperature in the treatment part is about 10–12°C.

● No meals are provided by the Health Resort in the Eastern Mountains' Stable Chamber. Guests can buy hot drinks from the vending machine – coffee, tea, and hot chocolate at the price of 1.50 Polish zloty (PLN)/drink.

● You can complement your stay with a visit of the Tourist or the Mining Route.

**Source: www.wieliczka-saltmine.com**

# Holidaying deeper underground

If the salt-mine experience gave you a taste for going underground, you may like to consider caving.

 **Track 6.4** Listen to caver Juan Roig talking about life under the surface and what he has discovered there.

## Check your understanding

1 Why did Juan go into the caves as a boy?

2 Who rescued Juan and his friend?

3 What had Juan's father done as a young man?

4 How does Juan describe seeing a new chamber for the first time?

5 What two things does Juan say he does not like about caving?

6* Think of three things you might need to go caving.

Would you like to go caving? It's probably one of those things that have great benefits but big disadvantages, too. A lot of decisions we make in life are based on "pros and cons" – good things and not – good things.

Come up with five pros, and then five cons, for a day spent in a cave. You would have an experienced instructor with you, though – so you wouldn't be on your own.

| Pros | | Cons | |
|---|---|---|---|
| 1 | | 1 | |
| 2 | | 2 | |
| 3 | | 3 | |
| 4 | | 4 | |
| 5 | | 5 | |

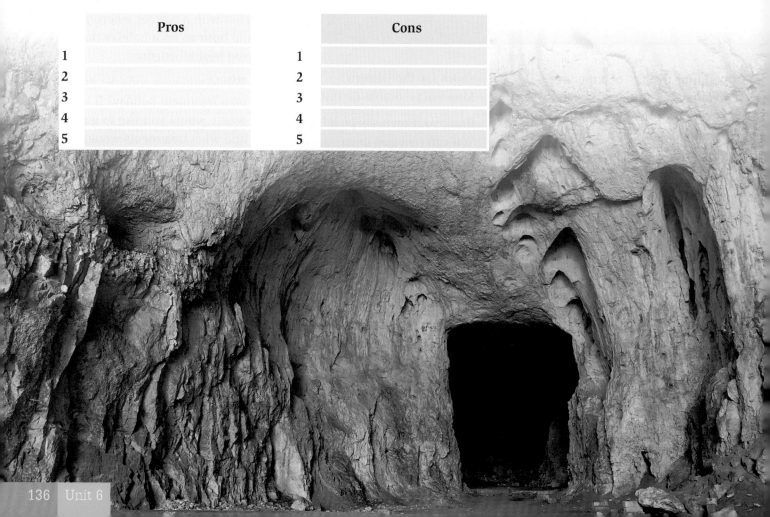

# The Digital Nomad

For generations, there have been groups of people and animals across the globe who have had to move around from place to place to survive. People who move around in this way are called **nomads** and their lifestyle is said to be **nomadic**.

## Thinking out loud

Is it a way of life you would like to have? Why or why not? Perhaps you would like this way of living for just a short time. Can you think of any advantages of being a nomad?

Although we may think of the nomadic lifestyle as being traditional, there are modern nomads, too, and others who use the name to show the travelling nature of their job.

 Read what the Digital Nomad wrote on his Twitter feed @WheresAndrew when he visited Tanzania.

In the space of an hour, I watched ten chimpanzees engage in about every behavior possible: fighting, sleeping, eating, and grooming. For the first twenty minutes or so, the chimpanzees remained high up in the trees, elusive in the shadows. And then, as if bored with teasing my camera, they all dropped down, ran past me, and then found a nice patch of sunlight and began lounging about, moving poses as I snapped my shutter, *click, click, click*

The slower I walk, the better it will be—I keep telling myself this. *Pole, pole*—slowly, slowly—they say. And so I take my time, enjoying the rich and earthy mountain air, the dripping forest silent except for the sound of clear waterfalls and the occasional shy bird.

Madete Beach is a giant nursery—64 sq. km. of protected nesting ground for the green sea turtle. Every year, several dozen sea turtles arrive on this sandy stretch of Saadani National Park, dig giant, Jacuzzi-size pits on the beach and then fill them up with their ping-pong-ball-sized eggs.

**Source: www.digitalnomad. nationalgeographic.com**

 ## Writing an email to express interest in a job

You have the chance of a dream job but it will mean having a nomadic lifestyle as it will involve constant travelling around your country with the *Nomadic Traveller*. Write an email to the *Nomadic Traveller* explaining why you would be perfect for the job. Be sure to include some skills and some experience you have that you think would be useful.

 ## Tweeting

Send a tweet message saying what you think about the nomadic lifestyle; it has to be 140 characters or fewer. You may find that someone will retweet the message, before adding their own comment, again, of no more than 140 characters.

# The Big Issue – space travel, but at what cost?

## Felix Baumgartner

Now, read about **Felix Baumgartner** and what he has done:

| Thinking out loud | Are some people braver than others? Are people born brave or are they taught how to be brave? How brave are you? Is being brave sometimes just being stupid? |
|---|---|

## Building your vocabulary

Here are some words you will see in the next article about Felix Baumgartner – a man who jumped out of a plane at 39 000 metres (128 000 feet) – with a very special parachute. Match them to the correct definitions using the crossword clues.

**helium     ambition     capsule     humble**

**harness     inspire     skydive     hero**

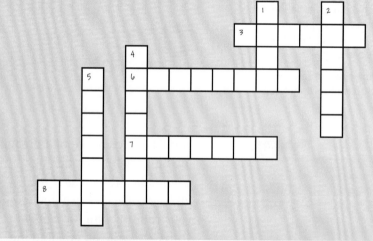

| 3 across | a light gas |
|---|---|
| 6 across | what someone would like to be or do in the future |
| 7 across | a jump from very high up |
| 8 across | a strap fixed to keep you in the same place |
| 1 down | someone who is admired by others for what he or she has done |
| 2 down | feeling modest |
| 4 down | a small compartment to carry someone into space |
| 5 down | to get a good idea from another person or event |

The former military parachutist ascended in a purpose-built **capsule** beneath a giant **helium** balloon to a height of more than 128 000 feet – almost four times the height of a cruising passenger airliner. After a salute to the millions watching around the world, Baumgartner jumped from the capsule and fell to Earth, reaching a speed of 833mph – or Mach 1.24 – faster than the speed of sound, according to his spokesman.

His achievement came exactly 65 years to the day after Chuck Yeager became the first man to break the sound barrier in an aeroplane, and it was one of three world records Baumgartner set with his jump. He also smashed the records for the highest manned balloon flight and the highest **skydive**. Minutes before his historic leap, which was broadcast on television around the world, the 43-year-old sat anxiously on the edge of his capsule, looking down at Earth.

As he was instructed to cut his oxygen supply and release his safety **harness**, mission control in Roswell, New Mexico, told Baumgartner that an "angel was with him".

He addressed the world with a short speech ahead of his leap. "I know the whole world is watching right now and I wish the world could see what I can see. Sometimes you have to go up really high to understand how small you really are."

# Check your understanding

1 What job did Felix Baumgartner have before attempting this jump?

2 Baumgartner beat the existing records for the highest skydive and highest manned balloon flight, but which word tells us that he beat these records by a long way?

3 Give two details of what Baumgartner did at the very end of his descent.

4 Give two examples of what he hopes to do in the future.

5 Why did he not press the button while falling to Earth?

6* Explain why it is important what Felix has achieved.

Baumgartner's family and friends, who had travelled to New Mexico, cheered and celebrated as it became clear he was safe. As he fell to Earth, Baumgartner complained that his visor was steaming up before he pulled his parachute cord. After two or three minutes he appeared against the cloudless blue sky before steering himself to safety, just nine minutes after jumping. Baumgartner looked calm as he landed. Only once his parachute had fallen behind him did he drop to his knees and punch the air in celebration.

After reaching such heights, Baumgartner's next **ambition** is to take to the sky once again. Although this time his ceiling will be much lower. He hopes to move to the country with his girlfriend, dividing his time between the US and Austria, where he plans to fly helicopters, performing mountain rescues and firefighting. In a press conference after the jump, he said "When I was standing there on top of the world so **humble**, you are not thinking about breaking records. I was thinking about coming back alive. You do not want to die in front of your parents and all these people. ... I thought 'please God, don't let me down.'"

Baumgartner had a button which would activate a parachute which would stop his spin but would mean that he could break no speed records. When asked what he is going to do next, he said he wanted to "**inspire a generation**". His team last night paid tribute to him. Dr Jonathan Clark, Red Bull Stratos Medical Director said: "The world needs a **hero**, and now we have one".

**Source: www.telegraph.co.uk**

## The bigger issue – achieving our goals

To achieve, we sometimes have to go the extra mile to reach our goals. What are your goals and how far would you go to achieve them? Spend a few minutes thinking about this. In a few more minutes you will need to explain what your main goal in life is, and what you will try to do to achieve it.

**Putting you in the hot seat** means that you take centre stage – but just for a few minutes. The idea is that you are asked a series of quick questions and that you give quick and sharp responses; there's no need to talk for a long time, explaining everything. Hot seating tests your quick response skills – and also tests the questioning skills of your audience!

# Recognizing and using relative pronouns

There are certain words we can recognize in a reading passage that tell us they are related to other information in the text; these are called relative pronouns.

When reading a text, you will see words that are used to refer to another part of the sentence. The writer does this so that shorter, more concise, sentences can be constructed.

Words including "this", "it", "he", "she", and "they" tell the reader that people, animals, items, ideas and so forth are being referred to. Look at the sentence below:

- As *he* fell to Earth, Baumgartner complained that *his* visor was steaming up just before *he* pulled his parachute cord. As *it* was released, however, things improved.

"He" at the start of the sentence refers to Baumgartner (who we can work out from context clues is in the middle of a parachute jump). "It" clearly refers to the parachute cord. We should always be able to scan a sentence to see who or what is being referred to when these types of pronouns are being used in this way.

Looking out for these words will help you understand the text more easily and find the answers you are looking for more quickly.

In the next two sentences, pick out the relative pronouns and the nouns they refer to:

1  The man had left his bag on the train, which had already moved off from the platform.

2  Jan phoned his best friend, who had broken a leg while on a skiing holiday. It had been placed in plaster as it was badly broken.

And these two sentences need to be completed using relative pronouns:

1  As Dan was walking along the road ...................

2  The plane was about to take off ......................

Finally, write a couple of similar sentences and remove the relative pronouns. Give these to a friend and see if the friend can make sense of the sentence, and maybe re-insert the missing words.

## Living in Space

**Thinking out loud**

In the future, we may not just visit Space, but live and work there for longer periods. At the moment, there are people in space living on the International Space Station, completing space-related experiments while orbiting Earth, often for months at a time. How would you feel if you were able to do this job for a year? What would you find exciting about the job? What would you miss about your life on Earth?

 **Writing a letter home**

Imagine you have been on the International Space Station for nine months. You decide to write a short letter to a friend or relative at home on Earth. Include:

- what it looks like where you are

- what you have been doing for the past nine months

- how you feel about the job.

Show your letter to a friend. What similarities are there? How are they different? Ask your friend to suggest one or two improvements to your letter.

# Reflection

In this chapter, we have looked at various forms of transport, as well as some reasons for travelling to faraway places. The place furthest away, however, which may become a regularly visited tourist destination in the future, is Space.

Which planet in our Solar System would you most like to visit? A billionaire has agreed to pay for a trip to the planet of your choice for one small group of people. However, the catch is that you need to present your case for going with arguments as to why it should be your group that receives these very special tickets.

In small groups, prepare your bid. The billionaire has insisted on four requirements before she will consider the bid:

1. A strong set of reasons for the particular planet chosen and why each of you wants to go on this trip.

2. An "Earth capsule". While on the planet you will need to leave a capsule. So think of four or five things you would put in the capsule that you think would represent life on Earth.

3. A television report to the people back home. You have been given a video camera, but only 2 minutes of film time. So you will need to describe how you will use the 2 minutes.

4. An explanation about what you will be searching for on the planet that you can bring back home to study; include reasons why it is important that this research is done.

You can present your bid in any form you like.

## ☑ My progress

Each chapter includes four study skills. These are skills that will feature in your final examinations. So let's check your progress with these key skills in mind.

| Where am I now? | Very pleased – I think I'm good at this | OK – but I do need more practice | One of my weaker areas – so I need a lot more practice |
|---|---|---|---|
| Locating specific details in a written information text | | | |
| Talking about my experience of a topic and expressing my views about it | | | |
| Listening to a talk and picking out the relevant information | | | |
| Filling out a form accurately | | | |

Now pick out one skill that you would like to prioritize for improvement and produce a short action plan to help you become stronger. Use a template similar to the following one, which is filled out for you with an example.

## Action plan

Skill I want to improve filling out a form accurately.

- *planning* – how I will try to improve this skill
  Analyse a wide range of forms from different sources.

- *implementing* – what I will need and what my exact strategy is
  Collect ten different types of forms and look at the different ways they ask questions and get information.

- *monitoring* – how I will know I am improving and what evidence I may keep
  See if I can pick out form-filling conventions similar to the form in this chapter and then create a small portfolio of IGCSE E2L-type forms.

# 7 Leisure and entertainment

## In this chapter you will:

- visit Norway, the UK, and India
- read about a Norwegian trumpet player, an Indian athlete, and a detective
- write a story and write about a festival
- listen to an actor, a writer, and a fundraiser
- talk about a local festival and your capital city.

## Key study skills

- *Speaking* successfully in the early part of the examination discussion
- Using linking words when *writing* a summary
- *Reading* to recognize numbers and figures with accuracy
- *Listening* to a follow-up discussion

# Music

Imagine that you want to join a band. What instrument would you play? What type of music would you play? How many musicians would be in your band? Or would you be the lead singer maybe? What may you like about being in band? What may you dislike? Think about all of this for a few minutes.

## Building your vocabulary

Look at the words below and make sure you know what they mean. Then use them to fill the gaps in the paragraph that follows:

**generation    soloist    highlights    fusion    quintet    awards    outstanding    ensemble**

The guitarist grew up enjoying playing in front of an audience. So when he was an adult, he became a ............................., playing all around the world. He soon became regarded as one of the best players of his ........................., and started to receive ......................... for his incredible music as well as his ......................... contribution to music in schools. One of his career ......................... so far has been playing at Soundwave, the Australian rock festival. He developed an interest in different types of music, which resulted in his playing more ......................... . He also made more friends who also played the guitar and eventually asked four of them to join him to form an ......................... . This ......................... has just released its first album, which is selling fast.

## Language focus

### Using prefixes to indicate numbers

Sometimes we are able to use a word to prefix a noun as a way of indicating a number. For example, "quin" relates to the number five, so "the guitarist played in a quintet" tells us that there were five people in the group. "Tri" relates to the number three, so a tricycle has three wheels.

Look at the prefixes below and decide on the number that each one relates to:

**bi    quad    uni    duo    hexa    quart    pent**

Look at the words below. Decide which number is being referred to, and then define the word. The first one has been done for you.

| Word | Number | Definition |
| --- | --- | --- |
| quartet | the number 4 | a group of four people |
| pentagon | | |
| triplets | | |
| unicorn | | |

We can use these prefixes to make our writing more concise. Compare the sentences below:

- She was very fortunate to have had three babies at the same time.

- She was very fortunate to have had triplets.

It also gives us the freedom to create new words when appropriate to do so:

- I have created a new pen that is also a pencil and an eraser in one; I call it my tri-pen.

Now you have a go. You are also an inventor. What would you call these inventions?

- a cycle that has four wheels

- a cup that has two handles

- a dress that can be worn in five different ways

- a rose that has red and white flowers

- a camera that is also a compass, tablet, and phone

Maybe just for fun you could make up some words that incorporate these types of prefixes, and then see if a friend can guess what they may mean.

Tine Thing Helseth, 25, started to play the trumpet at the age of 7, and is one of the leading trumpet soloists of her generation. Her mother was an amateur trumpet player and Tine grew up in a house with a wide range of music to influence her.

Highlights for Tine include performing in Australia, Monte Carlo, Germany, and Hong Kong. With her ensembles, Tine made a 15-date concert tour of Norway and undertook a 10-day tour of China, playing at the Beijing Music Festival with tenThing.

Rather than trying to impress listeners with her technique, Helseth embraces a digital age of communication. She has her own app which she has found exciting. It shows where she is playing and she also uploads videos, messages, and news using social media.

Onstage, she makes a point of talking to the audience and supplying some background about the pieces.

Tine was the first person to play a new concerto by Britta Byström with the Nordic Chamber Orchestra; and in celebration of the 150th anniversary of the birth of fellow Norwegian Edvard Munch, Tine was in charge of *Tine@Munch* – a three-day festival in Oslo's Edvard Munch Museum in June 2013.

In recognition of her outstanding performing abilities, Tine has received various awards including the 2009 Borletti-Buitoni Trust Fellowship, "Newcomer of the Year" at the 2007 Norwegian Grammy Awards (the first classical artist ever to be nominated), and the Luitpold Prize as the most outstanding and interesting young artist of the year.

tenThing was formed in 2007. Tine and three trumpet-playing friends were watching a string orchestra performing and decided they wanted to be part of a similar group for brass. So six others joined them and the group was born.

Tine has released her debut solo disc, *Storyteller*, and the debut album of her all-female brass ensemble tenThing, *10*.

**Source: www.tinethinghelseth.com**

# Check your understanding

1 For how long has Tine been playing the trumpet?

2 Give two examples of where Tine has performed on her own.

3 What was the reason for the Edvard Munch festival?

4 How many people are there in Tine's ensemble?

5 What is the name of the ensemble's first album?

6* What do you think Tine has been able to achieve in a group that she could not have done as only a solo player?

# Crime fiction and drama

## Sherlock Holmes

The British television series *Sherlock* has become a huge success in the entertainment industry in recent years and is now seen all over the world. Watch the actors talking about their roles in the video available at **www.youtube.com/watch?v = 5faHSZ0kNEY**

## Check your understanding

1 In which road does Sherlock live?

2 How does Steven Moffat describe Sherlock?

3 Who takes care of the forensics in *Sherlock?*

4 Where does Sherlock deduce that the girl has been?

5 What annoys Watson about Sherlock?

6\* Why is it interesting to watch a detective and his sidekick solve mysteries on television.

## Interviewing an actor

Which actor would you interview if you had the chance and what would you ask them?

Make a list of five actors who you would like to interview. Now compare your list with that of a partner. Are they completely different? Looking at both lists, decide on two actors you would like to interview. Now comes the tricky part. You will each play one actor while being interviewed by your partner. So you may both need to do some research to find out more about these people. If you are the interviewer, you'll need to think of about ten good questions to ask. One could be: "So what's your next film going to be about, then?"

---

### Study tips

#### Speaking – sequencing the early part of the conversation

The first part of the assessed phase of your Speaking test uses three prompts to help you settle in. The first two prompts ask you to talk about your own experiences and views relating to the topic, and maybe the views of people close to you. The third prompt moves into general areas and asks you to comment on how the topic affects society. So moving from the personal to the general is the aim of this part of the test.

Let's see how this works in the context of a discussion about films and acting. If the main topic under discussion was "The affect of films on society", you may be presented with these first two prompts:

- What types of films you like to see and why

- Films that you feel are unsuitable, or even harmful in some way

When you respond to the first prompt, it's likely that you will talk about particular films you have seen, probably the most recent ones, and then you will start to think about any genres that you seem to prefer. This is fine and your teacher/examiner will ask you about your favourite films, exploring your particular interests. Prompt two is more of a challenge as it asks for your views and asks you to support those views. It is *developing* the content of Prompt one.

Have a go at this with a partner. Write your own Speaking test. Choose a topic that is connected to leisure and entertainment, and write the first two opening prompts. Remember, Prompt one must ask about any direct experience of the topic, and Prompt two then asks about views, thoughts, or ideas connected to it, that is, "What I did", followed by "What I think".

Prompt three then moves into general matters. For our topic about films, it may look like this:

- that some countries or cultures seem to make more films than others – for example, Hollywood and Bollywood – and why this may be so.

So in the third prompt, you don't talk about your own experience at all. The main focus here is on society: groups of people, cultures, or even whole nations. In Prompt three you are nearly always considering one group of people's views, actions, and ideas against another's. This could be stated as "pros and cons", or advantages and disadvantages.

Now let's go back to your own topic and add a third prompt. Remember, it has to move into general matters and it should have the chance to present opposite or different actions, views, or ideas.

You could perhaps think of the development of the early part of the discussion therefore as:

- what I do or have done

- what others do and my views about that

- what everybody does and how this usually creates different views.

Prompt three usually focuses on what a particular group of people think and asks you to respond to their suggestions or ideas.

See if you can develop your topics along these lines, so, with your partner, practise going through the three prompts you created.

# Literary focus

Read this extract from a "Young Sherlock Holmes" novel *Black Ice* by Andrew Lane. Then answer the questions.

## Summary

The year is 1868 and 14-year-old Sherlock Holmes faces his most baffling mystery yet. Mycroft, his older brother, has been found with a knife in his hand, locked in a room with a body. Only Sherlock believes that his brother is innocent. But can he prove it?

In a chase that will take him to Moscow and back, Sherlock must discover who has framed Mycroft, and why.

Sunlight sparkled on the surface of the water, sending daggers of light flashing towards Sherlock's eyes. He blinked repeatedly, and tried to keep his eyelids half closed to minimize the glare.

The tiny rowing boat rocked gently in the middle of the lake. Around it, just past the shoreline, the grassy ground rose in all directions, covered in a smattering of bushes and trees. It was as if it were located in the middle of a green bowl, with the cloudless blue of the sky forming a lid across the top.

Sherlock was sitting in the bows of the boat, facing backwards. Amyus Crowe was sitting in the stern, his weight causing his end of the boat to sink lower into the water and Sherlock's to rise higher out of it. Crowe held a fishing rod out over the lake's surface.

"Now – what have you learned so far?"

Sherlock considered for a moment.

"The important thing is the temperature of the water, and the thing that drives the temperature of the water is how hot the sun is and whether it's shining straight down on the water or at an angle. Think about where the sun is, work out where the water is warm but not hot, and that's where you'll find the fish."

"Quite right."

They landed and Crowe started off walking, pushing through the undergrowth. Sherlock wondered briefly how the man knew which way

to go without a compass. He was about to ask, but instead tried to work it out himself. All Crowe had to go on was their surroundings. The sun rose in the east and set in the west, but that wasn't much help at lunchtime when the sun would be directly overhead. Or would it? A moment's thought and Sherlock realized that the sun would only be truly overhead at noon for places actually on the equator. For a country in the northern hemisphere, like England, the nearest point on the equator would be located directly south, and so the sun at noon would be south of a point directly overhead. That was probably how Crowe was doing it.

"And moss tends to grow better on the northern side of trees," Crowe called over his shoulder. "It's more shaded there, and so it's damper."

"How do you do that?" Sherlock shouted.

"Do what?"

"Tell what people are thinking, and interrupt them just at the right moment?"

"Ah," Crowe laughed. "That's a trick I'll explain some other time."

It took half an hour to reach the gates of Holmes Manor.

"A letter for you, sir," the maid said without making eye contact with Sherlock. She set the tray down on a table.

"Will there be anything else?"

"No, thank you." As she left he reached out eagerly to take the envelope. He didn't get many letters at Holmes Manor, and when he did they were almost always from – "Mycroft!"

"Is that a fact or a deduction?" Crowe asked.

Sherlock waved the envelope at him.

"I recognize the handwriting, and the postmark is Westminster, where he has his office, his lodgings and his club." He ripped the envelope open, pulling the flap from the grip of the blob of wax that held it firm. "Look!" he said, holding the paper up. "The letter is written on the headed stationery of the Diogenes Club."

"Check the postmark on the envelope," Crowe murmured.

"What time does it show?"

"Three thirty yesterday afternoon," Sherlock said, puzzled.

"Why?" Crowe gazed imperturbably at Sherlock.

"Mid afternoon on a weekday, and he's at his club, writing letters, rather than at his office? Does that strike you as unusual behaviour for your brother?"

Sherlock thought for a moment. "He once told me that he often walks across to his club for lunch," he said after a moment.

"He must have written the letter over lunch and got the footman to post it for him. The post would have been collected in the early afternoon, and the letter would have got to the sorting office for around three o'clock, then been stamped half an hour later. That's not suspicious, is it?"

Crowe smiled.

"Not in the slightest". He started reading:

*My dear Sherlock,[]*

*I write in haste, as I am awaiting the arrival of a steak and kidney pudding before I return to my office. I trust you are well. I trust also that our aunt and uncle are well. You will be pleased to hear, I am sure, that arrangements have been made to allow your education to continue at Holmes Manor. The news*

*that you will never have to return to Deepdene School will, I presume, not come as too much of a shock. Amyus Crowe will continue to school you in the more practical and sporting aspects of life, and Uncle Sherrinford has agreed to become responsible for your religious and literary education, which only leaves mathematics. I will think about that, and let you know when I have reached a decision. The aim, of course, will be to prepare you for university in a few years' time.*

*This morning, by the way, a letter arrived from our father. He must have posted it in India the moment he arrived, as it summarizes everything that happened to him on the voyage.*

*I am sure that you would rather read the letter than have me tell you about it, and so come and have lunch with me tomorrow. Please pass the invitation on to Mr Crowe: I have some details I wish to discuss with him about your education. The 9.30 a.m. train will bring you to London in good time. I look forward to seeing you tomorrow, and to hearing all about the events that have happened since we last met.*

*Your loving brother, Mycroft.*

"Anything interestin'?" Amyus Crowe asked. "We're going to London," Sherlock replied, grinning.

**Source: www.youngsherlock.com**

# Check your understanding

1 How old is Sherlock Holmes in this extract?

2 What is Amyus Crowe teaching Sherlock?

3 How does Crowe know the way he needs to go without a compass?

4 What is the name of Sherlock's brother?

5 When is Sherlock next meeting his brother?

6* How do you feel the story could continue? What will happen when Sherlock meets Mycroft?

# Common characteristics

What makes Sherlock a typical detective? Which things are less usual? A table has been started for you below.

| Typical | Not typical |
| --- | --- |
| He is interested in finding out reasons for things that have happened. | He is 14 years old. |

Now think about other fictional detectives you know about. Do they have any similar characteristics? In which ways are they different? Make a list and then compare your list with that of a partner.

# Lemony Snicket

Daniel Handler wrote *A Series of Unfortunate Events* under the pseudonym Lemony Snicket. He has also penned several books for adults under his own name.

 **Track 7.1** Listen to the interview with Daniel where he is talking about his work.

# Check your understanding

1 How does Daniel describe Lemony Snicket? Give two details.

2 To whom does Daniel compare detectives?

3 Which musical instrument does Daniel play?

4 Give one example of what Daniel enjoys about his work.

5 Why does Daniel enjoy reading paper books rather than electronic readers?

6* What qualities do you think Daniel needs to write a character like Lemony Snicket?

Would you like to be a detective? Or work for the police force? Why or why not? Have a think about the life you would lead if you were a detective. In what ways would you enjoy the role? What might cause you to not enjoy it? Think about other detectives you have read about or seen on television. In reality, is it maybe not as thrilling as they make it out to be?

## Building your vocabulary

**Match the words to the definitions.**

| | |
|---|---|
| theft | try to solve a mystery by finding facts |
| investigate | a secret place where it is hard to be found |
| hiding place | wanting to know too much information |
| curious | a narrow pathway between two buildings |
| alley | the taking of an item that is not yours to take |
| hired | unusual or strange |
| nosy | employed |

## Writing a job description

You are setting up a detective agency. Write a job description for new detectives. Include:

- previous experience you are looking for in applicants
- what particular qualities you want applicants to have
- availability, working hours, and so on
- any other things you are especially looking out for in applicants.

## Who could that be at this hour?

There was a town, and there was a girl, and there was a theft. I was living in the town, and I was hired to investigate the theft, and I thought the girl had nothing to do with it. I was a teenager and I was wrong. I was wrong about all of it. I should have asked the question "Why would someone say something was stolen when it was never theirs to begin with?" Instead, I asked the wrong question — four wrong questions, more or less.

You'll see her soon enough in any case, I thought, incorrectly.

Then the steam from my cup of tea cleared, and I looked at the people who were in the cafe with me. It is curious to look at one's family and try to imagine how they look to strangers. I saw a large-shouldered man in a brown suit that looked like it made him uncomfortable, and a woman drumming her fingernails on the table, over and over, the sound like a tiny horse's galloping. She happened to have a flower in her hair. They were both smiling, particularly the man.

Another woman came into the cafe. She did not look at me and brushed by my table, very tall, with a lot of very wild hair. Her shoes made noise on the floor. She stopped at a rack of envelopes and grabbed the first one she saw, tossing a coin to the woman behind the counter, who caught it almost without looking, and then she was back out the door. With all the tea on all the tables, it looked like one of her pockets was steaming. I was the only one who had noticed her. She did not look back.

There are two good reasons to put your napkin in your lap. One is that food might spill in your lap, and it is better to stain the napkin than your clothing. The other is that it can serve as a perfect hiding place. Practically nobody is nosy enough to take the napkin off a lap to see what is hidden there. I sighed deeply and stared down at my lap, as if I were lost in thought, and then quickly and quietly I unfolded and read the note the woman had dropped there.

Climb out the window in the bathroom and meet me in the alley behind this shop. I will be waiting in the green roadster. You have five minutes. — S

"Roadster," I knew, was a fancy word for "car," and I couldn't help but wonder what kind of person would take the time to write "roadster" when the word "car" would do. I also couldn't help but wonder what sort of person would sign a secret note, even if they only signed the letter S. A secret note is secret. There is no reason to sign it.

I stood up and walked to the back of the cafe. Probably one minute had passed already. The woman behind the counter watched me look this way and that. In restaurants they always make you ask where the bathroom is, even when there's nothing else you could be looking for. I told myself not to be embarrassed.

"If I were a bathroom," I said to the woman, "where would I be?"

She pointed to a small hallway. I noticed the coin was still in her hand. I stepped quickly down the hallway without looking back. I would not see the cafe again for years and years.

**Source: www.npr.org**

# Check your understanding

1  Where is Lemony Snicket?

2  How does Lemony describe the woman's drumming?

3  What does the woman buy in the cafe?

4  What does the woman give to Lemony?

5  How long does Lemony have to reach her?

6*  Give an example of something Lemony sees or does which might indicate he is a good detective.

# Writing an outline for a detective novel

You are going to plan the content for a detective novel. You have to plan five areas:

- Plot – outline briefly what is going to happen in the story.

- Characters – who is going to be in the story? What are their names? What do they do?

- Setting – where does the story take place? When – past, present, or future?

- Atmosphere – is it going to be serious? Is it going to be humorous? Is it going to be a mixture of the two?

- Ending – try not to give an ending that we have heard many times before. It is the last impression the reader has of your story, so you need to make sure it is interesting!

Once you have planned your story, share your plan with some of your classmates.

## Language focus

## Varying your conjunctions

When we give a reason for something, we often use "because":

- I wanted to give her some flowers *because* I needed to say sorry.

- I decided I would lend her my favourite book *because* I thought she would really like it.

However, it can be better to use other words, to make the writing more interesting for the reader:

- I wanted to give her some flowers *since* I needed to say sorry.

- I lent her my favourite book *as* I thought she would really like it.

Sometimes, using the one-syllable "since" or "as" can improve the overall flow of the writing.

We may wish to use alternatives for "because" to add variety to our writing:

- Seeing that it was raining, she decided to wear her long coat rather than her jacket.

- He studied physics rather than chemistry, the reason being he found it more interesting.

- He said he would donate five pounds to the charity in memory of his mother.

Now have a go yourself. Link the events and the reasons below by using words other than "because":

- Her favourite colour was pink/she was six years old.

- He was late for the concert/his watch had stopped.

- She was going on a two-week holiday/she had been working very hard.

- He really liked the film/his favourite actor was in the film.

- He wanted to be a mail carrier when he was older/he thought it was an exciting job to have.

## One-minute challenge

Challenge a partner to talk for a minute about a topic that you suggest. Ideally, this will be a topic that involves something that needs to be explained. See how long it is before he or she uses the word "because". Pausing is not allowed!

# Going out

We can also go out to be entertained. One area that has become increasingly popular in recent years has been the theatre.

Books, film, and the theatre have also become more closely linked. Books and theatre productions have been made into films, and films have been later put on stage. Both types have been equally popular. There are many examples: *Mamma Mia*, *The Lion King*, *The King's Speech*, *War Horse*, and *Billy Elliot*.

## Thinking out loud

Would you like to be on the stage? Do you get nervous in front of people? Could you overcome that to find fame and fortune? Or would you rather be a film star maybe? Think about being an actor. What would you like about it? Is fame always a good thing? Think about whether you could really handle being famous.

## Building your vocabulary

**Match the words to the definitions.**

| | |
|---|---|
| stage show | take the place of something |
| represent | a section of a stage show |
| act of a show | a performance in a theatre |
| Hollywood | an area famous for theatre in New York |
| stampede | the cause of the idea for something |
| Broadway | the central part of something |
| inspiration | an area famous for film-making in California, USA |
| essence | the fast movement of many animals of the same type, often through a desert |

## Adapting a film for the stage

Listen to the people who have adapted the animated film of *The Lion King* for the stage in the clip available at **www.youtube. com/watch?v = ScFWa-RwC3Y** (start at 0:56 up until 5:11).

## Check your understanding

1   How long is Act 1 of the stage show *The Lion King*?

2   What was the biggest challenge they faced in putting *The Lion King* on stage?

3   How many Broadway musicals had Julie done before *The Lion King*?

4   How many different ways are used to represent Simba?

5   What forms the essence of *The Lion King*?

6*  What stage adaptation do you like the most? If you have not seen one, explain why you would enjoy the chance to go and see The Lion King.

# First impressions

Imagine you have just been to see a musical on the stage. Write about it for your friends. How did the music make you feel? How did you feel as soon as you came out of the theatre? Write it all down as fast as you can. Aim for about 100 words. Don't worry about correct spelling or grammar – just scribble away!

Now pass this piece of impression writing to a partner. He or she is going to do two things:

1 Give you a mark out of 10 for enthusiasm and energy.

2 Show you where your spelling and grammar mistakes may be!

## Hollywood or Bollywood?

Which types of film do you enjoy watching? Why? With a partner, add to this list of genres: Biography, science-fiction, comedy …

Now think of a film that represents each genre. Share your finished list with another pair. Do any films appear in both lists?

## The role of films in society

Some films are based on events that have happened in the past. These films can be inspiring, as they tell how people have overcome problems to succeed, found fame despite coming from a poor background, or have been able to have a positive affect on a community around them.

Milkha Singh was able to do just that, becoming a world champion runner having overcome difficult personal circumstances. Milkha Singh's life has now been made into a film.

Read the extracts and then answer the questions.

---

## Milkha Singh: The man who never gave up

For the number of Indians who for over half a century have replayed a race again and again in their mind hoping it would some day throw up a different result, Milkha Singh's 400 metres final run at the Rome Olympics should be among the greatest heartbreaks in global sporting history.

However, continued adulation for the man decades later is a tribute to the scale of effort by India's greatest track athlete on that September day in the Italian capital, though he still missed out on becoming India's first Olympic track medallist.

As he was growing up, he used to run barefoot daily on hot sand to school, which was situated 20 kilometres from his house. He thinks this was good training but knows it is not possible to ask children to do this today. However, he does feel that the early identification of talented individuals is also important for India's athletic teams to shine.

India has in the last few years judged success purely in terms of medals, but looking into the past reveals how a more generous generation saluted Milkha as a pioneer. Milkha is India's finest track athlete of all time. He remains the only Indian male to win an individual Commonwealth Games athletics gold – he won the 400 yards at Cardiff in 1958, the first athlete from independent India to do so.

Despite that shattering miss, "The Flying Sikh" was a feared contender in the late 1950s and early '1960s, thanks to his punishing regime that reflected his will to win.

His national 400-metre record stood for 38 years, inspiring many world-class athletes who have followed him.

Since retiring from athletics, the former champion athlete has set up the Milkha Singh Charitable Trust, which helps poorer families survive if an athlete in their family has died. A percentage of the profits from the film *Bhaag Milkha Bhaag* are going to his trust.

Finally, let's read a quote from Milkha himself: "There is no shortcut to success. A scene in the film shows Milkha Singh running with wounded feet – this actually happened. I haven't found an alternative to hard work. You need to be patient, dedicated and true to yourself and your work."

**Source: www.hindustantimes.com**

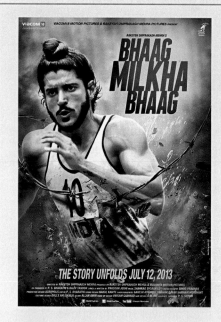

This isn't just a film about a sports person who brought untold glory to our country. *Bhaag Milkha Bhaag* is the story of an individual's journey from nothing to the peak of success.

In Prasoon Joshi's interpretation of Milkha's amazing success story, longing is the key to achievement. The "run" as a metaphor of life's circumstances runs through the narrative.

The screen time is taken up with Milkha's record-breaking achievements on the field. Milkha is played by Farhan Akhtar, who is not just playing Milkha; he is Milkha.

He gets tremendous support from other actors, specially Divya Dutta, who is very sincere in her role. Pavan Malhotra as Milkha's coach is, as usual, first-rate.

Unlike other period films in recent times that have conveniently and lazily resorted to antiques, artefacts, and vintage songs, *Bhaag Milkha Bhaag* simply and effortlessly emerges from the character.

Binod Pradhan's camera glides across Milkha's inner and outer world, telling it like it is. There's a complex design to the seeming simplicity of this story. The beautiful irony of Milkha Singh's life that this biopic captures so ably, is that he really didn't aspire to anything. He ran simply because he had to. The rest, as they say, is history.

*Bhaag Milkha Bhaag* is the kind of cinema that doesn't tempt us to share the main character's life with any false hopes. We the audience are driven into a desperate urge to share Milkha's life not only because he ran fast, but because he wasn't afraid to stumble, falter and, fall. Ironically, this film on Milkha rarely slips up, if ever.

**Source: www.dnaindia.com**

## Check your understanding

1 Which distance did Milkha Singh run as an athlete at the 1960 Rome Olympics?

2 For how long did his national record stand?

3 What is the main focus of the story in the film version of Milkha Singh's life?

4 What is the reason Milkha Singh ran, according to the film?

5 Overall, what does the reviewer think about the film?

## Writing a presentation

The national film council have offered your school the chance to propose a full-length film based on the life of one of your heroes. But only one film will receive the support and funding to be actually made.

In pairs, agree on a person who you would like to feature in your film. You will be giving a presentation to the class to persuade them to vote for your film. You therefore need to include plenty of reasons why your chosen person needs to be on the big screen, as well as giving examples of significant points in his or her life that will appeal to the cinema audiences.

Once all of your proposals have been viewed, have a secret ballot on which should go forward for the funding.

# Bollywood Oscars

The Bollywood Oscars — the four-day International Indian Film Academy's Weekend and Awards — has left India and, in 2014, been held in the US for the first time. The ceremony has an estimated global viewership of more than 800 million. That is quite an achievement for an industry which started quietly in 1913.

Tampa's competition for the 2014 event reportedly included Melbourne, Australia, as well as Dubai and Abu Dhabi in the United Arab Emirates.

Tampa has hosted major sporting events, including four Super Bowls, as well as political events like the US Republican National Convention in 2012. For Mayor Bob Buckhorn, Tampa's selection reflects its ability to host huge events and thousands of visitors without a hitch. Buckhorn said, "We can compete for these international and global events, and we can win."

With a monsoon season from June to September, Mumbai might be one of the only places on Earth where a trip to Tampa could seem like a summertime treat. Mumbai had a high of 85 Friday, with haze and a feels-like temperature in the 90s.

"I kind of can't believe it," said Shephali Rele, who writes about Bollywood for a newspaper for Indian-Americans in Florida. "People from all over America attended." Buckhorn said the area always extends "the warmest welcome that Tampa can possibly manage" to all visitors, including hundreds of Bollywood stars.

Buckhorn credited the success of the IIFA bid to two things. One, the city has handled political conventions without any problems. Also, the bay area is home to an active and organized Indian-American community of more than 23,500 and he says, "This is probably a winning formula".

The Tampa awards weekend was the 15th annual version of the IIFA celebration. Previously, it has gone to cities including London, Johannesburg, Amsterdam, and Bangkok. Local officials say IIFA weekends generate in the neighborhood of 24 000 hotel room nights with a local economic impact exceeding $11 million for the host cities.

"By all standards, this is a huge event," said Dr Kiran Patel, the Tampa cardiologist, philanthropist and insurance entrepreneur who is among the effort's backers." To get this to Tampa is really cool because nobody believed it could be done."

The Indian film industry is huge, turning out 1,255 movies in 2011 — more than Hollywood. (Still, Hollywood's big budgets and high ticket prices generate five times the revenue of Bollywood's $2 billion film industry.)

"Bollywood" originally referred to movies made in Mumbai (formerly called Bombay), and the term was probably first used in the 1970s, but it has become associated with films that can unfold over three hours, with an intermission, combining romance, comedy, action, drama and song-and-dance.

The Indian film industry as a whole also encompasses Kollywood, which turns out Tamil cinema, Tollywood, which makes Telugu films, as well as many others; and there are also many independent film producers.

The IIFA also sent representatives to check out Tampa on at least two occasions. Buckhorn was not surprised they liked what they saw. "It just reinforces what we tried to do throughout the RNC," he said, "which is to tell the world that, in Florida, there are places other than just Miami and Orlando."

**Source: *Tampa Bay Times***

# Bollywood Oscars

Read the extract and then answer the questions.

## Check your understanding

1 How many people watch the Bollywood film awards?

2 Give an example of another large event that has taken place in Tampa.

3 What is the weather like in Mumbai in June?

4 How many Indian-Americans live in Tampa?

5 Name a part of the Indian film industry apart from Bollywood.

6* How has Bollywood become international?

---

## Study tips

### Using linking words in a summary

Sometimes you need to change notes that you have written into full sentences, and paragraphs. This is how you create a summary. You will at some point have to write a short summary, using details that have already been given to you. It is much more interesting to the reader if you can use linking words to add variety to what you write. Some examples of linking words could be "also", "therefore", "furthermore", and "first".

Work with your partner and see how many more linking words you can think of. Give yourselves a time limit of two minutes. Then look at the sentences below. You will agree that they are very short and boring. How could you make them more interesting? Try using some of the linking words that you have chosen, or others that may be suitable.

> *The day was very hot. We decided to go to the beach. Our friends came with us. We had a good time. I didn't like the big waves. I did not go into the sea. We went to the cafe. I was glad we did. I ate some delicious cake. The day soon ended. I was very tired. I was pleased that I met my friends.*

Here are some notes that have been taken on the article about the Bollywood Oscars and Bollywood films.

- Oscars ceremony is a four-day event
- More than 800 million viewers worldwide
- The event held in Tampa, USA
- Bollywood films originally from Mumbai, India
- Indian film industry made more than 1,000 movies in 2011
- Films have romance and song and dance

Now on your own, write a summary to include all the information in the notes. Try to include linking words to make the summary more interesting. Compare your summary to your partner's – how similar are they? How do they differ?

### Sample student responses

Let's have a look and see how two other students attempted to write a summary about the choice of Tampa, USA to host the Bollywood Oscars.

**Student A**

The city of Tampa has hosted many major sporting events. People from all over America attended the Bollywood event. There were hundreds of Bollywood stars there. It was very successful. The harbour area in Tampa is the home to an active and organized Indian-American community. There are about 25 thousand of them. They supported the event with enthusiasm. One sponsor of the event said "Nobody believed it could be done."

**Student B**

In the past, the city of Tampa has hosted many major sporting events and, on this occasion, people from all over America attended the Bollywood event. In addition, hundreds of Bollywood stars were there and therefore this helped to make the event very successful. Furthermore, the harbour area in Tampa is the home to an active and organized Indian-American community, with more than 25 thousand inhabitants, who supported the event with enthusiasm. At the end, one sponsor of the event said that nobody believed that it could be done.

Discuss with your partner which of the two students showed the best summary-writing technique and would have scored the most marks. Give your reasons why.

# Organizing large-scale events

Watch the promotional videos for Rio and Tokyo below; their presentations resulted in them being awarded the Summer Olympic Games. As you are watching, write down the parts of the videos that you find appealing and that you think would have helped each city win its bid. Think about content, music, commentary, and other visuals.

Use the chart to help you.

|  | Content | Music | Commentary | Other visuals |
|---|---|---|---|---|
| **Rio 2016** | | | | |
| **Tokyo 2020** | | | | |

The Rio 2016 Olympic bid video is available at **www.youtube.com/ watch?v = uTVNr5mmaq8**

The Tokyo 2020 Olympic bid video is available at **www.youtube.com/ watch?v = zHSUz26fAIM**

## Hosting an international event

With a partner, choose an international event that appeals to you both.

This event is looking for a new host city for two years' time. Your city or town is applying to be the host, and you are in charge of the application.

What are the main positive features of your city or town? Why would it be the best place to hold this international event?

You are going to give a presentation on these positive features, so that the event comes to your capital city. You need to focus on convincing the event organizers that you are ready to hold such a large event. You can certainly add some music and pictures to make the presentation more attractive.

# The Big Issue – using celebrity to raise money

Increasingly, people working in the entertainment industry have used their position to raise money for good causes around the world. Since George Harrison, The Beatles' guitarist and singer, made the first charity single in 1971, donating what he raised to the United Nations Children's Fund (UNICEF), musicians, actors, and models have given their time and used their talents to raise money.

Live Aid in 1985 was one of the first global concerts, taking place in London, UK and Philadelphia, USA.

Comic Relief is a British charity that holds a big fundraising event called Red Nose Day every two years. It was started in 1985 by Richard Curtis, the film director, and Lenny Henry, the comedian.

## Building your vocabulary

What makes you donate money to a charity? Seeing pictures of suffering? The thought of finding a cure for a disease? A celebrity doing something amazing in return for a donation?

Look at the list of words and phrases below.

**fundraisers     fun run     relief     crisis     sponsored walk**

**treat     raising money     sponsorship     aid**

**sponsored     skydive     cure     help**

Which of these are things done by a charity? Which are done by others wishing to help that charity?

Look at the passage below and use the words and phrases from the list to complete it. (Not all the words appear in the passage.)

"As there are more and more charities, all competing for money, so they have to find increasingly creative ways to capture our attention and encourage us to donate to them. They need money to give ........................... to those most in need. A popular form of ................... is doing a ..........................., often in the local park, where it is safe from traffic and therefore suitable for all age groups. More adventurous ........................... may be more daring; some have done a sponsored bungee jump, while others have gone up in an aeroplane and done a ............................. However, the money is raised, however, the most important thing is that the charity is able to ........................... others."

## How it all began

Comic Relief was launched from a refugee camp in Sudan on Christmas Day in 1985, live on BBC One. At that time, there was a terrible famine in Ethiopia and something had to be done. That something was Comic Relief.

The idea was simple – Comic Relief would get a whole bunch of much-loved British comedians to make the public laugh while they raised money to help people in desperate need.

As well as doing something about the very real and direct emergency in Ethiopia, Comic Relief was determined to help tackle the broader needs of poor and disadvantaged people in Africa and at home in the UK.

## Red Nose Day arrives

It all began with a few live events and, before too long, Red Nose Day was created. The first ever Red Nose Day in 1988 took the nation by storm – bringing together comedy and charity like never before on live national TV. It raised an incredible £15 million.

The money raised by all Red Nose Days since has helped, and is helping, to support people and communities in dire need both in the UK and Africa.

## Sport Relief kicks off

In December 2001, Comic Relief launched a second major fundraising campaign – Sport Relief – that takes place in alternate years with Red Nose Day. The idea is that everyone gets active, raises cash, and helps to change lives.

## Others we've helped

As we've grown over the years, we've also lent a touch of expertise to other organizations who are also working hard to help transform the lives of disadvantaged people across the world. Comic Relief has been central in many projects and campaigns from Make Poverty History and Live8, to America Gives Back and the United Against Malaria coalition.

## What we've raised and how it's helped

Since 1985, Comic Relief has raised more than £900 million to tackle poverty and social injustice across the UK, Africa, and some of the world's poorest countries.

It's thanks to the public's amazing fundraising for Red Nose Day and Sport Relief, as well as astounding support from our friends and partners, that we've been able to do this.

Over the years, our cash in Africa has educated people about human immunodeficiency virus (HIV) and acquired immunodeficiency syndrome (AIDS) and taught women to read. It has helped street children from Bangladesh to Brazil and supported communities affected by terrible conflict and natural disasters.

Source: www.comicrelief.com

# Check your understanding

1. What is the exact date that Comic Relief was started?
2. Which event prompted people to create Comic Relief?
3. How much money did the first Red Nose Day raise?
4. What began in 2001?
5. Name two causes that Comic Relief has helped.
6* Which relief fund would you ask Comic Relief to help with and why?

# Study tips

## Working with numbers and figures

Numbers and figures appear so often in many forms in our daily lives that we hardly notice them. We sometimes overlook them. It is vital, however, that when we use numbers we use them precisely. Imagine the problems that could be caused if, for example, we added too many zeros to a figure.

You will be tested on your understanding of numbers and figures, but don't worry, you will not be tested from a mathematics perspective, so you will not be asked to add anything up, or to find the square root of something. However, you will be asked to locate a specific detail, which may be a date, or an amount, or the cost of something, or the length of something, for example.

Think of as many uses of numbers as you possibly can and create a list. Here are two to start you off: dates and times. How many others can you find?

Now work with a partner. Swap lists. Now create a question based on one of your partner's uses of numbers. For example, you may see "distance" on the list, so you could ask, "How far away is the nearest train station from your school?" The key skill in answering these types of questions is to be precise. So if the station is 20 kilometres away, you may write this in four ways:

a) 20 kilometres     c) 20 kms

b) Twenty kilometres     d) Twenty kms

You'll be pleased to know that all of these would be accepted as correct. However, our advice is to use the numbers when writing a number and not the full word – option c) from the list above.

Practise these number questions some more with your partner by creating some more questions from each other's lists of the various uses of numbers. Here are three examples:

1 How much does the box weigh?

2 What is the height of the tower?

3 What time did the accident happen?

## Sample student responses

1 How far is the station from the school?

**Student A** – 5 kilometres

**Student B** – 5

Student A has the correct answer. Why does Student B not get a mark?

2 How much did the e-book reader cost?

**Student A** – One hundred and fifty.

**Student B** – 150 dollars

Which student has the correct answer?

Look at these eight questions and answers. The student got three of these wrong. Which ones are they?

1 What time does the train leave tomorrow?

10 o'clock

2 How far is it to the beach?

4

3 How many kilometres is it to the beach?

4

4 What is the date of her birthday?

May 20

5 How long did the film last?

2 hours

6 How much was your new watch?

One hundred and fifty

7 How much do you weigh?

65

8 How many kilogrammes do you weigh?

Sixty five

It may be interesting if you go back to your number questions now and, with your partner, come up with some correct and some incorrect responses to them.

# Eddie Izzard

Read the blog and web extract. Then answer the questions.

## Eddie's Blog

I had always wanted to do a big physical running challenge, and this seemed a great way to do it and also raise money to help Africa and the poorest countries in the world as well as projects that Sport Relief fund in the UK I was also going to be advised by Olympic experts who have worked with Sport Relief before. They would help me keep running in the right direction.

So I told them I wanted to try to run around the whole of the UK. London to Cardiff to Belfast to Edinburgh and back to London, running through as many parts of the UK that lie in between our four capitals.

Comedian Eddie Izzard has completed one of the most incredible challenges in Sport Relief's history. Eddie arrived in Trafalgar Square, London, marking the end of his 43rd marathon in only 51 days – all in aid of Sport Relief.

He'd run at least 27 miles a day, 6 days a week for 7 weeks straight, covering more than 1,110 miles across the UK.

Eddie set off at 6.30am from Trafalgar Square on July 27th and headed off though all four nations of the UK in support of Sport Relief.

As he ran, Eddie carried the flag of each country he ran through. His mad adventure saw blisters popping and toenails falling off, he took ice baths each evening and was determined to run, walk or crawl his way back to London. He ate over 6,000 calories a day just so he could keep going. And he did it all to raise money for charity.

A few months after completing his amazing run, Eddie got an actual prize to show for it.

Eddie Izzard, went on to win a Sports Personality of the Year Special Award for his extraordinary efforts. He was presented with his award by world marathon record-holder Paula Radcliffe and fellow comedy actor James Corden in front of a huge crowd at Sheffield Arena.

Eddie's incredible challenge raised hundreds of thousands of pounds for Sport Relief.

# Check your understanding

1  Why did Eddie want to do his amazing run?

2  Who advised Eddie while he was preparing for the run?

3  How many marathons has Eddie completed?

4  How many calories a day did Eddie have to eat?

5  What special prize has Eddie been awarded?

6*  What would you ask Eddie if you ever met him?

## Language focus

### Using adverbs

When we wish to emphasize how good something was, we can, quite simply, add more words to do so:

- That was really amazing – the best I have ever seen.

- It was incredibly good finally getting to meet my idol.

- I felt completely exhausted having finished such a long run.

However, sometimes, looking back at our work, we can see the same words repeated so we need to make sure the words we are using in our writing are not repetitive:

- It was a thoroughly memorable experience, finally getting to meet him.

- It was truly the best experience of my life.

- I was utterly exhausted at the end of the day.

Using less common words makes the writing more interesting and more memorable for the reader.

We can use words like these to emphasize what we wish to say:

*especially, wholly, categorically, absolutely, entirely*, and *unquestionably*

Now you have a go. Add some of these words to the sentences to make them more interesting:

- The film I saw last week was exciting.

- Nick's party was the best I have ever been to.

- I thought the video of their latest single was good.

- It is a book I would read again as I enjoyed it.

- It was made up and I can say there is no truth in it at all.

In pairs, imagine you have just seen a film that you both liked. Role play this and build in some of the adverbs you have seen here, but also some new ones that you have perhaps not used before. Do some research on adverbs and then use them to describe films, actors, plots, characters, and so on.

# Apps

## Thinking out loud

Part of modern life is the mobile phone. And, increasingly, part of mobile phone use is the app (software application). There are thousands of apps that you could download to your phone. Some are free while others require a small charge. However, which ones are worth having? Spend a few minutes thinking about how you use your mobile phone and the apps you have. Do you really need them? Could you survive without a mobile phone?

## Building your vocabulary

**high resolution    high tech    GPS    interface    interactivity    terrain    database    reinforce**

Check the meaning of these words, phrases, and abbreviations and then put each one into the correct gap below:

When it comes to buying the latest smartphone, the features it has can be its greatest selling point and need to be ................................ as well as cutting edge. The pictures need to be ................................ so they can be clearly seen on a small screen; and the whole ................................ needs to be user-friendly, so the consumer can easily find their way around the phone. Useful additions are the inclusion of ................................, so owners can find their way around unfamiliar ................................ without the need of a map, compass, or any other location device. There needs to be fast ................................, so results can be found quickly, as well as a large ................................ from which the phone can pull results. Finally, the whole design of the phone needs to be such that it will ................................ the idea to the consumer that what they have just purchased is value for money, as well as being an object that will be positively commented on by their friends.

# Apps

Read the below text.

## Solar System for iPad

As the name suggests, this app is a digital book about our solar system, including facts about the sun, planets, moons, and more; you can learn about gravity, patterns (such as rotations around the sun), and each planet and moon. This reference app comes to life with high-resolution photos, videos, animation, music, and text, and some interactivity as well. Bring stargazing to life with this far-out collection of astronomy facts, photos, and animations.

## Geocaching

Common Sense Media says that this expensive but very cool GPS app makes it possible for the whole family to go geocaching, a high-tech treasure hunt game. Geocaches can be hidden in rough terrain and other public locations. This app makes it unnecessary to buy a dedicated GPS device. The app taps directly into a database with more than 2 million locations, some within walking distance, and gives you everything you need to find treasures hidden by other

enthusiasts. Search by your current location or specific address, and get hints, photos, and step-by-step navigation. All that's missing is a torch.

## SkySafari

*SkySafari* is a powerful mobile planetarium that uses GPS locations to view the night sky. The app comes in multiple versions. The databases, even on the entry-level versions, are large, requiring up to 940 MB of free space depending on the platform. You can learn about astronomy by viewing planets and stars; searching for specific objects of interest; or looking at astronomical sightings in that night's sky. You can view movements by the year, month, day, hour, minute, or second for 100 years into the past and future. *SkySafari* is a breathtakingly beautiful and amazingly rich resource for you to learn about, see, and appreciate astronomy.

## Historypin

Historypin is a great tool to bring families together to share stories.

Users pin historical photos to a mapped location and add a note explaining the image. You can learn about the history of any area by searching Historypin's world map by place, time, or subject. You can learn what your neighbourhood looked like in 1862, 1962, and 2002, or view photos of, say, summer camps across the world. Because there are a few different ways to use Historypin's bank of user-contributed knowledge, as well as ways to add content, you can learn how to access and create digital content that's meant to be shared with the general public. Historypin makes it easy for you to share your own stories while discovering the past.

## GarageBand

*GarageBand* is powerful digital music workstation and multitrack recorder. You can create songs in a number of ways: by sequencing high-quality prerecorded loops; by playing virtual instruments (guitars, basses, strings, keyboards, and drums); or by recording live instruments and vocals, all in an interesting interface. An added bonus is the great editing tools that tighten up any musical performance. You can share your *GarageBand* songs via social media, email, or text. The visual interface helps teach multitrack recording and song structure, and the virtual instruments reinforce music theory and aural skills. *GarageBand* is designed to give everyone an amazing musical experience – and it delivers.

Source: www.commonsensemedia. org/mobile-app-reviews/ historypin

# Making an individual presentation

Which apps have you used that you would recommend to others? Prepare a talk of about 3 to 4 minutes' length about a useful app. (It really does need to be useful and not a game-playing app.) You may need to research the available apps, and you will of course need to use spoken persuasive language and other devices in your presentation to convey just how useful this particular app is.

## Study tips

## Listening to a follow-up discussion

Listening to a talk about a topic often features in the listening test. However, you may also be asked to listen to a follow-up discussion, usually between two people who have listened to the talk as well. Here's how this may work.

A talk is given by a mobile phone saleswoman about how her company's new phone features more and better apps than any of the competitors.

This is followed by a discussion between two people attending the sales conference who discuss the details of the talk further.

Let's practise these two connected listening skills. With a partner, decide on an app that you know well and that you want to promote. Give a two to three minute talk on aspects of the app and why it is so good. You can both share the talking. You will be speaking to another pair of students selected by your teacher.

As a pair, note down five key aspects of the app that you have just heard about. Now, let's develop the skill of recognizing views and attitudes. Have a discussion about the app with your partner. What do you like or dislike about it? Do you think it will be popular with other people? How useful is it? What would you change about it to improve it? Do you think it will pass the test of time?

Now go back to the pair who gave the talk and re-enact your discussion about their app. They need to listen to you quietly and you need to discuss the app for about 3 minutes.

This exercise is intended to familiarize you with the format of the follow-on discussion. It's like listening to a talk about a talk!

**Track 7.2** Listen to the follow-up discussion about the effect of the growth of mobile phones and decide which of the three students below has understood that discussion best.

## Sample student responses

### Student A

It's clear that mobile phones and the various apps you can get for them is having a negative impact on most of the users. A lot of people become addicted and as a result, the government is going to investigate this growth area. The two people discussing phones were generally in agreement about this.

### Student B

One of the people accepts that she should be stronger in saying no. The other person has stronger views and feels that mobile phones are necessary but that people should think carefully about how and how much they use them.

### Student C

It's all about getting the latest phone. And the latest app. Nothing else matters, really. You'd look silly among your friends with an out-of-date phone, and that's too much embarrassment. I think the person with the negative views is wrong.

# Gaming

1940 – Edward U. Condon designs a computer for the Westinghouse display at the World's Fair that plays the traditional game Nim, in which players try to avoid picking up the last match. Tens of thousands of people play it, and the computer wins at least 90% of the games.

1966 – While waiting for a colleague at a New York City bus station, Ralph Baer conceives the idea of playing a video game on television. On September 1, he writes down his ideas that become the basis of his development of television video games.

1968 – Ralph Baer patents his interactive television game. In 1972, Magnavox releases *Odyssey*, the first home video game system, based on his designs.

1972 – Nolan Bushnell and Al Alcorn of Atari develop an arcade table tennis game. When they test it in Andy Capps Tavern in Sunnyvale, California, it stops working. Why? Because people played it so much it jammed with quarters. *Pong*, an arcade legend, is born.

1975 – Atari introduces its home version of *Pong*. Atari's founder, Nolan Bushnell, cannot find any partners in the toy business, so he sells the first units through the Sears Roebuck sporting goods department.

1981 – Video game fans go ape over Nintendo's *Donkey Kong*, featuring a character that would become world famous: Jumpman. Never heard of him? That's because he's better known as Mario, the name he took when his creator, Shigeru Miyamoto, makes him the star of a later game by Nintendo.

1991 – Sega needs an iconic hero for its Genesis (known as Mega Drive in Japan) system and finds it in Sonic the Hedgehog. Gamers, especially in the United States, snap up Sega systems and love the little blue guy's blazing speed and edgy attitude.

2001 – Microsoft enters the video game market with Xbox and hit games like *Halo: Combat Evolved*. Four years later, Xbox 360 gains millions of fans with its advanced graphics and seamless online play.

2006 – Nintendo Wii gets gamers off the couch and moving with innovative, motion-sensitive remotes. Not only does Nintendo make gaming more active, it also appeals to millions of people who never before liked video games.

2009 – Social games like *Farmville* and mobile games like *Angry Birds* shake up the games industry. Millions of people who never would have considered themselves gamers now while away hours playing games on new platforms like Facebook and the iPhone.

Source: www.icheg.org

## Check your understanding

1 Where was Ralph Baer when he came up with his gaming idea?

2 Why did the Atari table tennis game stop working in 1972?

3 In which year did Mario first appear?

4 When was the Nintendo Wii first launched?

5 Name a modern platform for gamers that has been available since 2009.

6* Which game in the article appeals to you the most and why?

# Reflection

In groups of four, you are going to adapt a book you all love for the stage. You first need to decide which book you are going to adapt. You then need to agree on which part of the book to adapt and plan out one scene. You're not adapting the whole book – just a few pages to create a single scene.

Now decide which role each of the group members will play – you will be working on different aspects of the adaptation before combining your ideas at the end.

**Director**: You need to decide how many actors are needed for your adaptation; remember, you can ask one person to play more than one role. Then decide who plays who. You will play the role of director.

**Writer**: You will write the dialogue for the scene. Remember to add stage directions for your actors to follow.

**Sound manager**: You will provide the music for the scene. It does not have to be continuous, but it does help set the scene, create and maintain atmosphere, and fill any gaps while scenery is being moved.

**Extra role**: Think of any of additional tasks that may be needed to plan and act out a scene.

Now go ahead and rehearse your scene, and when you are ready, perform it. Before the performance, ask one cast member to announce to the audience where the scene has been taken from and why you have chosen it.

 **My progress**

Each chapter includes four study skills. These are skills that will feature in your final examinations. So let's check your progress with these key skills in mind.

| Where am I now? | Very pleased – I think I'm good at this | OK – but I do need more practice | One of my weaker areas – so I need a lot more practice |
|---|---|---|---|
| Speaking about myself and my experiences and then talking about the views of others | | | |
| Writing clear summaries and linking the sentences together | | | |
| Dealing with numbers and figures in a reading text | | | |
| Listening to two people who are having a follow-up discussion | | | |

Now pick out one skill that you would like to prioritize for improvement and produce a short action plan to help you become stronger. Use a template similar to the following – that is filled out for you with an example.

# Action plan

Skill I want to improve dealing with numbers and figures in a reading text.

- *planning* – how I will try to improve this skill:
  do some research about where numbers and figures are more likely to appear in written articles

- *implementing* – what I will need and what my exact strategy is:
  a couple of articles that feature a lot of numbers and figures, and then extract the phrases or sentences that focus on the numbers; what exactly is being measured?

- *monitoring* – how I will know I am improving and what evidence I may keep:
  if I keep a list of the different ways that numbers and figures are used, and I update that list, I should eventually cover all of the uses that the examination tests

# 8 Hobbies and interests

## In this chapter you will:

- visit the UK, Paris and Myanmar to meet people engaged in a variety of interests

- read about a royal hobby and about a Nobel Prize winner's favourite music

- write to a newspaper about collecting as a hobby; give your suggestions as to what you would take to a desert island

- listen to a music lover explaining why he listens to music and follow instructions in an instant lesson on playing the ukelele

- talk about autograph hunting and debate the rights and wrongs of fishing

## Key study skills

- Using paraphrasing and examples when *speaking*

- *Listening* to recognize opinions and attitudes in a group of speakers

- Using paragraphs and topic sentences in your *writing*

- *Reading* to locate appropriate content for a summary

# Hobbies

What are your hobbies? Do you collect things? Or perhaps you prefer to make things? Maybe you enjoy being out in the countryside, or the town? Are you a keen sportsperson? Your hobbies are what you do in your spare time. They are things that help you escape or get involved in something different. Think about some hobbies that you'd like to explore.

## What's my hobby?

In small groups you are going to take it in turns to mime one of your leisure-time activities for the rest of the group to guess. They can have up to five minutes to try to guess your hobby. If they succeed, they win the round, but if they can't guess after five minutes, you are the winner. Here's a hint – choose the most unusual of your hobbies or an unusual aspect of a hobby.

In your groups talk about the hobbies that you were miming. Which hobby was the most difficult to guess? Why? Which was the most unusual? Take it in turns to say a little bit about your hobby and why you think others may like to take it up. Discuss hobbies you may like to try.

## Study tips

### Speaking – using paraphrasing and examples to work with prompts

Let's take this opportunity to look at a full Topic Card, based on the theme of Hobbies and interests. We will explore how a Topic Card is created and what each card contains.

Here's how it may look:

> **A Hobbies and interests**
>
> *Most people have a hobby or an interest that gives them pleasure and allows them to escape from the daily life of school, college, and/or work.*
>
> Discuss this topic with the examiner.
>
> **The following ideas *must* be used in sequence to develop the conversation:**
>
> - what hobbies or interests you have
>
> - any hobbies or interests that your friends and family have
>
> - the pros and cons of having a hobby
>
> - the suggestion that some hobbies can become life-changing and that this is usually a bad thing
>
> - the idea that hobbies are of no real use to anyone other than the people doing them.
>
> You are free to consider any other *related* ideas of your own.
>
> Remember, you are not allowed to make any written notes.

You can see that the prompts are designed to follow a pattern. With your partner, use your own words to describe this pattern. Make a list of 1 to 5, matching what each prompt is trying to cover. Compare your list to another pair. How similar are they? Our list is at the bottom of this section. But don't look until after you have written yours!

Remember that each prompt *must* be used. You can't miss one out if it proves to be difficult, but you can paraphrase it (that is, use your own words to say a similar thing) and this usually helps. Let's see how this works by looking at Prompts four and five from the card above. First, Prompt four:

- the suggestion that some hobbies can become life-changing and that this is usually a bad thing

How would you explain this to someone who didn't quite understand it? Here are two useful ways: 1) paraphrasing, and 2) by giving examples. For the above prompt:

1   When a hobby takes over someone's life it can have a negative effect.

2   For example, my friend was a keen cyclist. But he started to ride too many hours each day, and was soon riding for four hours a day. His wife was very upset at this as she never got to see him.

See if you can do the same thing now with Prompt five:

- the idea that hobbies are of no real use to anyone other than the people doing them.

Now you have a go at constructing your own Topic Card. Think of a topic with your partner and write five prompts. Don't worry about an introduction; focus strictly on the prompts.

Can you paraphrase some of the prompts? Can you give some examples that help explain what is meant by the prompts? If you can, then your prompts are working as they should be.

To test your Topic Card fully, why not hand it to another pair and have a four-way discussion? The aim of this activity is to familiarize yourselves with the pattern and to engage with the prompts actively to make them work for you.

Our first list:

1   Personal – about you.

2   Personal – about people you know well.

3   General – everyone's views; the views of society as a whole.

4   A suggestion made by one person; usually arguable.

5   A broader idea – usually abstract.

Our second list:

1   Easy – gets you talking.

2   Still easy – talking about people you know.

3   A bit harder – have to think about the different views and so on of lots of people.

4   Getting harder – need to respond to one person's strong view.

5   As hard as it gets – need to talk about "what if…" and other creative scenarios.

# Collecting

## Building your vocabulary

How many of these words do you know? Check their meaning in a dictionary and then try to solve the crossword below. When you've entered all the words across correctly, what word appears in the shaded column?

**philately    honorary    album    rarity    auction    courtier    confine    succeeded**

**accession    renowned**

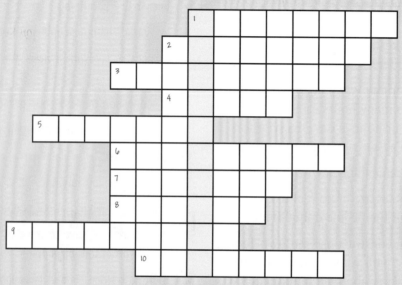

| | |
|---|---|
| **1** person attending royalty | **6** followed |
| **2** unpaid | **7** sale to the highest bidder |
| **3** stamp collecting | **8** something very uncommon |
| **4** in which photos or stamps are put | **9** coming to the throne |
| **5** restrict to | **10** famous |

# A royal collector

In 1856, the Prince of Wales (later King Edward VII) and his younger brother Prince Alfred, Queen Victoria's second son, were given copies of the soon-to-be issued new 6d stamps. Alfred became a serious stamp collector. He put together a small collection and served as Honorary President of what is now the Royal Philatelic Society London from 1890 until his death.

Before his death in 1900, he sold his collection to his older brother, who in turn gave it to his son, the Duke of York. He was already a very keen collector, and once wrote: "I wish to have *the* best collection and not *one of* the best collections in England."

In March 1893 he was elected Honorary Life Vice-President of the Royal Philatelic Society. On his marriage later in the year, fellow members of the Society gave him an album of postage stamps as a wedding present. It contained nearly 1,500 contributions from more than 100 of the Society's members.

In 1896 the Duke of York accepted the invitation to become President of the Society, a position he held until 1910 when he came to the Throne.

He recognized rarity and made every effort to obtain the rarest stamps at the first possible opportunity. By 1904 he had acquired both the Penny and Two Pence "Post Office" Mauritius of 1847 – the first stamps issued by a colonial post office and probably the most prized stamps that any collector could wish to acquire. The 1d was bought from another collector, while the unused Two Pence "Post Office" Mauritius was acquired at auction in 1904 for a then-record price of £1,450.

A courtier asked the Prince if he had seen that "some fool had paid as much as 1400 pounds for one stamp". "Yes," came the reply. "I was that fool!"

In 1906 he decided to confine his collection almost entirely to the stamps of Great Britain and the Empire.

The Duke of York succeeded his father as King George V on 6 May 1910. As the 70th anniversary of the penny black, it was perhaps an appropriate date for the accession of a king who became one of the most renowned philatelists of his time.

The strength of his collection lies in its completeness. Regardless of how attractive or unattractive the stamps were, King George V never neglected a stamp issue provided that it was of good status.

Tradition has it when King George V was in London he spent three afternoons a week with his stamp collection. He was very rarely interrupted.

Today King George V's collection is housed in 328 red albums, each of about 60 pages.

**Source: adapted extract from www.royal.gov.uk**

# Check your understanding

1 Who did Prince Alfred give his stamp collection to?

2 What position did his son later attain?

3 What did he spend £1,400 on in 1904?

4 What is the strong point about this royal collection?

5 How much time did the king spend looking after his stamps?

6* From the evidence in the passage what do you think the king enjoyed about stamp collecting?

# Planning for writing

Other famous stamp collectors have included musicians Freddie Mercury and, from the English rock band The Beatles, John Lennon. Perhaps you are a philatelist. If so, discuss with a partner why it appeals to you. However, stamp collecting is not the popular hobby that it used to be. Discuss with your partner why this may be so. Here are some potential reasons for you both to consider:

- competition from other interests – television, the Internet, and virtual entertainment

- the change in communication methods – email, cell phones, and chatrooms

- printed labelling of goods and packages.

Make some brief notes on the points mentioned in your discussion.

## Key skills

## Persuasive writing

One of the best ways to find examples of persuasive English is to study advertisements. Almost any advert will do, because the sole reason for an advert is to persuade.

Notice the following features:

- the positive tone – "take advantage", "improved flavour"

- the warm recommendation – "82% of caterers", "approved by caterers"

- the personal invitation – "please call ... or visit"

- the use of comparatives and superlatives – "best loved", "the choice"

- the appeal – "better add".

Find some examples of your own and see what techniques you can identify.

You may not make use of all of these techniques when writing a persuasive letter but they will certainly help. Now look at the following short statement:

I began collecting stamps last month and wondered if you are going to do so as well.

It contains the bare minimum of information and has no persuasive tone. How may you change that? Could you add the following?

- Positive tone: *I have really enjoyed ...*

- Warm recommendation: *having something to look out for has really helped me*

- Personal invitation: *Join me in a great new experience*

- Use of comparatives/superlatives: *... the best way for me to relax*

- Personal appeal: *Why don't you try it?*

Including words and phrases like these in your writing will really begin to persuade your reader. Most important is the approach. Think of your writing as trying to sell something. Now give it a go.

# Writing to a newspaper

Using the notes you made earlier as well as any other ideas you have, write one of the following persuasive letters:

- a keen collector writing to a newspaper complaining that collecting is being overlooked and urging people to discover its attractions

- in response to an invitation from a friend to take up a particular hobby, explaining why you *won't* be doing so.

## May I have your autograph?

**Track 8.1** Stamps are not the only things that can be collected. Listen to another collector talking about her collection and then choose the best fit in answer to the questions that follow.

## Check your understanding

1 The interview is taking place

   A   at a football match

   B   at a tennis tournament

   C   at a motor racing track.

2 The tennis fan's hobby is

   A   travelling the world

   B   playing tennis

   C   collecting autographs.

3 Whose autograph had she got that day?

   A   Ferrer's

   B   Ronaldo's

   C   Serena's

## Role playing – guess who I met today?

In pairs imagine a scene in which a famous person – from your country perhaps – is approached and asked for his or her autograph. How is the star going to respond? What else may they talk about? Have some fun and act this out.

4 Whose autographs does she most enjoy collecting?

   A   Sports' stars

   B   Film stars

   C   Pop stars

5 According to the tennis fan, do the stars mind being asked?

   A   They hate it

   B   They love it

   C   They agree reluctantly

# So you want to be an autograph collector?

## How to get started

A collectible pastime that many people enjoy is collecting autographs of famous people (stars). Add to this the fact that stars' autographs will be likely to increase in value over time, and you now have two of the essential elements of any collectible activity – fun and value. If this sounds like fun, but you don't know how to go about starting your autograph collection, the following are some useful tips on collecting stars' autographs:

## 1. Fan mail

Most famous people enjoy receiving fan mail. Almost all will take the time to reply to any fan mail you send them. As such, sending a famous person fan mail is normally one of the easiest and least expensive ways to obtain their autograph. If you want to try to increase your chances of getting a response from a star, you should also include a self-addressed envelope with your fan mail. One word of caution with fan mail: If you are writing to a star to get their autograph it is not good practice to let them know that you are an autograph hunter as this is generally frowned upon by stars who are resentful of fans asking for autographs that they later sell. Consequently, it is probably best to stick to the "fan mail" story when asking for the autograph.

## 2. Hunt them down

Sometimes you can be in the right place at the right time and stars will appear and will be willing to give you their autograph. At other times you need to be a little more aggressive and read the newspapers and magazines to see if any star is going to be appearing in your local area, so you can then go and ask for their autograph. Either way, it is useful to remember that some stars do not like members of the general public coming up to them and invading their privacy by asking for an autograph. Indeed, some stars try to avoid this situation arising by hiring personal security. Consequently, you should always err on the cautious side by making sure the star is going to be happy to give you their autograph, rather than just sticking a piece of paper and a pen under their nose.

## 3. Buy them

Unfortunately some stars simply refuse to give autograph hunters their autograph. If you want to add such a star's autograph to your collection then your best bet may be to try to purchase the autograph on eBay or a similar website.

## 4. Swap them

Autograph hunting and collecting is a hobby enjoyed by millions of people around the world. With the increasing popularity of the Internet, more and more forums are opening up where autograph collectors can chat among themselves about useful tips on how they obtain the autographs of certain stars. Sometimes you find that these forums have a section where autograph collectors are willing to swap an autograph they have for one you have. Consequently, if you are looking for an autograph to add to your collection and all other possibilities available for you to obtain it have failed, why not try swapping some of your autographs for the one you really want?

## Check your understanding

1 What two reasons does the writer give for collecting autographs?

2 The writer suggests that you send fan mail to the star whose autograph you want. What is it suggested you include to make it more likely that the star will reply?

3 What should you avoid saying if you decide to send fan mail to ask for an autograph?

4 When you go to meet stars to ask for their autograph what should you always check first?

5 Other autograph collectors can help by giving useful tips. How else may they help?

6* Whose autograph would you like to have? Explain briefly how you might follow the advice given to obtain it.

# Giving a talk

Using the magazine article, and adding ideas of your own, prepare a talk of two to three minutes' length on autograph collecting. Think about what information you could include and what questions may be asked afterwards. Give your talk to the class and, with your teacher, discuss the strong points of the presentation and ways that it could be improved.

## Language focus

### Prefixes

Many words in English are made up of a root – the main part of the word – and a prefix that adds to or adapts the basic meaning. "Autograph" is an example of a word formed in this way: -*graph* is the basis or root, meaning "writing" or "to do with writing", and *auto-* is the prefix meaning "self", "to do with self", or "personal". So "autograph" is "writing one's self".

Other words prefixed with "auto" include: "autobiography", "automatic", "automobile", and "autonomy". Can you guess, from knowing what the prefix means, what each of these words means?

Common prefixes that change the root meaning to its opposite are "un-" and "dis-". It is important to get these right. Think of the difference between the words "necessary" and "unnecessary" and the difference between the words "appear" and "disappear".

Noting the prefix can help us to work out the meaning of complex words. Here are some prefixes for you to think about:

| | | |
|---|---|---|
| *anti-* | "against" | for example, antidote ("that given against" poison or harm) |
| *bio-* | "life" | for example, biography ("writing about a life") |
| *mis-* | "badly" or "wrongly" | for example, misunderstand ("wrongly perceived") |
| *phil-* | "loving" | for example, philately ("love of tax paid", or of the stamp showing that postage has been paid) |
| *poly-* | "many" | for example, polygon ("many angles", so many sides) |
| *pro-* | "for" | for example, pro-life |
| *sub-* | "under" | for example, substandard (under the level of quality expected) |
| *trans-* | "across" | for example, transfer ("carry across") |

### Investigate

In small groups, see how many examples of prefixes you can find. Use a dictionary to check them out. Be careful; not all words that look as though they begin with a prefix actually do so.

# Listening to music

## Building your vocabulary

All of these words and phrases can be used when talking about listening to music. Check their meaning in a dictionary and then see if you can fill in the spaces in the sentences that follow.

**vocals    genre    addiction    passion    lilting beat    sentimental    tranquillity**

**resilience    augury    presenter    appreciate**

1   I am very fond of jazz, I really ........................................ it. You may call it my ........................................ .

2   He was hoping that the day would go well and when the programme ........................................ chose his favourite number he thought it an ........................................ that it would.

3   The ........................................ were rather ........................................ but the music had an uplifting ........................................ .

4   The music reminded her of peace and ........................................ that helped her overcome her

........................................ .

5   She showed great ........................................ in defending folk music, her favourite ........................................ against the claims of the pop music made by all her friends.

## Music and me

 **Track 8.2** Of course collecting things is only one kind of pastime. Maybe listening to music is your hobby. Perhaps you can identify with the author of "Music and me". Listen to what he has to say and then answer the questions that follow.

## Check your understanding

1   How often does the speaker listen to music?

2   What is his favourite kind of music?

3   What words does he use to describe the extent of his interest in music? Jot down as many as you can recall.

4   Why doesn't he sing?

5   Do you share his love of music? In what ways do you agree or disagree with what he says?

 Comment

What comment would you post? Write out your own response to "Music and me".

# Desert Island Discs

A popular radio programme in the UK is called *Desert Island Discs*. Famous people are invited to talk about their life and choose eight pieces of music that they would like to have with them if they were stranded on a desert island. The choices are typically a mixture of favourite pieces and ones that remind them of a special time in their life or of someone special to them. In January 2013 the special guest was Aung San Suu Kyi, the Burmese pro-democracy campaigner who was awarded the Nobel Peace Prize in 1991.

## Aung San Suu Kyi picks Beatles and Tom Jones on *Desert Island Discs*

After years of house arrest listening to Dave Lee Travis's pop picks, the Burmese pro-democracy campaigner Aung San Suu Kyi became the selector on Desert Island Discs on Sunday, mixing Burmese folk songs, the Beatles and Mozart before becoming the first guest in the show's 71-year history to choose a record they had never heard before – Tom Jones's Green, Green Grass of Home.

She picked the song after asking her secretary what she would like and after hearing its lilting beat, she concluded: "I like it. There's nothing wrong with loving one's home and family and feeling sentimental about it."

The 67-year-old Nobel peace prize winner had been approached to appear on the programme after she mentioned in her Nobel prize lecture last year that she listened to Desert Island Discs while a student in Oxford. The broadcast took six months to negotiate and fell through on several occasions, before the presenter Kirsty Young travelled to Naypyidaw in Burma after "swotting for this interview like I was doing an exam".

Aung San Suu Kyi said she had asked friends, colleagues and family to help her with her picks so she would be reminded of them on the desert island. Her classical selections included the overture to Mozart's Magic Flute and the Largo movement of Dvorak's New World Symphony, which she first heard in New York.

"It reminds me of the people in the States and elsewhere who helped us in our cause for democracy," she said.

Tom Jones's Green, Green Grass of Home features on the playlist.

She chose Pachelbel's Canon because she played it on her piano during house arrest and it represented "tranquility and resilience".

Here Comes the Sun, by the Beatles, was chosen for her by Britain's ambassador to Burma, Andy Hayn, who said it was "a good augury of a time when we can all look forward to a better life in Burma", and her younger son Kim selected John Lennon's Imagine. She said Kim had "tried to educate me musically and tried to make me appreciate Bob Marley and the Grateful Dead".

She spoke about her relationship with her father, a Burmese army general who led the struggle for independence and was assassinated in 1947 when Aung San Suu Kyi was two. She said he was "my first love and my best love".

Aung San Suu Kyi made clear she still had ambitions to lead her country by winning the next round of elections. "I would like to be president," she said. "If you are the leader of a party then you should want to get government power in your hands so you can work out all these ideas that you have harboured for your country."

Of her mother she said: "My mother was very disciplined and she was very courageous and she was very strict. I thought at times she was far too strict. But I have to say that when I was in a position of having to cope with things such as imprisonment, I was very grateful for her having brought me up in such a disciplined way."

Her recollections of her time in the UK included life as a student at Oxford, trying alcohol for the first and only time in the toilets of the Bodleian library and of how her perfectionist streak came out baking complex cakes for her children, one, ironically, in the shape of a tank, and using a hair dryer to get the skin crispy for Peking Duck. When the presenter suggested she was "an astonishing looking creature ... like a Bond girl" as a student, she admitted: "I turned a few heads."

Aung San Suu Kyi chose a compendium of Buddhist philosophy as her book and a rose bush that changes the colour of its blooms every day as her luxury after insisting "luxuries are not something I indulge in".

She said she would be happy to take the Bible too because her grandfather had converted to Christianity and she often read him passages when he started losing his sight.

She attributed her calmness to "upbringing, Buddhist faith and meditation". She said meditation heightened her awareness, particularly of rising anger and the need to control it which "is a great help when you have to cope with what most politicians have to cope with".

Source: www.guardian.co.uk

# Check your understanding

1 Why did Aung San Suu Kyi choose "Green Green Grass of Home"?

2 Who is the presenter of *Desert Island Discs*?

3 What did Aung San Suu Kyi choose to remind her of the people of the USA?

4 What music did her son try to persuade her to like?

5 How did Aung San Suu Kyi use a hairdryer to improve her cooking?

6* Summarise Aung San Suu Kyi's memories of her mother in one sentence.

## Selecting particular information

You will often be asked to locate and select particular information for a particular reason; this is therefore a key generic skill that you will use whether reading or listening. In this case, let's focus on the skill of identifying only which pieces of music were featured.

## What pieces did Aung San Suu Kyi choose?

Copy out and complete the following form. Some of the items have been filled in for you. You may enter the musical pieces in any order.

DESERT ISLAND DISCS

Presenter: _____     Guest: _____

*Choices: Music*

1. Burmese Folk Song                      5.
2. Burmese Folk Song                      6.
3.                                        7.
4.                                        8.

*Book:*   Compendium of Buddhist Philosophy

*Luxury:*

*Date:*                              *Location:*

## What would you take with you to a desert island?

You are soon going to be a guest on *Desert Island Discs*. Prepare for this by writing down your choice of records. For this activity, however, let's restrict it to four tracks. Don't make your selection simply on the basis of what you are currently listening to. You may wish to include the latest release but also aim to make your list representative of your life. You will also need to choose a book to take and one (but only one) luxury item.

Think about:

- music that reminds you of key events – *your first day at a new school perhaps*

- music that you associate with particular people – *family members, or a close friend*

- variety – *try to provide an entertaining range*

- not all "easy listening" – *perhaps choose one record that you need time to get to know*

- maybe even follow Aung San Suu Kyi's example and choose one you haven't heard!

Don't forget your book and your luxury item.

Next you need to work in pairs to prepare for the show. In turn, you are going to be both the presenter and the guest.

1  Exchange lists.

2  Go through your partner's list, making sure you understand the selections that he or she has made as well as the reasons behind them.

3  Add some notes to help you conduct the interview, thinking of questions you could ask.

Now conduct your very own *Desert Island Discs* programme.

# Learn to play an instrument

Read the web extract and then answer the questions.

## Ukeplayle

Something possibly even more delightful than an evening spent learning to play the Ukulele with a group of strangers, was finding out that "Ukulele" actually means "*Jumping flea*" in Hawaiian – so named due to the quick movement of the fingers (not mine).

After paying £20 for my racing red uke at a Denmark Street music shop, I happily took this along. Funny then that I didn't actually end up playing it.

I turned up to the "Ukelele Hootenany" (Monday nights; free) at a venue near Liverpool Street on a Monday evening, uke in hand. The kind host, a gnarled old man, came and tuned it for me. I went to get a drink, was joined by my friend, and was about to start playing when the little man approached again and said, "Let me tune that for you." I hesitated, but he scooped it up and was off faster than his age should have tolerated. He returned minutes later saying, "I've tuned it, but it won't be worth it – use this one instead," and handed me a racing red version of a more expensive uke that I happily fumbled with on the night.

You can cover the basics online – the strings, the numbers relating to finger tips, and so on – and come along expecting to be able to play the most commonly used chords (for the songs we covered). Just don't expect to fluidly flip between them without missing a few strums – that is easier said than done.

What makes this hobby unique is the fact that the ukulele is not seen as a "serious" or "proper" instrument, and so it attracts those more likely to be picking it up for fun. Monday night's crew were a haphazard collection of about 30 people ranging from 20 to 60, with various shaped and sized ukes and various levels of ability (or in some cases inability, but this mattered not).

We sat around a table, with two song books in front of us. The "leader" called out a page number as we flipped through to a well-known Johnny Cash or Queen tune and did our best to keep up. Later on we got to haggle – a Lady Gaga here, an Eric Clapton there.

But the part I enjoyed the most that I wasn't expecting was the sing-a-long. Everyone sings, and as no one cares about your singing abilities, people have a lot of fun with harmonizing, and putting on a heavy Southern accent even if it's not a country song. What resulted was a hobby

with a unique mix and hence one of my favourites; cheap, social, learning a skill, and above all great fun. Bear in mind, it won't sound anything much like the real thing!

Best thing with places like this, you don't even need to buy a uke ahead of the occasion as they're happy to lend them out, so nothing to lose and only Mondays to improve. That said, please don't go – I kind of like the event and need to ensure there's a spare uke to join in!

**Source: adapted from www.pursuitofhobbyness.com**

# Check your understanding

1   What musical instrument did the girl want to play?

2   Why did she choose to go to the club on Monday evening?

3   Why didn't she play on her own instrument there?

4   How had she learned to play the basic chords?

5   Besides playing the ukulele together, what else did the people do at the club?

6*  According to the article, what is the appeal of learning to play the ukulele?

 How to learn to play "Let it be" on the ukulele in two minutes

Watch the video available at **www.youtube.com/user/ukulelecenter?feature = watch**.

## Study tips

# Listening – recognizing the opinions and attitudes of several people

One of the key skills that you will need to practise and develop is that of recognizing and understanding the ideas, opinions, and attitudes that speakers have – particularly in a context where there are related ideas, for example, in a group of people discussing the same topic. It is a useful life skill to be able to quickly recognize people's views towards a topic, as well as forming part of your course.

 **Track 8.3** Listen to the recording of several people talking about which musical instruments they each play and why they like it.

Each person has a different view on what music means to them. Some take it very seriously; others are more light-hearted about their lives as musicians. Let's explore their various attitudes, opinions, and ideas.

With a partner, see if you can match these comments to each person. You can listen to the recording again.

**Guitarist    Drummer    Conductor    Violinist Xylophone player    Pianist**

1   He doesn't like to be made to practise.

2   He thinks that playing is the best way to learn an instrument.

3   She thinks that she is the driving force of a band.

4   She thinks that music is not about achieving perfection.

5   He thinks that music is about achieving perfection.

6   She thinks that teaching music is not very fulfilling.

Now make up your own bank of "attitude statements". With your partner, sift out the various views, opinions, attitudes, and ideas that these six musicians have about music. Now create a list similar to ours above and hand this to another pair to match up with the musicians in question.

Now to make things a little more interesting, come up with six additional statements that each person may make. By now, you should know something of each person's character. What other things may they add as this discussion among fellow musicians develops? Share these six additional statements with another pair.

## Sample student responses

Three students listened to these six people and they came up with the following recommendations. Which of these three students' advice would you take? Or would you take the advice of none of them and choose another musician to learn with?

### Student A

My advice is to take lessons from the pianist. He is hugely successful now. But if I were you I'd stay well away from the xylophone player as she makes mistakes.

### Student B

If you want to learn an instrument well you need to enjoy it. So maybe you should meet up with the xylophone player for inspiration. But – for the actual playing, I'd suggest the violinist.

### Student C

The drummer is the most focused. He keeps good time, too, which is really important in music. I'd learn with him.

When the same three students were asked to describe a musician, this is what they said. Which is the most accurate?

### Student A

The conductor is the most patient. He listens carefully to people and responds very sensitively to their needs.

### Student B

The guitarist is the one who takes his music the least seriously. He doesn't bother with reading music and plays only cheap and cheerful guitars.

### Student C

The violin player is the most knowledgeable player. She knows the instrument inside out and has dedicated her life to her music.

 ## Writing

In small groups, discuss the two-minute lesson you have just watched. Now go back to the article "Ukeplayle" and make notes on the ukulele and how to play it. Write a blog or an email to a friend, beginning, "I have just watched an amazing video and, guess what, I've decided to learn the ukulele!"

## Creating an advert

You have decided to set up a "sing along" evening at your school. In small groups, work out what you are going to do that evening. Will you invite people to bring instruments? Or will you sing along to recorded music only? What songs will you sing? What other activities will you include in your "festival of music" evening?

Create an advert for the evening.

# The language of music

Listening to music or playing an instrument is one of our most popular leisure activities and is well represented in imagery and figurative language in English.

To help you to get into the groove, here are some examples. See if you can work out what the expressions mean. "To get into the groove", by the way, is to get into the right mood or frame of mind. It comes from the act of playing a record (a vinyl disc) on a record player. In order to hear the music properly you have to place the needle correctly in the track or groove.

What do you think these highlighted expressions mean?

1   The music was really *groovy* and inviting.

2   The home team was *on song*, winning 5–0.

3   Everything continued *in harmony* with the wishes of the family.

4   The new office manager soon had everyone *singing off the same song sheet*.

5   The whole show was carefully *orchestrated* to avoid any mistakes.

6   He was 80 years old and *as fit as a fiddle*.

7   She refused *to play second fiddle* to her younger sister.

8   We have to fill in lots of details – name, date of birth, address, and *all that jazz*.

9   He was very proud and always *blowing his own trumpet*.

10  Some were genuine supporters but some had just *climbed on the bandwagon*.

All have musical origins. See if you can work out what these origins are.

See how many other musical figures of speech you can come up with in five minutes. Compare notes with your neighbour. Be prepared to explain the origin of each figure of speech.

# Literary connections
## Reading

One of the most popular and enduring pastimes is reading.

### Surveying your class

Carry out a survey of your class to find out:

- what they are currently reading
- their favourite author
- their favourite book
- any characters they particularly like or identify with.

In pairs, design a questionnaire. Include short-answer questions and ones that require a little more thought. If you have been reading a book together as a class, then add some questions specifically about that book.

Once you have agreed on the questions, pass copies of the questionnaire to another pair for them to fill out. Completed questionnaires should be returned to the people who devised them so that the results can be collated.

### Writing up the results of your survey

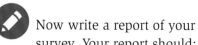 Now write a report of your survey. Your report should:

- say what the survey was about
- include charts to show popular titles and authors
- include a conclusion on the findings and any implications.

# Leisure pursuits

Our hobbies and pastimes are opportunities to escape from the busyness of daily life. As the poet W.H. Davies put it:

**Leisure**

WHAT is this life if, full of care,

We have no time to stand and stare?—

No time to stand beneath the boughs,

And stare as long as sheep and cows:

No time to see, when woods we pass,

Where squirrels hide their nuts in grass:

No time to see, in broad daylight,

Streams full of stars, like skies at night:

No time to turn at Beauty's glance,

And watch her feet, how they can dance:

No time to wait till her mouth can

Enrich that smile her eyes began?

A poor life this if, full of care,

We have no time to stand and stare.

**Source: *Collected Poems of W.H. Davies*.**
**Messrs Jonathan Cape Ltd**

Think about the poem you have just read. What is he saying about the importance of leisure? What does he take time to stand and stare at? Is Davies right? Are we simply too busy? What would you take time out to watch and reflect on?

#  Writing an article

Write an article for your school magazine or web page in reply to Davies's poem.

- Do you agree with him? If so, explain why you think taking time out is important.

- Or is he out of date? The world has simply moved on. "We live in the techno-age and chill out in the virtual world.'

## Study tips

### Writing – using paragraphs and appropriate verbs

When you write an extended piece, such as an article or a letter, there are two key areas that are very important for success.

The first is using paragraphs appropriately. It is important that you have a balance to the piece as a whole, with an introduction and a conclusion, and paragraphs will help you to achieve this.

The second is using verbs accurately. The main points to remember here are to learn as many irregular verbs as possible and to try not to mix tenses when you write.

Think about these questions:

1 If you have to write a letter to a friend and there are three bullet points that you need to address, how many paragraphs do you think you should use? Discuss this decision with a partner.

2 If you have to write a balanced argument for and against a topic, how many paragraphs do you think you should use? Discuss this decision with your partner as well.

Planning a piece of writing by using topic sentences and paragraphs is a useful way to ensure that you remain focused on the main theme. A topic sentence indicates to the reader what the paragraph is about and what they can expect to be reading about in terms of content and examples.

If you had to write an article for your school magazine with the title "It is better to have a busy life than a life with plenty of time for leisure" how would you go about doing it? With your partner, come up with four or five sentences that indicate how each paragraph may look. We've done the first one for you:

There are many advantages of keeping busy.

See if you can plot your way through this essay by just using topic sentences.

Now with your partner, think of another essay title – one that can also have opposing points of view – and write the topic sentences. Pass these over to another pair who should see if they can make sense of your essay. Let them tell you what kind of essay content they think you will be including. Is it what you had in mind?

## Sample student responses

Let's have a look at two students who are writing an email to a friend about a new school activity club. They have both made some verb errors. How many can you find in each email? Which one of the students made fewer verb mistakes? Make a list of all the wrong verbs and see if you can put them right.

**Student A**

I write this letter to tell you about some very good news. Last week the school introduced a new activity club and invited all the students over the age of 14 to come along. There were more than fifty students who take part. There were three different groups, one for sports, one for music and one for art.

I chose the basketball group and we played non-stop for one hour. I was very tired at the end. On the way home I talked to my friends about the evening and they all agree that it was a big success.

We want to go along again next week and try a different activity.

**Student B**

I am writing this letter to tell you about some very good news. Last week the school introduce a new activity club and invited all the students over the age of 14 to come along. There were more than fifty students who took part. There were three different groups, one for sports, one for music and one for art.

I choose the basketball group and we played non-stop for one hour. I am very tired at the end. On the way home I talk to my friends about the evening and they all agreed that it was a big success.

We will want to go along again next week and try a different activity.

# Getting away from it all

Outdoor pursuits are among the most popular of hobbies and there is an impressive range of pursuits to choose from. How many you can think of? Which ones appeal to you? Do you spend enough time outside? If not, why not? Are you an outdoor type or do you prefer to be indoors?

## Building your vocabulary

Do you know the following words and phrases? Use a dictionary to check the meaning of any you are not sure of. See if you can match them to the definitions.

| | |
|---|---|
| bond | someone fishing with rod and line |
| immersed | of the water |
| hustle and bustle | eating |
| serenity | range covered |
| picturesque | got bigger |
| aquatic | participate |
| consumption | peace |
| accumulated | placed in the middle of |
| expanded | strikingly beautiful |
| scope | steadily built up |
| engage | form a close relationship with |
| angler | hurry and confusion |

# The Big Issue – to fish or not to fish

## Fishing as a relaxing hobby

Hi, my name is James and I really enjoy fishing. My dad taught me to fish when I was young and I have now taught my son and daughter to fish, and they love it! It is a way of relaxing in nature and spending time together as a family doing healthy outdoor activities.

People fish for different reasons. Recreational fishers, like myself, fish for pleasure or sport, while commercial fishers fish for profit. Recreational fishing does have conventions, rules, licensing restrictions and laws that limit the way in which fish are caught. These forbid the use of nets and the catching of fish with hooks not in the mouth. I fish with a rod, reel, line, hooks and baits or lures like artificial flies.

Fishing is a great hobby and an estimated 3 million people fish in the UK alone. Not only is it relaxing but it's also really satisfying. I work indoors so I love to get some fresh air first thing in the morning or after a hard day at work. You forget about the hustle and bustle of city life. I commute to work and live near the coast so I'm very lucky. It definitely promotes a healthier lifestyle as I often walk for ages to find the best spot.

Fishing offers you the chance to improve your self-esteem through respect for the environment, mastering outdoor skills and achieving personal goals. Fishing is a lifetime skill and activity that can be enjoyed at any age.

You do need patience when fishing as it might take a while to catch something but it is worth it. Sometimes it comes down to luck but you do learn where the best spots are with experience. It's also a hobby that you can either enjoy with your friends or by yourself. It's a really fun way to socialise! My son has entered lots of competitions and I'm really proud of him. I don't understand why people are against such a great hobby.

## Check your understanding

1   Why do people fish?

2   What does recreational fishing prohibit?

3   Why is fishing good for city workers?

4   Why does James enjoy this hobby?

5   What quality is needed to ensure that you catch a big fish?

6*  Briefly, what is the appeal of fishing, according to the passage?

# Or maybe it isn't so appealing after all!

## Don't go fishing!

Hi, my name is Ricardo and I am strongly against fishing. I don't understand how this can be considered to be a hobby or a sport.

Fish die unnecessarily just for the pleasure of humans. A lot of people are unaware that fish also get stressed and out-of-breath just like us. A fish breathes by moving water over the gills, and if it's used up all of its energy, it can't move to get the water flowing. Just like a person, if a fish can't breathe, it will die.

I think that we should protect fish in the same way that we protect other animals. Fish numbers continue to decline for many species and yet the number of people fishing for sport still rises every year. The 'catch-and-release' method is a practice within recreational fishing intended as a technique of conservation. Having been caught, the fish are unhooked and returned to the water. I have serious concerns about this as I think that the fish can experience serious exhaustion or injury during the process.

Fish are also not the only victims. I live near the coast and reports have estimated that hundreds of thousands of birds die each year in gillnets around the world. The birds get tangled in the nets and simply drown because they can't get out.

I strongly believe that we should put a stop to fishing. Fish are beautiful and intelligent creatures that have the right to be protected just like any other animal.

## Check your understanding

1. Why is Ricardo against fishing?

2. What happens to a fish when it is distressed?

3. Why is Ricardo against 'catch-and-release'?

4. How does fishing impact on sea birds?

5. Briefly, what are the arguments against fishing, according to the passage?

## A class debate

Would you go fishing? Is it a great opportunity to enjoy natural surroundings or cruel exploitation of nature for fun? Is it the busy person's relaxation or the lazy one's huge waste of time? What do you think?

Discuss these two opposing points of view. Your teacher will help you set this up as a debate.

---

### Study tips

## Reading to locate appropriate content for a summary

When you are asked to write a summary, it often involves two aspects – for example, the *disadvantages* and the *advantages* of a certain topic. It is important that you produce a balanced summary and find examples of both aspects. It is a good idea to show that you are moving from one aspect to another by creating a new paragraph.

Now let's have another look at the two articles on fishing. You will find that the first one is positive about fishing whereas the second one is negative. With your partner, decide which article you are going to study again in more detail. If you are reading the first article, then make a list of the advantages, while your partner makes a list of the disadvantages from the second article. Swap them and check to see if you can find: a) anything you disagree with, or b) other ideas that could be added.

Summaries are unusual in that they integrate reading and writing skills. However, we can practise both elements separately: reading for appropriate content, and conveying this content accurately and concisely.

So far, you have been practising your reading skill in scanning through the articles to locate the information you want. The next step would be to try to write the summary.

The most important skill, however, is probably to locate the points or examples that you will then link together to produce your written piece. For the summary, you will probably need from six to ten separate points to create a successful piece. If these points are not in a logical order, your summary will not be as successful. However, sometimes you

can re-arrange the points or examples to suit your preferred approach. This is fine, as long as your summary makes sense and has a logic running through it.

With your partner, re-arrange your final agreed list of the "advantages and disadvantages of fishing" in a way that makes the summary less effective. Can you see what we mean? Sequencing in a summary is the most important skill.

## Sample student responses

Look at each of the three student responses to the same summary title we just gave you. Decide which one you think is the best, the second best, and the least successful. You could discuss your findings with your partner and see if you agree.

To help you make up your mind, think about the following:

Does the student write about both the advantages and disadvantages? Does the student include any details that do not answer the question? Does the student attempt to use his or her own words or just copy the expressions in the original text? Are there linking words? How about paragraphs? Is there a logic to the points being covered?

**Student A**

People fish for different reasons. Recreational fishers fish for pleasure or sport, while commercial fishers fish for profit. It is a way of relaxing in nature and spending time together as a family doing healthy outdoor activities. Fish die unnecessarily just for the pleasure of humans. A lot of people are unaware that fish also get stressed and out-of-breath just like us. Just like a person, if a fish can't breathe, it will die. Fishing is a lifetime skill and activity that can be enjoyed at any age. Reports have estimated that hundreds of thousands of birds die each year in gillnets around the world.

**Student B**

There are both advantages and disadvantages of fishing as a hobby. Firstly, one of the benefits is that it is a way of relaxing in nature and spending time together as a family doing healthy outdoor activities.

However, there are equally many disadvantages. Fish die unnecessarily just for the pleasure of humans. Furthermore, reports have estimated that hundreds of thousands of birds die around the world each year as they get trapped in the nets.

**Student C**

These days people not only fish for profit but also for pleasure. Firstly, one of the advantages is that it is a way of relaxing in nature and spending time together as a family. Fishing offers you the chance to improve your self-esteem through respect for the environment, mastering outdoor skills and achieving personal goals. However, the fish may suffer when they are caught and fish numbers continue to decline. The fish experience exhaustion or injury during the 'catch and release' process. Birds also get tangled in the nets and drown because they can't get out of the nets.

# Reflection

Which of the hobbies featured in this chapter appeal to you? Why? Have you been persuaded to take up a new hobby or to change what you do? In small groups look back through the suggestions in this chapter and discuss some of the activities, pastimes, hobbies, and interests mentioned. Here are some ideas for further discussion:

- Are you a collector? What is the appeal? How do you go about it?

- If you are not, why not? What may persuade you to start?

- Music – are you a listener? A performer? Both?

- Or do you prefer outdoor pursuits?

## ✏ Write your own lesson plan!

As a group, choose one leisure activity or hobby that hasn't featured in this chapter and develop a short series of lessons (a scheme of work) about it.

Once you have made your selection you'll need to do some research.

- See what you can find on the Internet or elsewhere in the media – pictures, articles, and videos.

- Select what you want to use – it should not to be too complicated: one informative piece and one more light-hearted piece perhaps; something that can be listened to, or watched.

- Decide how best to introduce the activity or hobby – a game perhaps.

- Put together a "Building your vocabulary" list.

- Try to build progression into your plan – working towards a conclusion.

- Put together some exercises; try to cover a variety of skills.

- Think of ways to work in pairs and groups.

- How are you going to end your scheme of work?

Assign roles to each group member. Each member should produce a single lesson idea/plan that would take about 30 minutes of class time. Remember, this is English, so you have to cover all four main skills: reading, writing, speaking, and listening.

 **My progress**

Each chapter includes four study skills. These are skills that will feature in your final examinations. So let's check your progress with these key skills in mind.

| Where am I now? | Very pleased – I think I'm good at this | OK – but I do need more practice | One of my weaker areas – so I need a lot more practice |
|---|---|---|---|
| Being able to paraphrase and use examples when speaking | | | |
| Recognizing opinions and attitudes when listening to a group of people talking | | | |
| Using topic sentences and paragraphing when writing | | | |
| Locating appropriate and logical content when reading an article to summarize | | | |

Now pick out one skill that you would like to prioritize for improvement and produce a short action plan to help you become stronger. Use a template similar to the following – that is filled out for you with an example.

## Action plan

Skill I want to improve <u>being able to paraphrase and use examples when speaking</u>

- ***planning*** – how I will try to improve this skill:
  <u>focus on explaining myself more when I am speaking</u>

- ***implementing*** – what I will need and what my exact strategy is:
  <u>I will need to use more expressions like: What I mean by that is, Let me give you an example</u>

- ***monitoring*** – how I will know I am improving and what evidence I may keep:
  <u>I will be able to say the same thing more often using different words. My conversations should flow more naturally as a result</u>

# 9 Customs and cultures

## In this chapter you will:

- visit North America, South America, and China
- read about greetings around the world, traditions linked to the birth of a child, and traditional marriage customs.
- write an article for a wedding magazine
- listen to people talking about coming-of-age rituals
- talk about the rituals we would like to save.

## Key study skills

- *Writing* accurate and controlled sentences
- *Speaking* with strong opinions and taking control of a conversation
- *Listening* carefully in order to work out what is being implied
- *Reading* to recognize a balanced argument

# Greetings all!

**Thinking out loud**
What do you say when you meet someone? How does what you say differ according to whether the person is a friend or an acquaintance? What about when you are introduced to someone for the first time? What would you say to someone from a different culture? What message are you trying to convey in your greeting and the way you say it?

## Greetings

Look at the greetings in different languages shown on the right. Can you find your language? How many others can you identify? In pairs, make a list of all the greetings and languages you can identify, adding the name of the country and where you have come across the greeting. Are any that you know missing?

But we don't always say the same thing when we greet people; it depends on who they are. What we say to our best friends is likely to be different from how we greet those we don't know so well. Every culture has a number of different ways in which people are greeted. "Hello" or its equivalent is just the start. What else do we say when we meet people?

In pairs, compile a list of greetings that are used in your language with explanations of how and when

they would be used. Give the original and its English equivalent in each case. Now go on to develop a conversation with someone you have just met for the first time.

---

## Building your vocabulary

Do you know the following words or phrases? They are all used in the passage you are about to read. Use a dictionary to check the meaning of any that you are unsure of and then see if you can pick the correct meaning from the choices given. Check that the meaning is accurate for the passage.

| collaborative | | | | | |
|---|---|---|---|---|---|
| A | working together | B | complicated | C | colourful |

| contributors | | | | | |
|---|---|---|---|---|---|
| A | partners | B | those who have given money | C | writers (of the article) |

| tactile | | | | | |
|---|---|---|---|---|---|
| A | touching one another | B | sensitive | C | cautious |

| peck | | | | | |
|---|---|---|---|---|---|
| A | light nibble | B | light kiss | C | light smack |

| Anglos | | | | | |
|---|---|---|---|---|---|
| A | English | B | English speakers | C | religious people |

| freaks them out | | | | | |
|---|---|---|---|---|---|
| **A** | disgusts them | **B** | disturbs them | **C** | annoys them |
| **effusive** | | | | | |
| **A** | shy | **B** | unrestrained | **C** | fussy |
| **beaming** | | | | | |
| **A** | smiling broadly | **B** | crying loudly | **C** | big and strong |
| **conservative** | | | | | |
| **A** | respectful | **B** | shy | **C** | traditional |
| **blushed** | | | | | |
| **A** | were angry | **B** | were amused | **C** | were embarrassed |

# Kiss, hug, or shake hands?

That was a question that a website asked its readers. Here are some of the answers that were posted.

## Greetings around the world

This is the first in a new series of collaborative posts, where we explore different social situations from the point of view of our contributors around the world.

Today's topic: how to greet people in different countries.

## Argentina

In Argentina, people are fairly tactile: we hug and kiss and hold hands all the time. We give one peck on the cheek when we greet friends and family and even acquaintances. When we're introduced to new people, say at a party, we tend to kiss too, especially women. Men hug and kiss their friends too (both male and female). In a more formal situation, we shake hands (at least the first time we meet).

This men-kissing-men (on the cheek) takes a lot of getting used to, especially for Anglos. It's been my experience that they take to kissing girls like fish to water but having to kiss other men freaks them out, although it eventually comes naturally to them.

*By Ana, Regional Contributor in Argentina.*

## Brazil

Brazilians are really well-known for the warm, latin-american-like greetings, very effusive, with lots of kisses and hugs. Among men, if they are friends, there's generally a light hug and a tap on each other's back. Among men and women or women/women, kisses are the norm.

How many? Well, that's where the problem comes in! It will depend on the region. In Brasilia, my home town, we kiss twice on the cheek. If you go a bit farther, more to the south of Brazil, let's say, São Paulo, then one kiss is the routine. So, you'd better check in advance how many kisses and how tight you should hug a Brazilian! Anyway, with Brazilians, everything will do, kisses, hugs, taps. Leave shaking hands only to formal situations.

By Carla, *Regional Contributor in Brazil.*

# Great Britain

We British are usually not very tactile, although we're getting better at it. On meeting someone for the first time, we would normally shake hands if it's a formal situation (at work, for example), or even just smile at each other. If it's a friend or casual acquaintance, we would hug or (between two women or a man and woman) make one kiss on the cheek.

By Lucy, *editor*

# Romania

As for hugging and kissing: people hug and kiss on the cheek often – women with women, women with men or even men with men, but less frequently if they are very young or if they are close and sometimes if they are colleagues. Older men used to kiss a woman's hand instead of shake hands when they were introduced or when they met in the street.

By Carmen, *Regional Contributor in Romania.*

# India

In India, greetings indicate the relative position of individuals in society.

Close friends hug. Man hugs man, woman hugs woman. Older uncles and aunties hug younger children.

Grandparents are not to be hugged, you are supposed to touch their feet and receive blessings for a long life, a speedy marriage, numerous children, etc. Kissing is a big no-no. Only infants are to be publicly kissed.

The touching feet business, especially in large family gatherings, leads to funny situations. Within the space of a few seconds, I have to decide whether the beaming relative headed my way is my senior or my junior in the family. Age has got nothing to do with it. I have got "uncles" who are half my age. So, I watch his body language. Is he bending forward to touch my feet or is

he preparing to raise his right arm in greeting? Most of the time this works. When it fails, I just move on to another pair of feet I am sure of!

By Sanjay, *Regional Contributor in India.*

# Singaporean Chinese

We Chinese tend to be more conservative. On meeting someone for the first time, we would usually nod our heads and smile or shake hands (in formal situations). Kissing on the cheeks might make those who are not used to Western practices rather uncomfortable.

(My parents blushed when they came to Spain for the first time and my boyfriend's parents kissed them on both cheeks! ha!)

By Nellie, *Guest Contributor*

# The Philippines

These rules on physical contact are conservative, but guaranteed not to get you into any trouble!

Kissing (on the cheek) is only for family and close friends. Hugging is for family, close friends, or a friend you haven't seen for a long time. You shake hands when you're formally introduced or you just got acquainted.

There's also the customary placing one's cheek against the other's or air kisses between women in some circles. Between men and women, this has been adopted over time but between men in the Philippines this is a no-no. A firm handshake would do just fine.

The explanation behind this is quite simple: it's just not "manly" for most Filipino men.

By Bryan, *Regional Contributor in the Philippines.*

**Source: www.pocketcultures.com/2010/07/14/ kiss-hug-or-shake-hands**

# Check your understanding

1. What greeting do Englishmen in Argentina find difficult?
2. How do men and women greet one another in São Paulo?
3. What are the British getting better at, according to the web page editor?
4. In India how is respect for grandparents shown?
5. Who embarrassed Nellie's parents when they visited Spain?
6* How are habits changing in the countries surveyed?

##  Developing a discussion

There is quite a wide variation in practice described here. In pairs discuss each contributor's comments in turn. What greeting style is most similar to that of your culture? Would you (or your parents) find any country's greeting embarrassing? Did you like the collaborative post? Work out what comment you would add in reply.

##  Writing a web page entry

The articles posted on the collaborative website were in response to the question: "Kiss, hug, or shake hands?" Following the pattern of the extracts, write an entry for your country. If your country is already included, then say whether your greetings would be exactly the same as the original entry. How may it differ? Give examples. Your entry should include:

- how you greet family members or close friends
- how you greet people you are introduced to for the first time
- the difference (if any) between formal and informal greetings
- if there has been any change in recent times.

##  Māori greetings

Watch the video available at **www.vimeo.com/8419032** In this video some visitors to New Zealand are taught the greeting that native New Zealanders, the "Māoris", use.

# Check your understanding

1. Why do the Māoris rub noses?
2. What does the action of touching foreheads signify?
3. What is your reaction to this unusual form of greeting?
4. Where does the tourist being told about this come from?
5. Do you think it is right that the Māori people and their customs have been made into a tourist attraction?

---

## Study tips

## Writing accurate sentences

In one exercise of the Reading and Writing test, you will need to write a full sentence or two about information in a text. Sometimes you can use as many words as you like as long as the sentence includes the content that is required. However, the instructions can be more specific – such as, you must write from 12 to 20 words. You need to practise writing sentences within a word range if you want to be successful.

Remember, your sentence must:

- be within the word-length requirements
- be written in the first person
- include the relevant content
- be a "proper" sentence.

This last point is interesting. What is a "proper" sentence? Let's work with a partner and see if we can create our own definition.

Here are three sentences. Different students are writing about the best moment in their holiday and why they liked it.

a) I liked the boat trip best because I saw lots of dolphins swimming close to us.

b) Because we were on a boat and we saw lots of dolphins swimming close to us.

c) And we went on the boat and saw lots of dolphins swimming close to us.

One of the sentences is a "proper" sentence. Which one do you think it is? Discuss with your partner why the other two are not "proper" sentences. Make a list of your findings and then discuss it with other members of your class.

Now let's look again at the article on how to greet people in different countries. There are seven countries mentioned in the article. You need to find your information in the correct part. For example, here is a student writing a sentence about greetings in Great Britain:

I normally shake hands with someone in a formal situation or when I meet them for the first time. (19 words)

Complete the following two tasks with your partner. Then hand the sentences over to another pair, who will mark them for accuracy.

1   Write one sentence from 12 to 20 words on your experience of greetings in Argentina.

2   Write one sentence from 12 to 20 words on your experience of greetings in India.

## Sample student responses

**Q.** Write a sentence from 12 to 20 words in which you describe meeting someone for the very first time.

Two students, Student A and Student B, have written these six responses between them. Can you tell which responses are written by Student A, and which are written by Student B? Hint: One student is much more accurate than the other, who makes more mistakes.

a) But you shake hands when you are formally introduced and hugging is only for families and close friends.

b) I always check to see how many kisses to give because it varies from region to region.

c) I tend to be more conservative and if I meet someone for the first time I usually nod my head and smile.

d) They used to kiss a woman's hand instead of shaking hands when they were introduced.

e) I have friends all over the world and I greet them as often as I can.

f) When I meet people for the first time, I tend not to be close. I just say hello.

# Birth customs

Many of our customs and traditions are part of our family life and relate to what we do at different times of the year, on particular days, or for special events. What events do you celebrate in your culture? For example, how is a new baby welcomed into the family and community and prepared for life?

## Building your vocabulary

These words and phrases occur in the passage you are about to read. See if you can match each one to its meaning.

| | |
|---|---|
| rituals | adapted for a particular purpose |
| charm | keep something away |
| fist | a party at which gifts are given for a newborn baby |
| ward off | baby's room |
| dew | hand |
| nurture | a lucky piece of jewellery |
| navel string | cord connecting mother and unborn baby |
| customized | caring |
| nursery | ceremonies |
| baby shower | moisture |

## Baby Customs, Traditions, and Rituals from Around the World

When a baby is born, there are various traditions, customs, or rituals that families participate in depending on their culture or country of origin. In the United States, for example, it's customary to visit the new parents and baby and bring already-cooked meals so that parents have one less thing to worry about as they

care for their newborn. What about other cultures? How do they celebrate the birth of a baby? I asked around and learned about several baby traditions from around the world, including customs celebrated in Trinidad and Puerto Rico, where my husband and I are from.

## Puerto Rico

Growing up in a Puerto Rican family, I always saw newborn babies wearing a bracelet with a black charm in the shape of a fist. I later learned it is called mano de azabache and is meant to ward off evil and bring good luck to the baby. Many people provide new parents with this bracelet for their baby.

## Trinidad and Tobago

I asked around to learn about some of the baby traditions in Trinidad, where my husband and his family are from. @SammyTAlexander mentioned that when people visit newborn babies, they usually put money into the baby's hand. I immediately remembered that my mother-in-law had actually done this when she first met our baby boy! Apparently, it is meant to bring prosperity and good blessings to the newborn. Another custom I learned about from @bytesdog is that some parents do not allow people to come in their house after 6 p.m., since the evening dew is believed to make the baby sick.

## Mexico

Silvia Martinez of Mamá Latina Tips shared that in many families in Mexico, the women of the family – grandmothers, aunts, sisters – nurture and take care of the new mum for 40 days after the birth of a baby. These women help with the cleaning, cooking, and older kids. The new mum's only job is to take care of the new baby.

## The Bahamas

"An old time tradition here in the Bahamas is burying the navel string of the newborn baby in the yard," said Michelle G. Roper of Sapphire Ridge Chronicles. "It is believed that you will always find your way back home no matter how far you may travel. Another tradition is to tie a black ribbon on the wrist of the newborn for several weeks to ward off evil spirits."

## Brazil

"In Brazil, a typical tradition is that the expectant mother prepares a basket with souvenirs that are given to each person that comes to the hospital to visit when the baby is born. These souvenirs usually match the chosen theme that has been picked for the baby's nursery. Some of the most often used souvenirs are refrigerator magnets, customized notepads, sachets, and even tiny bottles of perfume. Most of the time there's a tiny message saying the baby's name is thanking them for visiting. They are much like favors that are prepared for baby showers, only they are given to those who visit at the hospital," shared Eren Mckay of Embracing Home.

## Muslim families

Faiqa Khan of Native Born provided some insight into customs of Muslim families. "Soon after their birth, the heads of newborns born into Muslim families are shaved within their first month. The hair that has been removed is then weighed and the equivalent of the weight in silver is given to charity. For families, this tradition is extremely important as it signifies the inclusion of the child into the community as well as a reminder to always keep those in need in mind. Because Muslims live in all parts of the world, this is a custom practiced everywhere from Pakistan to France and in the U.S. as well."

## Canada

Susan Carraretto from 5 Minutes for Mom told me about similar traditions in Canada to those here in the U.S., including decorating a nursery ahead of the delivery and friends or family hosting a baby shower for the parents. She mentioned that, traditionally, only women attend the baby shower, but that recently some men like to get involved in the celebration as well.

*What additional baby traditions do you know about from other parts of the world? Share yours with us!*

Posted by Melanie Edwards on August 1, 2012.

**Source: adapted extract from www.disneybaby.com**

# Check your understanding

1   In which two countries is a black bracelet or ribbon put around the baby's wrist?

2   Why is money sometimes put in new babies" hands?

3   In which country does the baby's family give presents to visitors?

4   What happens to the baby's hair in Muslim families?

5   What happens at a baby shower party?

6*  How is the role of the mother recognised in some cultures described here?

## An oral presentation

You are going to give a short talk to your class on the subject of celebrating a birth in different cultures. You may make use of the information in "Baby Customs, Traditions, and Rituals from around the World" and add ideas of your own. You may like to consider:

● traditions to protect the baby, such as giving charms

● practical support for the family, for example, preparing meals

● ways that your birth may have been celebrated.

How are you going to begin? Try to think of a good ending, rather than a sudden stop.

# Coming of age

## The bullet ant test

Watch the video "Could you pass the bullet ant test?" available at **www.youtube.com/ watch?v = XwvIFO9srUw**

## Check your understanding

1  How does he feel about the test before he witnesses it?

  **A**  Keen to be involved

  **B**  Amused

  **C**  Scared

2  Why is the bullet ant also called the 24-hour ant?

  **A**  Because pain from its sting lasts 24 hours

  **B**  Because the ant is active 24 hours a day

  **C**  Because the ant only lives one day

3  Why are the ants drugged?

  **A**  To send them to sleep

  **B**  To make them even more fearsome

  **C**  To kill them

4  What purpose do the gloves serve?

  **A**  They protect the youths from the ants.

  **B**  They give relief from the pain.

  **C**  They are filled with the stinging ants.

5  What other effects do the ant stings have on the youths?

  **A**  They make them shake uncontrollably.

  **B**  They cause them to perform a ritual dance.

  **C**  They make them feel excited.

## A radio interview

You have been invited to appear on a radio programme to discuss the subject of coming-of-age rituals, like the bullet ant test. And you are an expert in this area! Do some research, and try to find some other examples of rituals that symbolize the passing from adolescence to adult life.

Are these harmless fun, not to be taken seriously, a little bit of cultural history to be maintained? Or are they a primitive behaviour best forgotten, sexist, and insulting?

What should mark the transition from child to adult?

- a family gathering
- a formal passing on of responsibility – a key perhaps
- something else

How would you like coming of age to be celebrated?

Now prepare for your interview. You will be interviewed by a classmate.

# Speaking – expressing your opinions and taking control of a conversation

The Speaking test will challenge you to meet two particular objectives:

1. To convey information and express your opinions effectively

2. To engage in and influence the direction of a conversation.

You will need to show that you can express your opinions confidently and that you can change the direction of the conversation at key moments. Let's practise these two skills together by focusing on developing a discussion about customs in your country. With a partner, have a five-minute discussion based on this theme. It doesn't matter if your partner is from a different culture with different customs from you or if he or she is from the same culture.

Did you notice that either of you took the initiative and tried to change the direction of the conversation? At which moments? Why do you think this happened? Did either of you show strong opinions? It is very likely that you did and that you were keen to inform your partner of those opinions. By changing the direction of the conversation, you were seeking to propose some new ideas and utilize some new information.

This is exactly how you should approach the Speaking test. The test is about you; it is about your experience, views, and opinions of a topic. So it is fine for you to convey your opinions strongly and to change the focus of the discussion where you feel that new areas are relevant. A warning, however – don't change the topic completely; you must remain on task. The five prompts will help you to do this.

Let's practise this a little further now. Here's a sample comment made by an Examiner during a Speaking test:

*"That might be so, but I don't think that we should take rituals too seriously. I mean, they are all just ways to repeat old-fashioned behaviour and to stick with tradition."*

How would you like to respond to this? Would you like to challenge what the Examiner is implying? We think you should. With your partner, think of two more statements that an Examiner may come up with during a test about "Cultures and Customs" and then present them one by one to another pair. See how they respond, and perhaps allow a brief conversation among the four of you to develop for a couple of minutes.

## Sample student responses

Here's how three students responded to the statement above. All three respond to the Examiner, but in different ways. Rank them in the order that you think is the most effective to the least effective.

**Student A**

I agree entirely. But rituals are only one aspect of tradition. People go to basketball games in America because of ritual type behaviour. They don't really want to go. Maybe they have nowhere else to go? I think they go out of habit and that's a ritual. So I do agree with you, except one thing – I think rituals are a serious matter.

**Student B**

People like to do the same things each day. It makes them feel at home. Like walking in the park or going round to see a relative. We'd all like to think that we could travel around the world, but we can't, so it's important to have a routine at home. Old-fashioned behaviour is fine. But so is doing new things. I like to go and see my 85-year-old uncle every two or three weeks but I also like to make new friends. So I think what you say is wrong, actually.

**Student C**

There's nothing wrong with repeated patterns of behaviour. I mean we all do this at times. We all need our comfort zones, don't we? I know what you're trying to say here … that people just don't think for themselves, that they follow others and take part in the ritual because they feel they have to. Well, it might not be for that reason. Rituals can provide a warmth and a feeling of belonging. That's why you see more rituals in traditional cultures – and these cultures nearly all have a strong sense of identity.

# Trick or treat?

How you describe something can show what your feelings about it are. Some people will be careful to observe tradition when a new baby arrives, while others don't care at all.

Look at these sentences:

*The brave man fearlessly put his hand into the glove and held it there without a sound.*

*The foolish man carelessly put his hand into the glove and held it there in grim silence.*

Both are describing the same moment but, while the first admires the bravery of the man, the second considers him foolish. It is not just that those two words are used; other word choices continue the impression.

| | |
|---|---|
| *brave* | *foolish* |
| *fearlessly* | *carelessly* |
| *without a sound* | *in grim silence* |

What other words would you add to each column? Try to think of contrasting examples.

Now see how many additional contrasting words you can find for these pairs:

delicious/horrible    interesting/boring    beautiful/plain
friendly/hostile

Use your pairs in sentences that describe the same things but convey opposite feelings.

What other pairings can you think of? Swap your list with your neighbour and see what words you can add.

In your pairs write brief descriptions of the following, showing contrasting feelings:

- a shopping trip
- a television show
- a pop group.

# Marriage customs in Europe

## Building your vocabulary

| | | | | |
|---|---|---|---|---|
| bride | crosses | doomed | groom | maintained |
| modifications | proposal | prospective | superstitious | susceptible |

These words all appear in the passage that you are going to read. Check the meaning of any you are unsure of. Then see if you can fit them into the spaces in the sentences that follow.

1 Tom was very ........................... . Every time he saw an ambulance he held his breath until he could touch something blue.

2 To be ........................... to something is to be likely to be harmed by it.

3 When you alter something you make ........................... to it.

4 These customs have been ........................... for thousands of years.

5 The ........................... and ........................... made a happy couple as they got married.

6 In some cultures the man makes his ........................... to the father of the girl he wants to marry.

7 He was called her ........................... husband as they were not yet married.

8 Everyone said that the last minute plans were ........... to fail.

9 She referred to her difficulties as her ........................... .

---

## Customs associated with weddings

There are many customs and superstitions associated with weddings. In the past a wedding was seen as a time when people were particularly susceptible to bad luck and evil spirits. Many are modifications of customs that began many centuries ago.

Some, such as the bride wearing something old, something blue … , or not being seen by the groom in her wedding dress before the ceremony are known throughout the country and many other parts of the world. Others may be regional or even maintained within families from generation to generation.

They are maintained in the belief that they will bring good luck and happiness to the couple at a time when their lives are changing, hopefully for the better.

### Proposal

In the past when the marriage proposal was a more formal procedure, the prospective groom sent his friends or members of his family to represent his interests to the prospective bride and her family. If they saw a blind man, a monk, or a pregnant woman during their journey it was thought that the marriage would be doomed if they continued their journey as these sights were thought to be bad omens.

If, however, they saw nanny goats, pigeons, or wolves these were considered to be good omens that would bring good fortune to the marriage.

During Medieval times in Brittany [France] the man proposed by leaving a hawthorn branch at the door of his beloved on the first of May. By leaving the branch at the door she accepted his proposal. She made known her refusal by replacing the hawthorn branch with a cauliflower.

### Surnames

It was thought unlucky for a woman to marry a man whose surname began with the same letter as hers, as summarized in the following rhyme:

*To change the name and not the letter Is to change for the worst and not the better*

The bride-to-be should not practise writing her new name before the wedding. This is thought to bring bad luck by tempting fate.

## Check your understanding

1 Traditionally, what is the bride supposed to avoid on her wedding day before the ceremony has taken place?

2 At one time, who often did the proposing?

3 It was thought that seeing what would bring good luck to the marriage?

4 In Brittany in Medieval times, how did a girl show that she was not interested in marrying a man who proposed to her?

5 According to tradition, what should a bride-to-be avoid doing before her wedding?

6* Which custom do you find the most strange? Explain why.

# Literary connections

## Traditional verse

Many of the old traditions and customs have been carefully preserved in rhymes and songs that give advice to young people in love and their families.

Choosing the day on which the wedding was to take place is the subject of one famous old rhyme:

*Monday for wealth*
*Tuesday for health*
*Wednesday the best day of all*
*Thursday for losses*
*Friday for crosses*
*Saturday for no luck at all*

While the following rhyme gives advice about which month is best:

*Married when the year is new, he'll be loving, kind and true.*
*When February birds do mate, You wed nor dread your fate.*
*If you wed when March winds blow, joy and sorrow both you'll know.*
*Marry in April when you can, Joy for Maiden and for Man.*
*Marry in the month of May, and you'll surely rue the day.*
*Marry when June roses grow, over land and sea you'll go.*
*Those who in July do wed, must labour for their daily bread.*
*Whoever wed in August be, many a change is sure to see*
*Marry in September's shrine, your living will be rich and fine.*
*If in October you do marry, love will come but riches tarry.*
*If you wed in bleak November, only joys will come, remember.*
*When December snows fall fast, marry and true love will last.*

Another traditional rhyme advises the bride on what to wear:

*Married in White, you have chosen right,*
*Married in Blue, your love will always be true,*
*Married in Pearl, you will live in a whirl,*
*Married in Brown, you will live in town,*
*Married in Red, you will wish yourself dead,*
*Married in Yellow, ashamed of your fellow,*
*Married in Green, ashamed to be seen,*
*Married in Pink, your spirit will sink,*
*Married in Grey, you will go far away,*
*Married in Black, you will wish yourself back.*

## Poetry please!

These rhymes were a mixture of fun and more serious advice. What would be your suggestions for days on which to get married? Try putting them into a rhyme. By leaving off Sunday (a day to rest), as the original rhyme does, it is more straightforward.

*Monday for fun*
*Tuesday for gain*
*Wednesday brings sun*
*Thursday rain*
*Friday is special, apart from the rest*
*But Saturday's wonderful, simply the best.*

Now it's your turn.

In small groups, read your poems to one another. Why not go on to a rhyme about the months to get married in, or what colour the bride should wear?

## Writing for a specialist magazine

The customs described in the previous passage are from western Europe. The wedding traditions may be very different from those of your family and culture. In pairs, discuss customs and traditions to do with the wedding day in your locality.

- How is the day prepared for?
- How are the bride and groom dressed?
- What happens at the wedding ceremony?
- What celebrations follow?

See what further information you can find on the day of getting married in your locality in the library or on the Internet. Are there are older members of your family – your grandparents perhaps – who you could ask about wedding customs and traditions?

Now use the information you have gathered to write an article for a magazine that specializes in weddings. You may like to look at such a magazine first to see the types of articles it contains.

# Chinese Wedding Traditions

Wedding customs in China follow a long and ancient tradition. Details vary from one region to another but some of the traditions go back hundreds of years. In modern times the wishes of the young couple might be taken into account but that is a very recent consideration. With the future well-being of the family at stake, who your son or daughter marries is far too important to be left to them. Indeed it was not unusual for the couple's first meeting to be at the wedding ceremony. Much of that ceremony involved giving the newly-weds the opportunity to get to know one another.

The bride and groom at their marriage ceremony

The new couple bows down to each other.

## Who shall it be?

The first thing to note is that this is a question for the parents. When they think that the time to marry off their son has come, they will begin to look around for a suitable match. They may enlist the help of a professional matchmaker, who will advise them in a number of ways:

- Is the girl's family of the right social status? *It is important that their son doesn't marry into a lower social order*

- How wealthy are they? *This is a delicate question that it is impolite to ask directly, so the matchmaker can make discreet enquiries, but it has to be just right:*

  - too rich and the proposal will be rejected

  - too poor and the family reputation will suffer

- Does the girl's birth sign match? *If not the marriage will be thought unlucky*

Woman matchmaker

## Betrothal

The parents then present a formal, written proposal to the girl's parents. The matchmaker goes along too, but no attention is paid to her (so as not to bring bad luck) until both sides have agreed to the match. She then receives lavish presents from both families and is given the responsibility of supervising preparations for the wedding.

The families exchange presents, with the matchmaker acting as go-between, and a date for the wedding is agreed. However, this is no simple matter of comparing diaries, as the most important thing is to ensure that the most propitious day for the ceremony is selected. Astrologers are consulted and the day chosen according to the stars.

**Presenting Wedding Gifts**

# Wedding

The actual wedding takes place over the course of three days, with a series of ceremonies marking the end of life with their parents and the beginning of married life together.

On the first day, the groom goes to the bride's family home to meet her and accompany her to the place where the main ceremony will be. She will be wearing the first of her three wedding dresses. This will be bright red, with gold trimmings and include a heavy veil, also red, completely covering her head. As she is led to her carriage she must cry loudly and cling to her mother to show sadness at leaving home.

The bride's dowry is proudly displayed at the wedding and indicates the wealth and status of the bride as well as including traditional symbols of good fortune and happiness: an abacus, a measuring vessel, a ruler, a pair of scissors, a set of scales and a mirror. As guests arrive, they add their money gifts to the display and a careful tally is kept.

Fireworks are let off and traditional music played as the groom, also in red, formally receives his bride and the celebrations begin. After showing reverence to both families and to his new bride, who is now revealed to him – possibly for the first time – he escorts her to the bridal chamber and festivities begin.

**Ancient Chinese Wedding**

# The wedding feast

The wedding feast traditionally is of six courses and includes a number of speeches and toasts to the bride and groom and their families. After the third course the bride leaves the banquet briefly to change into her second wedding dress, which is usually white, and which is in turn exchanged for a third as the feasting ends and the party begins.

On the final day a dinner party for close family and friends is held at the bride's parents' home. In some traditions the bride returns to visit her parents on the seventh and ninth day before the marriage is finally said to be complete and the couple leave to begin married life together.

# Comparisons

While there are many similarities between Chinese wedding traditions and the customs mentioned in the earlier passage about marriage traditions in Western Europe, there are also many differences. In pairs, note down what these similarities and differences are.

Make your notes under the following headings:

- parental involvement
- suitability
- proposal
- wedding day/date
- wedding ceremony.

Compare your findings with others in your class.

 Diary entry

Imagine that you have been the guest at a wedding. Write about it in your diary.

- Say something about what happened and why.
- Include your thoughts, feelings, and reactions to what was taking place.

## Key skills

### Punctuation

Correct punctuation is important if we are to be correctly understood. Look at the following:

marry you i will not wait a year or even a day

Has the girl said "Yes" or has she said "No"? It all depends on the punctuation! See how many different ways you can punctuate the sentence to change the meaning. Can you think of other examples where different punctuation affects what is said? Compare your examples with a partner. Sometimes wrong punctuation can lead to misunderstanding and frustration … or amusement! Take one of your examples and develop it into a short, amusing scene.

### Supply the missing punctuation

1 at one time friday especially the 13th was thought unlucky

2 in ancient china a boys parents would employ a matchmaker usually a woman

3 has a fortune teller asked to name the best day she enquired

4 a western bride wears white but red my favourite colour is worn at chinese weddings

5 where are the pictures of our daughters wedding she asked

# Reading – recognizing a balanced argument

We all have strong opinions about certain topics but it is always a good idea to take notice of other people's points of view. Sometimes we are asked to write about a topic and to consider it from both sides. It is important that we try to find ways to present it in a balanced form.

Let's consider the following topic: "Marriage is just as important in today's world as it was for our parents".

Think about the topic and come up with some ideas to support it and some ideas to oppose it. Now let's work with a partner. Compare your lists, and, together, write an article that covers both sides of the argument. Don't worry at this stage about the accuracy of the writing, the spelling, or the grammar. This is a reading activity, so let's focus on the key reading skills of being able to recognize different points of view in a piece of writing.

When you have written about 200 words, pass your first draft piece onto another pair. They will read it to see how balanced it is. Does the piece prefer one point of view to another? Does it contain about 50 per cent of views for one side and 50 per cent for the other? You are about to get some feedback from the two students who have just read your article, so sit back!

Now here's another task for you both: You are going to locate an article about marriage on the Internet. The article should be about 400–500 words. It may help to think of IFAC (Introduction, For, Against, Conclusion) while looking through potential articles to ensure that a balanced view is given.

**Introduction:** briefly stating what the topic is about.

**For:** developing some ideas that are for the argument.

**Against:** developing some ideas that are against the argument.

**Conclusion:** briefly stating that side of the argument is preferred.

You will certainly engage with plenty of topics while you study this course that present two sides of an argument, and this is a skill that will also feature when practising speaking, listening, and writing.

## Sample student responses

Let's look at how three students have planned an essay on the title in the task above. Which one do you think is likely to achieve the best balance? Which one will probably have the best content?

Discuss these points with your partner and then say which one you think is the best and why. Why are the other two not so good?

**Student A**

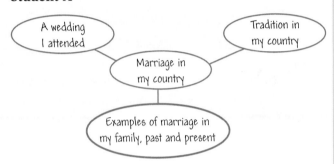

**Student B**

FOR: tradition, family stability is important

AGAINST: finance, costs too much cross-cultural marriages cause problems

CONCLUSION: there are both advantages and disadvantages

**Student C**

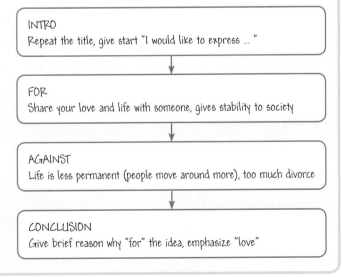

# Death customs

Perhaps the richest and most varied customs are kept for the last act of our lives. Why do you think that is? Death is treated with respect in all cultures and is something that we will all experience. What happens to people when they die in your culture? How are they said goodbye to?

## Building your vocabulary

Do you know the following words and phrases? Use a dictionary to check the meaning of any you are not sure of.

| concept | pyramid | suits of jade | deceased | cremated |
|---------|---------|---------------|----------|----------|
| novelty | plazas | antlers | decomposing | wake |

 **Track 9.1** Listen to the sentences as they are read out and decide which word or phrase is being referred to in each case.

## Caring for the dead

### Funeral practices around the world

In many countries in the modern world, the practice of burying the dead is common. However, it's a relatively new concept by some standards, and in some places, it's almost a novelty. In fact, many of today's contemporary funeral practices might be considered a bit strange by our ancestors. There is such a wide variety of funeral practice throughout history that it's worth taking a look at – in fact, archaeologists have learned that studying the treatment of the dead can actually give them a clue to how a culture lives.

Every society, throughout history, has found some way to attend to the proper care of their dead. Here are some different methods in which various cultures have said farewell to their loved ones:

- On the island of Sulawesi, in Indonesia, newborn infants who die are buried in the trunks of giant trees. The people there believe that the child's soul will rise up into the heavens through the tree.

- Many cultures, such as the Maya and the Egyptians, buried their dead in tombs that were part of ceremonial centres. Multiple burials were often contained in the same pyramid or plaza. Earlier burials were often built over by later generations, making these sites a bit of a puzzle for researchers.

- The ancient Chinese buried their rulers in suits of jade before interment.

- Archeologists have unearthed the tombs of Neanderthal man dating back over 60 000 years at the Shanidar Cave in Iraq. The graves included animal antlers placed on the body and remains of flowers nearby. This may indicate that some sort of ritual took place, even that long ago.

- Modern-day women of a New Guinea tribe, the Gimi, have a ritual that involves eating the flesh of deceased men. Gillian Gilson, author of *Between Culture and Fantasy: A New Guinea Highlands Mythology* indicates that this is partly because eating the body prevents it from decomposing, but there are some other, more complex, cultural reasons as well. In some ancient societies, the dead were cremated and then their ashes consumed.

- The burial of a Norse chieftain included all the things the man might need in the afterlife – a ship, weapons, horses, and food. In an account given by the 10th-century Muslim writer Ahmad ibn Fadlan, he describes a scene in which a slave girl is sacrificed in a chieftain's funeral.

- In some customs, funeral services consist of simply leaving the dead to rot, or be consumed by wild beasts. In Tibet, and in some Native American cultures, it was believed that those who were eaten by dogs were better off in the next world.

- Covering the face of the dead comes from the ancient belief that the soul escaped the body via the mouth. In some African tribes, it was common to tie the mouth shut. Many practices also come from the idea that evil spirits were hovering around the body to steal the soul immediately after death – this is where we get the ringing of bells, firing of weapons, and the holding of a wake.

**Source: www.about.com**

## Check your understanding

1 What do archaeologists say you can learn from studying the ways that people have treated their dead?

2 Why do archaeologists find some Mexican burials puzzling?

3 What was buried alongside Norse chieftains?

4 Why did some African tribes tie the mouths of the dead shut?

5 Where did the practise of ringing a bell at funerals originate from?

6* Which funeral practice mentioned here strikes you as the strangest? Why?

## A multimedia project

The article "Funeral Practices Around the World" gives several examples of burial practice from history. With a partner, choose an ancient civilization – that of your own country perhaps – to investigate. See what you can find out about that civilization's customs surrounding birth, marriage, and death. Gather as much information as you can and use it to assemble a digital presentation for the rest of the class. Use lots of visual images and cut down on the amount of text. It's going to be a multimedia project.

# Listening – understanding what is implied

One of the higher-level listening skills that is tested is to understand what is implied but not actually stated, for example, to be able to recognize gist, relationships between speakers, a speaker's purpose or intention, and a speaker's feelings. One of the questions on the examination paper tests this specifically, but there will be questions elsewhere that test this generic skill. Let's practise this skill, therefore, to see how it can be applied.

Imagine you are in a room with three other people and someone raises the topic of culture shock. By this, they mean how difficult it can be at times to get used to being in a new and different culture.

 Track 9.2 Listen to how the discussion develops

Now, with a partner, work out what each person's attitude is towards new places and new cultures. How would you describe each person? Compare your descriptions to another pair, and then another pair. Are you finding some very similar descriptions?

Here are three questions – see if you spot which person each is talking about.

1 Who would feel most comfortable in a room of people who do not speak the same language?

2 Which person would probably plan his or her trip the most carefully, working out details for every step of the way?

3 Which person would someone from the local culture be less interested in meeting?

In answering these questions, you are starting to use your inference skills – that is, you are trying to understand what is implied but not actually stated.

Have a go with your partner at one of the other skills in this area – recognizing the relationship between speakers.

You have just left the room after meeting the three people you listened to. Continue the discussion about culture shock with your partner for two to three minutes. Talk about what you liked and disliked about the three new people you have just met. You can add further things they may have said, but you should stay with their basic character traits. Include your own views on culture shock, too.

Now complete a table like this (see Worksheet 9.6), giving a mark out of 5 where 5 is the most likely to be a match, and 1 is the least likely. It will be interesting to add up the scores at the end! And it will be interesting to compare your table to your partner's, and to other people in the class.

|  | Person 1 | Person 2 | Person 3 | You | Your partner |
|---|---|---|---|---|---|
| Loves to meet new people |  |  |  |  |  |
| Keenness to travel and explore |  |  |  |  |  |
| Prefers own company |  |  |  |  |  |
| Understands cultural matters |  |  |  |  |  |
| Is open to learning |  |  |  |  |  |
| Totals |  |  |  |  |  |

# Reflection

As we increasingly become members of one "global village", it is inevitable that many of the customs dear to earlier generations will gradually die out … unless they are carefully preserved.

In small groups, discuss which of the cultural traditions featured in this chapter, or covered by you as part of your own investigation, you would seek to preserve. Select one to work on in your group. Be sure to be clear about:

- what the tradition is
- why you have chosen it
- why you think it is important
- what steps you are planning to take to help its preservation.

In your group you are going to mount a campaign to keep a tradition that is in danger of dying out. Your campaign is going to involve some or all of the following:

- posters and handouts
- letters to the media and any relevant authorities
- an exhibition space and what you will place in it
- a debate/discussion to be held on a TV news programme
- a special visitor
- a website page.

Assign each of these different areas to a member of the group to work on. You don't need to use them all, so choose what works best for you. Give your campaign a suitable title, or slogan – "Save the" – or whatever. Then present your campaign to the whole class.

Preserving
cultural heritage

 **My progress**

Each chapter includes four study skills. These are skills that will feature in your final examinations. So let's check your progress with these key skills in mind.

| Where am I now? | Very pleased – I think I'm good at this | OK – but I do need more practice | One of my weaker areas – so I need a lot more practice |
|---|---|---|---|
| Writing short, accurate, and controlled sentences | | | |
| Expressing opinions orally and taking control of a conversation at times | | | |
| Listening to infer what is being implied or suggested | | | |
| Recognizing a balanced set of views in a written article | | | |

Now pick out one skill that you would like to prioritize for improvement and produce a short action plan to help you become stronger. Use a template similar to the following – that is filled out for you with an example.

## Action plan

Skill I want to improve taking control of a conversation at times.

- **planning** – how I will try to improve this skill:
  seek out some people I can have focused discussions with who won't mind me expressing a strong view

- **implementing** – what I will need and what my exact strategy is:
  prepare myself with a set of strong views on a topic I am interested in; set up a 10 minute conversation

- **monitoring** – how I will know I am improving and what evidence I may keep:
  I should become less passive when speaking and more confident to promote my views and to be on equal terms with the other person. I could record some of the conversations to measure my progress over six months

# 10 The past and the future

## In this chapter you will:

- visit Egypt, China and the UK to relive the past and imagine the future

- read about life in 1912, and over 2000 years ago

- write a diary entry set 100 years ago; imagine daily life of someone in the future

- listen to an interview with two centenarians

- talk about when you would most like to have lived –past, present or future!

## Key study skills

- *Speaking* about abstract matters

- *Reading* a text to identify redundant material

- Using own words in *writing* a summary

- *Listening* to reproduce accurate grammatical and contextual details

# Progress

## What has been the greatest influence?

In pairs discuss why you think change has been so rapid. What have been the greatest influences? Here are some suggestions, but feel free to come up with more.

Television and radio

Communications such as mobile phones

Computers and IT

Road and air transport

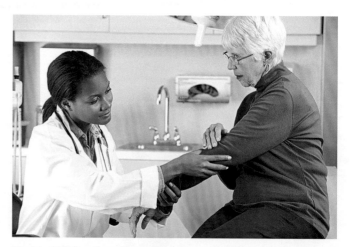

Healthy living and medical advances

With your partner, choose an influence and deliver a talk of three to four minutes' length on how you think it has brought about so much change.

# Ten things that have changed our lives

## 10 Television

The television or **colloquially** just "TV", has become commonplace in our homes, offices and institutions, particularly as a prime source for advertising, entertainment and news. Since the 1970s the availability of video cassettes, CDs, DVDs and now Blu-ray Discs, has resulted in the frequent use of TV for viewing recorded as well as broadcast material. In recent years Internet television has risen to **prominence** with websites like iPlayer and Hulu.

## 9 Mobile phone

There are more than five billion mobile phones in the world, and the number is growing rapidly in China and India. Mobile technology has changed how we communicate, as it allows us to make calls, send text messages or even update our Facebook status from any location.

## 8 Aircraft

How can one travel 7,000 kilometres in 8 hours? Fly! We all should be thankful to Orville and Wilbur Wright, commonly known as the Wright Brothers, who developed the three-axis control system with the incorporation of a movable rudder on their 1902 Glider. The glider was the basis for their **patented** control system still used on modern fixed-wing aircraft.

## 7 Automobile

Do you know there are **approximately** 600 million passenger cars worldwide? That is roughly one car per eleven people! We all know how important they are in our life and it would be hard to imagine a world without them.

## 6 Steam engine

The Industrial Revolution, which is possibly the greatest change over the shortest period of time in the history of civilization, was carried forward by the steam engine. Now, while the steam engine has been overshadowed by electric and internal combustion engines in the areas of transport and factory power, it is still incredibly important. Most power plants in the world actually generate electricity using steam turbines, whether the steam is heated by burning coal, natural gas, or a **nuclear reactor**.

## 5 Email

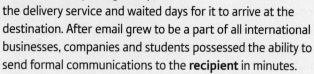

The worldwide spread of email affected the exchange of communications. Before email, a business in the US sending an important document overseas printed the document, packaged it, paid for the delivery service and waited days for it to arrive at the destination. After email grew to be a part of all international businesses, companies and students possessed the ability to send formal communications to the **recipient** in minutes.

## 4 Internet

The U.S. Department of Defense first used a service called ARPANET [Advanced Research Projects Agency Network] in the 1960s. Then, in 1989, Tim Berners-Lee invented the World Wide Web, which shrank the world like nothing else. Today more than 1.7 billion people, or 25 per cent of the world, use the Internet. It is such a powerful invention that we've probably only begun to see its long-term effects.

## 3 Computers

Computers have changed our lives in so many ways, from landing on the moon to simply browsing the web, none of it would have been possible without them. In fact, it's hard to think of any aspect of life that has not been improved by computers. They are able to make complicated mathematical calculations at an incredible rate of speed and when they operate under the instructions of skilled programmers, they can accomplish amazing **feats**.

## 2 Light bulb

If you are not sitting in the dark then you should be thankful to Thomas Edison for inventing the light bulb. Joseph Swan did similar work in Britain at the time, and eventually the two **merged** their ideas into a single company, Ediswan. The bulb itself works by **transmitting** electricity through a wire with high resistance known as a filament. The waste energy created by the resistance is expelled as heat and light.

## 1 Electricity

Probably one of the single most important things in our lives. If the power of electricity had never been **harnessed** we wouldn't have even a fraction of what we have in the world today. No TVs, no microwave ovens, no computers, no air conditioning, and most unfortunately – no List25.

Source: extract from www.list25.com

# Check your understanding

1   Of what three things is television a major source?

2   What were the first names of the Wright brothers?

3   How is most electricity generated?

4   How have computers helped mathematical calculations?

5   Electricity is not an invention but why was its discovery so important?

6*  Which of these inventions would you give top place to? Why?

# The definitive list!

Perhaps you noticed that these are the top ten items from a list of twenty-five life-changing things published on a website. They are just one contributor's suggestions. What do you think the other fifteen may be? Write down some suggestions and then compare them with a partner – have you found fifteen more between you? Discuss what the most important life-changing invention or discovery may have been.

---

# Study tips
## Speaking
### How to approach Prompt five in the Speaking test

The final prompt on the Speaking test card allows you to take the discussion into more sophisticated ground. This prompt can be quite abstract, which means that you need to explore areas that are not straightforward and that invite you to think at a higher level. Prompt five is therefore set to be challenging and it is where you can really show your higher-level speaking skills. The key skill is to be able to either defend an argument or oppose it – but whichever you choose, you need to be convincing.

But don't worry. If you are not a strong speaker, your teacher/examiner will try to paraphrase the prompt so that you can engage with the ideas it presents but at a more straightforward level.

Let's have a look at how it works in the context of this chapter's theme – the past and the future. Here's a Prompt five that could feature in a discussion about "Things that have changed our lives":

● the idea that there is nothing in the past that is of any use at all.

To engage with this prompt, you are being asked to consider the view that there is only the present and the future, and what life would be like if everyone was to adopt this view. We are all told that we should learn from the past, from our mistakes, for example, but this prompt denies us this and states that we only live from the present. So, it is an abstract idea in that it is only your response to a strong view that is needed. You can't usually use anything concrete in Prompt five, but you can put forward a strong argument.

With your partner, have a go at creating some other Prompt five questions, based on any topic or theme. Remember, it must be something that is presented as an idea to explore – and it does not, therefore, need to be factual or even rooted in reality!

Spend about 15 minutes creating and discussing some abstract ideas.

### Sample student responses

**Track 10.1** Listen to three responses to the Prompt five we used above. Which of the three is the strongest response, really grasping the abstract idea? Which is not really able to engage with the main idea? Which one shows some understanding of the abstract idea but lacks the confident and convincing approach needed to express it?

Now that you can see how Prompt 5 works, go back to one of the questions you discussed with your partner earlier and see if you can make it more abstract.

# Life in England 100 years ago

## Building your vocabulary

**gobbledygook   clerical   debutante   pungent   shrink
tight-knit   facilities   coveted   gossip   prioritized**

All of these words are in the passage that you are going to read about life in England at the beginning of the last century. Check that you know their meaning and keep a record of the terms and their meanings. Then see if you can fill in the blanks.

| nonsense | _ _ _ _ _ _ _ _ _ _ K |
|---|---|
| wanted badly | _ _ _ E _ _ _ |
| of office work | _ L _ _ _ _ _ _ |
| girl being introduced at court | _ _ _ _ T _ _ _ |
| strong smelling | _ U _ _ _ _ _ |
| public toilets, for example | _ _ _ _ L _ _ _ _ _ |
| close together | _ _ _ _ _ _-_ N _ _ |
| get less | _ _ R _ _ |
| idle talk | _ _ S _ _ _ |
| considered most important | P _ _ _ _ _ _ _ _ _ _ |

## Check your understanding

1   Why may you have been jobless in 1912 in England?

2   What determined career choices 100 years ago?

3   What advice did doctors give schoolgirls then?

4   How often did a maid get to have a bath?

5   Why were working-class girls not keen to remain unmarried?

6*  What description do you find the most off-putting in this article? Why?

In comparison to life 100 years ago, our lives are delightfully luxurious.

According to Jen Newby, author of *Women's Lives: Researching Women's Social History* 1800–1939, those born in the last century were more concerned with survival than living standards.

"If you travelled back in time to 1912, you'd probably find yourself out of a job, because many modern industries would not exist and your qualifications would be **gobbledygook** to a potential employer. If you're an office worker, then you would be lucky to land a **coveted** job as a typist or **clerical** assistant."

Newby says that a century ago, whether you were male or female your career options were entirely dictated by the social class you had been born into.

Without money, connections and a public school education, you would have an uphill struggle.

"While the professions were open to men – from the "right" background – almost all were closed to women. Women could not vote; they did attend universities, but at most institutions could not obtain full degrees; and doctors were still advising against schoolgirls competing with boys in examinations."

The good old days before cycling shorts

But if you were lucky enough to get a job, you'd then be forced to interact with the outside world. Not an entirely pleasant experience.

"One of the first things that you'd notice would be the smell of body odour. While we're used to putting on fresh clothes every day, in 1912 this was something that only the wealthy could afford to do."

While a **debutante** might have changed her clothes three or four times a day, a maidservant was lucky to get a weekly bath, and would have probably shared the water with at least one other person.

Only the better off enjoyed an indoor toilet, and poorer communities shared brimming, **pungent** outdoor **facilities** with the whole street.

And if you think they were **tight-knit** communities filled with laughter, fun and no work culture – shake that thought away.

"You would see your leisure time instantly **shrink**, as most workers, whether factory or office employees, only had Sundays off."

However, this might have been a blessing as in most towns there were limited sources of amusement for working people beyond parks, public libraries, or the

Servants were lucky to bathe once a week in the last century.

occasional trip to a music hall. All that most working women enjoyed was a cup of tea and **gossip** with a neighbour.

"The 1870 Education Act had provided a free elementary education for all. However, families usually **prioritized** education for boys. While their brothers were sent away to school, middle class girls might be taught decorative skills by a governess – needlework, music, water colour painting, a little French."

"Working class girls and boys would have stayed on at school until age 13 at most, then gone out to work. There were few scholarships available and most families needed every penny from their children's wages, as a working man couldn't earn enough to support his whole family."

So if people weren't learning, having fun or bathing – could you hope for a happy marriage?

"Like today, ordinary couples married later in their mid to late twenties, when they had saved up enough money to start their own household and the husband earned enough for his new wife to stop work." But to remain unmarried was undesirable as it would mean financial dependence on your parents for the rest of your life, and probably being used as a free child-minder and nurse by your family.

Right: we're fine in 2014, thanks!

Source: www.huffingtonpost.co.uk

Girton College was England's first residential college for women, established in 1869.

223

# Study tips

## Reading

## Identifying redundant material in a written text

When you make notes on an article, it is very likely that you will only be interested in certain parts of the text. The piece may have eight paragraphs and be 600 words long but the information you need is perhaps only in three of the paragraphs and you can ignore many of the other words. The details in the text that you do not need are called "redundant details".

Look again at the article "What was life like 100 years ago?". Imagine that you need to make notes on the following:

a   *problems that women faced*

b   *education for working-class and middle-class children*

c   *personal health and hygiene*

Which paragraph(s) would you need to concentrate on to address each area? How did you make your choice?

With a partner, write three more headings – **d**, **e**, and **f** – with *different* ideas to those above. Now show them to another pair and see if they can find the relevant lines or sections in the text. Just as importantly, decide which bits of material you don't need to use – the redundant material. A key examination skill is to have the confidence to ignore the redundant material and focus on what you think is relevant. The ability to select appropriate detail is what you are tested on in these types of exercises.

Here are some notes that have been taken on the article "What was life like 100 years ago?". Can you place the notes under the correct headings? **Be careful!** Some of the notes are wrong and cannot be placed under any of the headings.

**Headings:**

a   *problems that women faced*

b   *personal health and hygiene*

c   *education for working-class children*

**Notes:**

- *Poor communities shared outside toilets*
- *Almost all professions closed to them*
- *To remain unmarried was undesirable*
- *They could not vote*
- *Did not stay beyond 13 years of age*
- *Daily fresh clothes were for the rich*
- *Taught by a governess*
- *Not many scholarships*

With your partner, think of a question relating to the theme of the past or the future. An example could be: "Which event in the past influenced us the most?" Now write a paragraph that contains 50 per cent relevant material, and 50 per cent redundant material. Pass this along to another pair and challenge them to extract the redundant material.

## Sample student responses

Let's have a look and see how three students attempted to write notes on the article under a different heading.

Disadvantages of being unmarried

**Student A**

- the husband earned enough for his wife to stop work
- ordinary couples married later

**Student B**

- used as child minder by family
- financial dependence on parents

**Student C**

- to remain unmarried was undesirable as it would mean financial dependence on your parents
- used as a child minder and as a nurse by your family

Discuss with your partner which of the three students showed the best note-taking skills. Give your reasons why.

# Writing

You are going to compare the situation in England 100 years ago, as described in the passage above, with the situation for you in your country now. First, you need to note down the main points made in the passage. Do this under the following headings:

- Work
- Opportunities for women
- Hygiene
- Leisure
- Family life

## Chat show guest from the past

Using what you have learned from your note-making activity, work with a partner and create a chat show where one of the guests is someone who lived 100 years ago. Spend some time thinking about what questions you would ask – both the interviewer and the guest can ask the other person questions about the times they have lived through.

Discuss your notes with a partner and then take it in turns to interview each other. Think carefully about the questions you are going to ask and make notes on the answers that you are given.

# Writing a diary entry

So, what was life like 100 years ago? Supposing you had been there, what would you have been doing? What would you have looked forward to? What would you have longed for? What may your private thoughts have been?

It is a Saturday night. Before you retire to bed, exhausted, you sit down and write your diary entry for that day.

## Two 100-year-old ladies talk about their lives

**Track 10.2** Listen to these two ladies being interviewed and then answer the questions.

# Check your understanding

1 How many siblings did Hetty have?

   A ten

   B nine

   C eight

2 Where does Peggy have breakfast?

   A in her room

   B in the dining room

   C she doesn't have breakfast

3 Where did Peggy live as a child?

   A in China

   B in North London

   C in a hospital

4 Which of the old ladies still enjoys reading?

   A Hetty

   B Peggy

   C neither

5 Which word best describes their lives?

   A hard

   B tragic

   C fulfilled

#  A remarkable old lady

Imagine that you get to meet one of these two ladies. Write an article for a popular magazine describing how the day went. Where did you meet the old lady? What did she talk about? What impressions did you get of her? Did she have any complaints?

## Thinking out loud

If we go back into the past, not 100 years but several thousand years, we find civilizations very different from ours – but with some surprising similarities, too! What do you think the differences may be? What about any similarities? What would you have liked about living 1,000 years ago? What would you have disliked, or even feared?

## Building your vocabulary

influence   penalty   outright   artisan   nome

available   acrobat   household chores   hired   mourner

Check the meaning of the words and phrases above, noting down any that are new to you. Then see if you can solve the following puzzle.

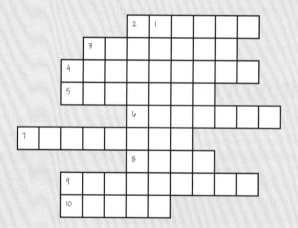

| 1 | down, 2 across | daily jobs around the house |
|---|---|---|
| 3 | | performer of gymnastic skills |
| 4 | | having an affect on |
| 5 | | craftsperson |
| 6 | | punishment |
| 7 | | totally, completely |
| 8 | | province in Ancient Egypt |
| 9 | | open to, obtainable |
| 10 | | employed for payment |

# Family life in Ancient Egypt

The people of Ancient Egypt highly valued family life. They treasured children and regarded them as a great blessing. In the lower-class families, the mother raised the children. The wealthy and the nobility had slaves and servants who helped to take care of the children by attending to their daily needs. If a couple had no children, they would pray to the gods and goddesses for help. They would also place letters at the tombs of dead relatives asking them to use their influence with the gods. Magic was also used as an attempt to have children. In the event that a couple still could not conceive a child, adoption was also an option.

Although women were expected to obey their fathers and husbands, they were equal to men in many ways. They had the legal rights to participate in business deals and own land and they were expected to represent themselves in court cases. Women even faced the same penalties as men. Sometimes wives and mothers of pharaohs were the "real" ruling power in government, although they ruled without the common people knowing. Queen Hatshepsut was the only woman who ruled outright by declaring herself pharaoh. Egyptian wives and mothers were highly respected in this ancient society.

Young boys learned a trade or craft from their fathers or from an artisan. Young girls worked and received their training at home with their mothers. Those who could afford it sent their sons, from about the age of 7, to school to study religion, reading, writing, and arithmetic. Even though there is no evidence of schools for girls, some were home-taught to read and write and some even became doctors.

Children were expected to look after their elderly parents. Upon their parents' death, the sons inherited the land, while daughters inherited the household goods, such as furniture and jewellery. If there were no sons in the family, there was nothing to prevent the daughters from inheriting the land. There is evidence of some women inheriting entire nomes.

Although women were expected to raise the children and take care of the household duties, there were some jobs available to them. Women ran farms and businesses in the absence of their husbands or sons. Women were employed in courts and temples as acrobats, dancers, singers, and musicians. Wealthy families hired maids or nannies to help with household chores and the raising of the children. A noblewoman could become a priestess. Women also worked as professional mourners and perfume makers.

Source: adapted extract from *Splendors of Ancient Egypt Educational Guide*, copyright 1999, St Petersburg Times

FRONTISPIECE.  THE ANCIENT EGYPTIANS.

SCENES FROM THE TOMB-PAINTINGS.—1. Reception of guests in a villa. 2. Kitchen. 3. Toilet of the women. 4. Procession of women with lyre, double flute, zither, and harp. 5. Egyptian house-plan, and garden with pond. 6. Female musicians. 7. Washing. 8. Weaving. 9. Spinning. 10. Cabinetmakers. 11. Wheelwrights. 12. Ropemakers. 13. Shipwrights. 14. Weigher. 15. Shoemakers. 16. Two-horse chariots. 17. Threshing. 18. Bird-hunting and spear-fishing. 19. Bird-catching on the pond. 20. Arms and armor.

## Check your understanding

1 Name three things that couples might do if they were childless.

2 What was the name of the only female pharaoh?

3 At what age did Egyptian boys start school?

4 Who looked after the elderly?

5 In addition to raising children and looking after the home, what jobs were open to women?

6* "The people of ancient Egypt highly valued family life." How is this best shown in the extract?

227

# Writing to a friend in the future!

Imagine that you are a teenager in Ancient Egypt and, using the information in "Family life in Ancient Egypt", send a letter to a friend from the future about your life.

## Study tips

### Summarizing in your own words

You may be asked to summarize two particular aspects of the text, so make sure that you find details from the text for both aspects; don't just concentrate on one part. One of the key skills in writing the summaries needed for the Reading and Writing test is to use relevant content only and to do this as concisely as you can.

Another very important skill in writing summaries is to try to *use your own words* and doing this well can convey very clear understanding. This does not mean rewording all the text but you should try to change some verbs, adjectives, adverbs, and nouns. These new words you will be bringing in are called "synonyms". However, words with very similar meaning but some difference are also useful to show that you have good understanding.

Look at the following examples of words that could be used to replace other words:

**Verbs:**   donate > give      halt > stop

**Adjectives:**   enormous > large      sad > miserable

**Nouns:**   trade > business      news > information

**Adverbs:**   slowly > carefully      fully > completely

How many of these words are true synonyms, with identical meaning? How many could have a different shade of meaning?

Now try it yourself. With a partner, make a list of some nouns, adjectives, adverbs, and verbs (let's say three of each). Give these to another pair and they will see if they can add some synonyms or words with a similar meaning. When you get your list back, place the words in two columns: true

synonyms; and close meaning but not quite the same.

Now look again at the text "Family life in Ancient Egypt".

Write a summary with your partner of about 80 words on how women were equal to men in Egyptian life.

When you have finished, swap it with another pair. Give each other your opinions on the summary. You should consider: Is the summary the right length? Are all the details relevant? Have any of the words in the text been changed? How successful was the use of own words?

### Sample student responses

Read the following three summaries in response to the same theme that you used to write yours. With your partner evaluate each summary. Which is the strongest? Which is the weakest? Which one is in-between?

Why is this so?

**Student A**

The peple of acient Egypt highly valued family. They treasured children and regarded them as a great blessing,iln the lower class families, the mother raised the children. Women were expected to obey their fathers and husbands, they were equal to men in many ways. women had the legal right. Women faced the same penalties as men, Women were expected to raise the childrens, there were some jobs avalable to them. woman ran farms and buisneses in the absence of their husbands or sons there was nothing to prevent the daghters from inheriting the land.

**Student B**

Although women were expected to obey their fathers and husbands, they were equal to men in many ways. They had the legal right to partipate in businness deals, own land, and were expected to represent themselves in court cases. Women even faced the same penalties as men. There were some jobs available to them. Women ran farms and businness in the absence of their husbands or sons. Women were employed in courts and temples as acrobats, dancers, singers and musicians.

**Student C**

Women were equal to men in many ways in Egyptian life. Firstly, they could legally take part in business deals and could represent themselves in court. In addition, it was possible for them to inherit and own land. Furthermore, they were active in businesses and sometimes managed farms. On occasion they entertained people in the temples as singers and musicians. However, one disadvantage of this equality was that they faced the same penalties as men if they disobeyed the laws.

## Language focus

### Homophones

"As we consider the *past* we are thinking about things that have long since *passed* into history".

This sentence illustrates an example of two words that sound the same but have different meanings. The technical term for these is "homophones". Getting them wrong can lead to confusion, so it is a good idea when you check (not cheque) your writing for possible errors to look out for these.

Can you select the correct words in each of the following?

1   The *deer/dear* had very *course/coarse hare/hair*.

2   *Their/There/They're* not *allowed/aloud passed/past* the barrier.

3   He chose to *wear/ware/where* a *pair/pare/pear* of dark *blew/blue* shorts.

4   She was *scene/seen* dressed as a *which/witch*.

5   Take the next *rite/right* for a *site/sight* of *wear/ware/where* the *sale/sail* will take place.

## Watt a bout ewe? [What about you?]

See how many homophones you can come up with. This can be great (grate) fun, but there is a serious point to this exercise, too. Using the wrong one is one of the commonest English language spelling errors, so any practice will help you to be prepared.

Swap lists with someone and use each word in a sentence to show the correct meaning.

## The past unearthed

 Watch the video "The Terracotta Warriors" available at **www.youtube.com/watch?v = RsUE-ZtcUFg**

In pairs, discuss the remarkable discovery that was made in 1974. How much can you remember of the find? See how many details about the statues you can note down in 2 minutes. Then watch the video again to see if you got them right.

# The Terracotta Army

The Terracotta Army is a collection of terracotta sculptures depicting the armies of Qin Shi Huang, the first Emperor of China. There are more than 8,000 life-size statues of soldiers buried along with the emperor. Emperor Qin wanted to live forever. He felt this huge army would protect him and help him to keep his power in the afterlife. He died and was buried in 210 BC, more than 2,000 years ago.

## Statues

The soldiers of the Terracotta Army are life-size statues and are all different heights, shapes and sizes. Despite there being so many statues, no two soldiers are exactly alike. There are soldiers of all ages with different ranks, facial features, and hair styles. The soldiers have different clothing. Some have armour and others don't.

The soldiers were even more impressive 2,000 years ago. The soldiers were painted to look even more realistic and then covered with a lacquer finish. They also held real weapons, such as crossbows, daggers, maces, spears, and swords.

## The project

Archaeologists estimate that more than 700,000 craftsmen worked on the project for several years. There were moulds for the legs, arms, torsos, and heads. These pieces were then put together and custom features,

A soldier

such as ears, moustaches, hair, and weapons, were added later.

There are from eight to ten different head shapes for the soldiers. The different head shapes represent people from different areas of China as well as different personalities of the soldiers. The heads were made from moulds and then customized and attached to the bodies.

**Archaeologists have had to reconstruct the soldiers from thousands of pieces**

## The discovery

The Terracotta Army was discovered by farmers digging a well in 1974, more than 2,000 years after it was covered over during the burial of Emperor Qin. The army was located about a mile from the tomb of the emperor.

## Facts

- Archaeologists have been trying to put lots of the statues back together as they were found broken.

- Terracotta is a common type of hard-baked clay. Once the soldiers were shaped with wet clay, they would have been allowed to dry and then baked in a very hot oven called a kiln so the clay would harden.

# Check your understanding

1  Why did the emperor want this vast terracotta army?

2  What would have made the soldiers look more impressive when they were first made?

3  Why were the soldiers given different head shapes?

4  How was the army discovered?

5  What is terracotta?

6*  From the information given here, describe one of the soldiers.

# Giving a presentation

You have been asked to make a presentation about the first emperor of China, Emperor Qin Shi Huang. What information about him was given in the video or can be found in the article? You will want to include details about the Terracotta Army but other facts about the emperor are also given, or can be inferred. In your groups see how much you can find. You may like to assign different tasks to individual group members. Points to consider include:

- his character
- his reign
- his beliefs
- burial plans
- his legacy.

# Study tips

## Listening

### Accuracy in gap-filling exercises

Your Listening test will feature a section or two where you have to fill in some gaps based on a scenario you have just listened to. In all cases, you will be limited to using only one or two words in the gap. It is very important, therefore, that you choose your words carefully. You should be able to achieve two things: 1) to convey that you have understood the context and have supplied the appropriate details, and 2) that you have done this with an accurate grammatical and contextual fit.

Let's have a look at how this works by using the video about the Terracotta warriors.

Early on in the clip, the narrator mentions some of the feats and achievements of the Chinese Emperor. The questions may, therefore, look like this:

1. Emperor Qin standardized writing, ............. ........................, weights and ................... ..............................................
2. He built a number of ................................ .................................
3. He paid for the early attempt of the ............ ..................................
4. His highest aim was to achieve immortality and he began building a ............................ to bring this about.

With a partner, see if you can locate the specific words needed to fill in these gaps. Remember, only one or two words are allowed.

Now using the same video, create **two** more sentences with gaps in where two words must be inserted. Pass these over to another pair and have a go at the two sentences you receive back. You are practising the key skill of selecting appropriate details, and, indeed, the appropriate number of details.

## Sample student responses

Let's use some sample responses to explore the second objective of this type of gap-filling exercise: to ensure correct grammatical and contextual accuracy. Here are some responses from three students that are all wrong, but can you say why are they wrong?

**Student A**

He built a number of "high and very straight ways"

He paid for the early attempt of the "Really good wall"

**Student B**

Emperor Qin standardized writing, "money" weights and "distances"

He built a number of "high roads"

**Student C**

He paid for the early attempt of the "wall that proved to be great"

His highest aim was to achieve immortality and he began building a "two empire" to bring this about.

Can you supply some responses to these sentences (or your other two sentences) now that would not be acceptable because they do not have a close enough grammatical fit or maybe because they use too many words? Hint: Sometimes just changing the tense of a verb will result in changing the meaning, and be careful with plurals as they can also change the meaning.

For example:

"The emperor likes to go swimming" is correct, but "the emperor likes to go swim" would not be allowed as it does not have an accurate grammatical fit.

"The emperor grew maize" is correct, but "the emperor grew maizes" would not be allowed as it becomes ambiguous.

# The future

## Thinking out loud

What will you be doing in ten years' time? How may life have changed for you? What about 40 years from now? Will things be as different from now as the early twentieth century was from the present? And what about 1,000 years? Can you even imagine that?

## Life in 2050?

## Forty years from now ...

**A glimpse of how daily life may look in the smartcity of 2050, as predicted by Michael Durham of *The Guardian***

It is the weekend, so it is time for some shopping and family organizing for Katy Smith, citizen of London in 2050.

Before leaving the house on Saturday morning, Katy switches on the vacuum cleaner and sets it to clean all four floors. Robot Vacs are fully mobile and come with sensors connected to local weather data, so they know how much dust is in the air.

Katy does not really need to do any food shopping beyond making a few simple checks on her house computer network. The barcode-enabled fridge and fresh-food delivery system linked to her chosen online supermarkets make sure the kitchen cupboards are well stocked.

She orders her clothes online – a virtual scanner system ensuring an exact fit to her body shape. Food, clothes, and most other household purchases are delivered by a driverless electric postal truck, directed by street sensors and global positioning system (GPS) tracking to her front door.

But Katy needs a day out and today she is going to Oxford Street to do some serious window shopping. Before leaving the house, she taps a code into her smartphone and is connected to the automatically controlled car pool, which locates the nearest suitable vehicle. A few minutes later, an electric car arrives.

With a touch of her smartcard the electric vehicle moves off.

At the tube station, Katy changes on to the Victoria line. In the West End a few minutes later, she doesn't need to fight the crowds – a sensor-controlled pedestrian-management system, first tested in European cities back in 2010, shows the least-congested route to the shop on her mobile phone.

But she is not actually going to buy anything. Shopping now means a half-hour holographic fashion show of selected product lines, where everyone has a front-row seat. Because it has all her stored details, the shop has picked items it knows Katy will want to see, and all the information is available online.

On Sunday, Katy and Alan do their weekly online digital health check, where they run sensors over their bodies for signs of ill health. The results are forwarded to a smart health network. Universality of data means their individual health patterns can be compared with millions of others worldwide, enabling analysts to instantly recognize rare conditions or new health trends.

If either are, say, overweight, the clinic will send instructions to the house system to modify diet and book extra gym sessions. If there are signs of illness, the clinic will prescribe medicines or special implants, delivered automatically along with the family foods, or book a virtual appointment with a doctor who will be the top specialist, wherever they may be in the world.

**Source: adapted extract from www.guardian.co.uk**

## Check your understanding

1  Who does the vacuum cleaning?

2  How is Katy's food shopping list kept up to date?

3  How is food delivered?

4  How does Katy travel to Oxford Street?

5  What does the house computer system adjust if Katy is overweight?

6*  What do you find particularly "smart" in the "smartcity" of 2050? Explain why.

 # Writing as if you were someone else

What do you think life may be like for the rest of the family in the "smartcity"? You are going to continue the predictions, based on the ideas contained in the article. Imagine other family members:

Alan (husband): an IT engineer
Alys (daughter): a university student
Seb (son): a school pupil
Mary Brown (Katy's elderly mother): a widow

*(You may like to add your own family members)*

Think about the kind of things that may be included – such as electronic aids, "virtual" entertainment, and automatic links with teachers. Now choose one of the family members and write from their point of view, that is, in the first person. Aim for about 150 words.

## Language focus

### Past and present tenses

I live in London – present tense

I lived in London – past tense

1  I am living in London

2  I lived in London

3  I was living in London

4  I have lived in London

5  I have been living in London

6  I used to live in London

All of these are saying something slightly different. Can you match the sentence continuations below to each one so that the completed sentences make sense?

*but now live in Paris.*
*and in Paris but not in Rome.*
*at the moment.*
*for two years.*
*for three years.*
*at the time.*

See if you can make up sentences of your own using different tenses to express:

1  something you used to do but have stopped doing

2  something you do every day

3  something you are doing temporarily

4  something you would like to do

Discuss your answers with your neighbour. In pairs, make up a language exercise in which different tenses have to be used. Try them out on other students.

To practise using the past tense, try changing the following from the present tense into the past.

> John is living in Paris, where he studies French and Art. He likes most French food but is not keen on snails. His favourite French artist is Edouard Manet and he has been to see the exhibition of his paintings three times. In addition to European art he is interested in Malaysian culture and plans to move to Kuala Lumpar when he finishes his studies though he is not sure where he will live.

Discuss the process with your neighbour.

Now have a go at putting it into the future tense.

# The Big Issue – a Golden Age?

## Thinking out loud

Have you ever wanted to escape from the busy, cluttered present to an ideal time? No trouble or sickness. No worries, just fun, fun, fun! Think about what you would like to be rid of, what you would want to keep. If only …!

You're not alone! In fact, we have all been there, haven't we? In our imagination, we've found the ideal world, or at least sought for it. El Dorado, the Spanish call it, or the Golden Age.

## The Golden Age

The term **Golden Age** comes from **Greek** mythology and legend and refers to the first in a sequence of four or five (or more) **Ages of Man**, in which the Golden Age is first, followed by **Silver**, **Bronze**, **Heroic**, and then the present (**Iron**), which is a period of decline. By extension, "Golden Age" denotes a period of **peace**, **harmony**, **stability**, and **prosperity**. During this age peace and harmony prevailed, and humans did not have to work to feed themselves, for the earth provided food in abundance. They lived to a very old age with a youthful appearance, eventually dying peacefully, with spirits living on as "guardians". The Classical Greek writer, **Plato**, writes of a golden race of humans who came first; they were not literally made of gold, but they were good and noble people.

There are similar concepts in other religious and philosophical traditions. For example, ancient **Hindu** culture saw history as cyclical, with alternating Dark and Golden Ages. Similar beliefs occur in the ancient **Middle East** and throughout the ancient world, as well.

European Pastoral literary tradition often depicted a time when people lived a life of rustic innocence and simplicity, untainted by the corruptions of civilization — a continuation of the Golden Age — set in an idealized **Arcadia**, a region of Ancient Greece. This idealized vision of the simple life, however, was sometimes contested and even ridiculed.

Source: adapted extract from www.en.wikipedia.org/wiki/Golden_Age

## When?

The big question is when was that Golden Age? Was it some time in the past, before wars and poverty and hardship and drudgery?

Or is it still to come, when technology has eased our lives?

Or maybe you think it is now! (Really?)

Or maybe you think it will never come.

##  What do you think?

In pairs, discuss when you think you would like to have lived or would like to live – past, present, or future. Try to establish clear reasons for your choice. And, remember, you don't have to look for perfection, just for a time when, if you had the choice, you think you would have most satisfaction. Make your selection and prepare to present the case for the period (and place) of your choice.

## Debate

Once you have come up with your ideal time, place, and setting, move to small groups to argue your point. In turn say:

- when your "Golden Age" is, was, or will be
- why you have opted for that time and place
- what life would be/have been like for you
- examples to support your argument.

Put the question to the vote and see what period wins the title "The Golden Age".

…

## Back from the future

 **Track 10.3** Listen to the interview with Minqq, a visitor from 1,000 years in the future. Suppose you met Minqq. What do you think he (or she) would be like? Give a brief description, or do a drawing perhaps.

##  Interview

Minqq was going to a sports event. Suppose Minqq returns to the studio to be interviewed about that trip. What was that event? In pairs, you decide. Then go on to produce that second interview. Take it in turns to be interviewer and Minqq.

# Literary connections
## Historical fiction

Writing about historical events and characters in a way that mixes fact and fiction is a popular form of literature. Especially interesting are stories that reconstruct everyday life in former times. They usually include famous people and events but focus on how these influenced the lives of ordinary individuals.

In small groups, discuss examples of historical fiction that you have come across.

It is as though the writers ask us to travel back in time to see for ourselves what life was like. Some have even taken the idea of time-travelling literally – like Dr Who and his Tardis.

One story that describes time travel is *The Time Machine* by H.G. Wells. In fact Wells can be said to have "invented" the idea of travelling not just through the three dimensions of length, breadth, and height but also the fourth dimension of time.

In this extract, the Time Traveller uses a model of his machine to demonstrate time travelling.

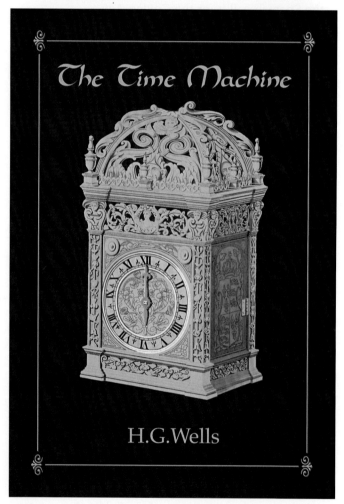

"It took two years to make and I want you clearly to understand that this lever, being pressed over, sends the machine gliding into the future, and this other reverses the motion. This saddle represents the seat of the time traveller. I am going to press the lever and the machine will go. It will vanish, pass into future time, and disappear. Have a good look at the thing. Look at the table too, and satisfy yourselves there is no trickery."

There was a minute's pause perhaps. Then the Time Traveller put his finger towards the lever. … We all saw the lever turn. I am absolutely sure there was no trickery. There was a breath of wind, and the lamp flame jumped. One of the candles was blown out, and the little machine suddenly swung round, became indistinct, was seen as a ghost for a second perhaps … and it was gone – vanished! Save for the lamp, the table was bare.

**Source: *The Time Machine* by H.G. Wells. Pan Books, p. 14**

The Time Traveller (we are not told his name) does indeed build a full-size machine. He makes several journeys further and further into the future. His reports of future life, of the year 802701, and the extinction of man are increasingly severe, until one day he departs, never to return.

# Reflection

In small groups discuss which period in history you would most like to have lived in.

- Is there a national hero you would like to have the chance to meet?
- Or a development (in medicine, perhaps) that you would like to have been part of?
- Or perhaps a great moment in political history that you would like to have been present at?

You decide. It may help if you think of some films you have seen or books you have read that are based on the past.

##  In the past

In your groups you are going to recreate a period from the past. You will need to research the period of your choice carefully, with each of you working on a different aspect of it. The aim is to put together a short scene that can be acted out for the rest of the class.

You will need to:

- select your scenario carefully – make sure that everyone in the group is fully involved
- agree on four or five characters – this can be a mixture of historical figures and others who are perhaps not so famous
- research the background
- be careful not to cover too much!

Remember, each group member should have a specific role and these should be roughly equal in terms of contributions.

# ☑️ My progress

Each chapter includes four study skills. These are skills that will feature in your final examinations. So let's check your progress with these key skills in mind.

| Where am I now? | Very pleased – I think I'm good at this | OK – but I do need more practice | One of my weaker areas – so I need a lot more practice |
|---|---|---|---|
| Speaking about abstract matters | | | |
| Identifying redundant material when reading | | | |
| Using my own words as much as possible when writing summaries | | | |
| Using accurate grammar when filling in gaps when testing listening skills | | | |

Now pick out one skill that you would like to prioritize for improvement and produce a short action plan to help you become stronger. Use a template similar to the following – that is filled out for you with an example.

## Action plan

Skill I want to improve "identifying redundant material when reading".

- **planning** – how I will try to improve this skill:
  "find 3 or 4 information articles on the Internet of about 500 words long and print them out"

- **implementing** – what I will need and what my exact strategy is:
  "articles with a specific theme; and I will then tell myself that I am only interested in one element that the article covers"

- **monitoring** – how I will know I am improving and what evidence I may keep:
  "I will be able to highlight the chunks or parts of the texts I think are relevant, and whatever remains, is not relevant, or redundant, for my purpose"

# 11 Communication

## In this chapter you will:

- visit Hungary, the USA, and France
- read about ways of communicating, in the past and today
- write to a communication company and write a newspaper report
- listen to a debate about computers, a deaf musician, and a sign language trainer
- talk about two people who cannot speak but who can communicate.

## Key study skills

- Using a formal register when *writing*
- Focusing on accuracy and range of structures when *speaking*
- *Listening* to responses that include follow-on information
- *Reading* a text to identify its themed detail

# Why do we need to communicate?

**Thinking out loud**

When did you last communicate something and how did you do it? Why do we communicate at all? Why is it important that we are able to communicate easily to those around us? How would you feel if you were not able to communicate?

## A collaborative activity

Here are four reasons that we communicate with one another.

1   We communicate to persuade: It means that we want someone to do something and this desire of ours is communicated. The mother patting the child to stop crying and the advertiser displaying a new T-shirt both wish to persuade.

2   We communicate to give or provide information: The science teacher demonstrating an experiment or the bank announcing a reduction in interest rates are both communicating to provide information.

3   We communicate to seek information: A passer-by asking you the way to the post office or the student asking the teacher for some explanation are seeking information by using this communication skill.

4   We communicate to express our emotions: These may be courage or fear, joy or sorrow, satisfaction or disappointment, with appropriate gestures and words. Public speakers commonly use emotions to emphasize their message.

Let's explore these reasons further with a pair-based collaborative exercise.

Pair one – you will be focusing on how to communicate to persuade. Which words may be used most often by people who wish to persuade? Add some more examples to those situations where people use communication to persuade.

Pair two – you will be focusing on how to communicate to give or provide information. What communication is there in your daily lives that gives you information and when do you give information? What specific language can be used to do so?

Pair three – you will be focusing on how to communicate to seek information. When else do you need information? When was the last time you were in a situation when you needed to ask for information? Tell the group. What language did you use to do so?

Pair four – you will be focusing on how to communicate to express emotions. When did you last hear something that was trying to use emotions to communicate a message? What effect did it have on you?

When you are ready, your teacher will form working groups and each group will share their findings.

# How do we communicate?

**Thinking out loud**

If you need to tell your best friend something but he or she is not near you, how do you do it? How quickly does the message reach them after you have sent it? Do they get the message straight away or is there some time in-between? Do they reply to you using the same method or do they use a different method to reply? Are there sometimes some misunderstandings?

## Ways that I communicate

What are the different ways you communicate? Write them down on a separate sheet of paper.

Did any of the ways you communicate match any of these?

- a message of up to 160 characters that you may send by phone

- a longer written message that can be typed on a computer or laptop before being sent electronically

- a form of social media that can be used on mobiles, tablets, or computers

- a gadget that allows you to dial a number and speak to a person

- a digital recording of a spoken message you may wish to leave if you have been unable to speak to them by phone

- a message of up to 140 characters, uploaded via a website, which can be seen by one or many thousands of followers

In olden days, and today at school, if we need to write something down, to communicate with another person using written words, we will probably use a pencil or a pen. If it is a pen, then it may well be a biro. And if you are not using one today, you may well have one at the bottom of a bag or at home. But why is it called a "biro" and when was it invented?

# Laszlo Bíró

Laszlo Bíró presented the first ballpoint pen at the Budapest International Fair in 1931. Bíró patented the invention in Paris in 1938. It took Bíró one year to build his ballpoint pen – a ballpoint pen is thus still widely referred to as a "biro" in many English-speaking countries, including the UK, Ireland, Australia, and New Zealand.

Ballpoint pens are everywhere in modern culture. While other forms of pen are available, ballpoint pens are certainly the most common and some households may have several. The fact that they are cheaply available and convenient to use means they are often to be found on desks and also in

pockets, handbags, bags, and in cars – almost anywhere where one could need to use a pen.

Ballpoint pens are often provided free by businesses as a form of advertising – printed with a company's name, a ballpoint pen is a relatively low-cost advertisement that is highly effective.

Laszlo, together with his brother George, moved to Argentina, where their newly formed Eterpen Company commercialized the Biro pen. The press hailed the success of this writing tool because it could write for a year without refilling.

In 1950 Marcel Bich bought the patent from Bíró for the pen, which soon became the main product of his Bic company.

László Bíró died in Buenos Aires in 1985. Argentina's Inventor's Day is celebrated on Bíró's birthday, 29 September.

Today, the highly popular modern version of Laszlo Bíró's pen, the BIC Crystal, has a daily worldwide sales figure of 14,000,000 pieces. Biro is still the generic name used for the ballpoint pen in most of the world. Biro ballpoint pens will produce more than 28,000 linear feet of writing – more than five miles, before running out of ink.

**Source: United States Patent and Trademark Office**
**www.inventors.about.com/library/**
**weekly/aa101697.htm**

# Check your understanding

1  Where did Laszlo Bíró first present his ballpoint pen?

2  Give two common places where you may keep a ballpoint pen.

3  Why do companies sometimes give out free pens?

4  Who bought the patent for Biro's pen? When?

5  Why is Argentina's Inventor's Day on 29 September?

6*  Why are biros so popular?

## Language focus

### Anecdotes

When writing a biography, we need to include details about a person's life. However, to make it interesting, we need to include more than just facts and dates. The reader will be more interested in the biography if we include anecdotes about the person.

Read the two extracts below and decide which is the more interesting and why. Compare your views to a partner's.

1  I was born in Hong Kong in 1998 but my parents moved to Shanghai when I was three. It is an amazing city to have grown up in – it literally grew around me when I was a child. It is a really special place to me and I think it always will be, even if I go to university in a different city.

2  Moving to Shanghai when I was three really changed my life. I was so inspired by the building going on around me, although I didn't really know it at the time. I found a real interest in how buildings were constructed and the different shapes skyscrapers could take. I used to play on the leftover bamboo scaffolding with my brother. I think it was living in Shanghai at that time that influenced my career choice and I hope to go to university to become an architect.

The second extract is perhaps the more interesting as it gives a better explanation of the influence the city has had on the author as he was growing up and it includes a short anecdote of his time playing in the city, making the writing more individual.

Think of an anecdote you would tell a biographer about your life – a short and funny story about an event that has influenced you in some way. Now email your anecdote to a friend and he or she will email one of theirs to you. What do you notice about the language of anecdotes?

**Track 11.1** Listen to the interview with Tommy Harrison, who works in a school and believes we should be using computers less and pens more.

# Check your understanding

1 Give two reasons why Tommy believes we should use pens more.

2 For how long does William think he can give up using a computer at first?

3 Give one thing Anni checks before starting work.

4 What does Dan use a computer for to tell his friends?

5 What last piece of advice does Tommy give?

6* Give an example of how you could use your computer less and a pen more.

## No Pens Day Wednesday

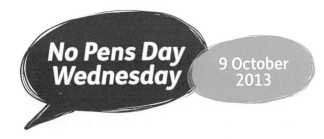

No Pens Day Wednesday encourages schools to put down their pens and to run a day of speaking and listening activities. Over 1,100 schools signed up to take part in this year's No Pens Day Wednesday which we suggested they run on 9th October.

No Pens Day Wednesday is a speaking and listening event organised by The Communication Trust. The Trust is a group of nearly 50 voluntary organisations with knowledge of speech, language and communication, who support the children's workforce to develop the skills of the children they work with.

The importance of speaking and listening for good teaching and good results is often being highlighted.

In its second year, No Pens Day Wednesday was originally developed for the Hello campaign (national year of communication). Hello sought to make children's communication development a priority in homes and schools across the country and had a special focus on identifying and supporting those with speech, language and communication needs (SLCN).

The aim of the day is to see a positive impact on all pupils and enable speaking and listening to be used as a vehicle for learning across the curriculum.

If you would like to run a No Pens Day Wednesday in your school, please register your school. Once you have submitted your details you'll be able to access all the resources. To get a flavour of what No Pens Day Wednesday is about, please download the Activity Pack. The resources will always be available on our website, once you have registered.

**Source: www.thecommunicationtrust.org.uk**

## Designing an application form

In pairs, design the application form that schools will need to fill in to register for No Pens Wednesday. You will need to include the following:

- text that requests basic details about the school – name, address, and telephone number

- text that requests details of the main contact at the school for No Pens Wednesday

- a box in which the person filling in the form has to say why their school would like to join No Pens Wednesday

- details of where they can get further information.

Once the forms have been completed, swap with another pair and fill in their form.

# Who are you writing to and what is your purpose?

What we are writing about and the way we use words to do it is determined by the target reader – who we are writing to. And this dictates the style and format we will use. These two elements are called *purpose* and *register*.

We could use email to tell a friend about our holidays, for example, or we may apply for a job in a local company by email. But we would not tell the local company director what we had done on holiday.

Getting the register for the target reader right can influence the overall effect the writing has on the reader. Read the sentences below and say whether the writer is writing to a friend (informal register) or to someone they do not know (formal register):

1   I can't wait to see you to tell you more; what a shame you had to go and visit your aunt last week instead.

2   I shall be available for interview any day next week.

3   I am hard-working and reliable. I also enjoy new challenges.

4   You know I love action films – well, the latest one I've seen is just amazing. You have to go and see it too.

When we have chosen the correct register for our writing, we are ensuring that the message we wish to communicate will be clearer. A business is more likely to be successful if the letters a company sends out use an appropriate register. Similarly, when we are writing to a business, it is important to use the correct register if we are going to make a positive impression.

Now, write two further sentences to follow on from the sentences below. You will need to use a different register for each one:

1   So, Mike, what do you think about meeting up to go to the cinema on Tuesday with the others? I thought we could go for a pizza first.

2   I went on holiday last month and you will never guess what! I have taken up a new hobby. Even more surprising, it is a new sport.

3   I am interested in visiting your company on the Open Day and would like some information first.

4   I have enclosed a copy of my application form and wonder if you could help me with some questions I have.

5   It was an amazing film; I really enjoyed it.

6   So first you need to take the flour and sieve it carefully into a large bowl.

# When were the first communication satellites used?

 **Track 11.2** Listen to the talk about early satellites.

## Check your understanding

Match the first half of the sentence to the second half according to what is said.

1   Satellites were used by armies       weather reports and telephone calls.

2   Today, satellites are used in         to find their way and to spy.

3   Newspapers use satellites             use GPS to find their way.

4   Some reliable taxi drivers            use satellites to find ships and planes.

5   Search-and-rescue teams               to speed up local distribution.

## Study tips

## Writing – using a formal register

When you write an email to friends or a family member you can use very informal language and you do not have to be too concerned about register. If you are writing a more serious piece, such as an article or a report, to someone you do not know, then your writing style must be different: It needs to be more formal.

It may help you when writing this type of piece to think of the three "Ws":  Who? Why? What?

In other words: Who are you writing to? Why are you writing the piece? What are you writing about? If you like, you could call these, respectively, the audience, the purpose, and the content.

You will gain more marks if you have a correct style and can develop your views in a persuasive way. There will be prompts in the examination paper to help you, but you should only use them as a guide and you should always try to introduce your own ideas. The worst thing that you can do is to copy the prompts.

You will certainly have opinions on things that are happening around you. They could be things that are happening in your school, your town, your country, or even in other parts of the world.

What issues or events do you feel strongly about? Work with a friend and make a list of three issues on which you both have strong opinions. Choose one of the issues from the list and discuss the main points. See if you can develop this and together present a balanced view with ideas from both sides, for and against.

One of you could then write three sentences about the positive aspects and the other person in the pair could write three sentences with opposite views.

Can you develop and expand any of the ideas?

Finally, as a pair, create a balanced argument on the whole issue. It would be a good idea to add an introduction and a conclusion.

Here's an example of how the task may look:

You are going to write an article for the school magazine about communication in today's world. Here are some different points of view about communication.

"Fast communications are so helpful in many situations."

"We are so obsessed with speed of communicating these days that I'm sure we're spending millions on improvements we don't really need."

"People spend too much time on mobile phones and social networks."

"Social networking has brought the whole world closer together."

What are your views on how we communicate today?

Your article should be from 150 to 200 words in length.

## Sample student responses

Let's read three sample student answers that all respond to the task above. Which one has the most developed content? What about the level and accuracy of language?

Discuss these points with your partner and then rank the articles in order. Which one do you think is the best? Why? Why are the other two not so good?

### Student A

So many people use communication nowadays and it's very useful. You can communicate by email, mobile phone and many other devices very quickly. The other person can reply to you very quick also.

One good point is that fast communications are good in many situations. Like in an accident or when you have lost your way. It is also useful if you want to meet someone. But I don't like it when people always use their phones in public places like cafes and restaurants because it annoys other people.

To sum up, modern means of communication have its good and its bad points.

### Student B

Do you like to talk to peple? Do you like to text peple? I think texting is very good cause it is quick and you get quick answer. Fast communications are so helpful in many ways. But people spend too much time on mobile phones and socal network. If I want to call the police or the doctor it is very good and this is the advantage of communication. We should use email and phone a lot but not too much if you becomes like an addict and not able to stop. In my opion peple should use communications in some places and not others.

### Student C

It must be said that means of communication have advanced considerably over the past twenty years. Does this always bring benefits or are there also disadvantages?

Emergency situations can be co-ordinated better when we can contact people wherever they are. The speed of communications can save lives in certain situations.

On the other hand, we spend so much time communicating with people for no real reason, just because it seems fashionable to have the latest e-device. We are so busy communicating at a distance that we forget the importance of meeting people face-to-face.

In conclusion, I think that we must communicate when necessary and not feel that we need to be in touch every minute of the day.

# Writing a letter

You have seen the following advertisement in your local newspaper:

---

## Wanted: Satellite communication expert

Are you interested in using the latest satellite communication?

Would you like to work for one of the best businesses in the town?

Write to us, telling us why you are interested in modern communication and what your qualifications are.

Mr David Smith
BD Communication Ltd

---

What register would you use if you were responding to this advertisement? Start the letter and write two short paragraphs. Compare these with a friend's and discuss the similarities and differences.

# Communication in the past

# The Pony Express

Watch the clip explaining the history of the Pony Express available at
**www.youtube.com/watch?v = y1R-GeEd95c**

## Check your understanding

Now match an amount of time or a date to each of the following statements:

| 19 months | April 1861 | 1,966 miles | 20 days | October 1861 |
|-----------|-----------|-------------|---------|--------------|

1   The distance of the Pony Express between Missouri and California.

2   The time it took to deliver mail by stage coach.

3   The date W.H. Russell transferred ownership of the Pony Express to Wells Fargo.

4   The date the transcontinental telegraph was completed.

5   The period of time in which 35,000 letters were delivered by the Pony Express.

# Homing pigeons

Pigeons have been used to carry messages for centuries. The earliest recorded reference to the use of homing pigeons comes from Egypt, in about 1200 BC, when they were used to carry messages between cities describing the flood level of the Nile. The Romans also used pigeons to carry messages across their empire, and their ships sent messages ahead telling the port of their coming arrival. Homing pigeons were also used in the Arab world, where they were called "The King's Angels".

In France in the 1800s, there was an official pigeon postal service and by 1870 this had expanded to include a route between Paris and London. Pigeons carried their messages either in special message containers on their legs, or in small pouches looped over their backs.

Pigeons used in racing as a sport started to become more popular in the 1900s, and continues to be popular in many parts of the world today.

Our fascination with the homing ability of pigeons has also attracted a lot of scientific research.

Scientists believe that homing pigeons use a range of skills to find their way home. The two most common theories are that pigeons use their magnetic and solar compasses to find a route. They can follow the magnetic curves of the Earth's surface, as well as the Sun, so their owners let them have a good look at where the Sun is before they are released.

Other scientists believe that pigeons follow landmarks such as roads and rivers; the pigeon can also use its sense of smell through the white bump on its beak.

The homing pigeon is likely to use a combination of these to get home. As well as carrying messages, they used to be used to carry blood samples across one city from a hospital to a laboratory.

**Source: www.rpra.org**

# Check your understanding

1  For how long have humans used pigeons to carry messages?

2  What has caused scientific research interest in homing pigeons?

3  There are two main theories on how homing pigeons return home; give one of these.

4  Give an example of a landmark that a homing pigeon may follow.

5  What else, apart from messages, did homing pigeons carry?

6*  How long did it take for the French pigeon postal service to become international?

## ○ Persuading your boss

You work for a shipping company that is planning to use homing pigeons in case vital satellite equipment should ever break down. It will be fairly cheap to keep them but your boss may see it as an unnecessary expense. You need to present your reasons for this choice to your boss and the board of directors, explaining why you feel the pigeons would be a useful addition.

 **Morse code**

Now watch the clip available at **www.youtube.com/ watch?v = L6gxfX4GrbI** for a brief demonstration of Morse code.

## Samuel Morse

Before phones, computers, and telegraphs were invented, messages would take months or even years to reach their destinations, taken by foot, pony or ship.

Samuel Morse was born in the United States in April 1791. One day, he wrote a letter to his parents from his college saying that he wanted to be a painter. Mr and Mrs Morse were afraid that he couldn't make a living as a painter, so they made him become a bookseller. He worked as a bookseller but at night he would paint. Finally, his parents realised how he loved art so they found the money for Morse to study art in London.

In class, he made a model of Hercules in clay. His professor liked it so much that he asked him to enter it in a contest. It won a gold medal. So Samuel Morse had finally found something that he was good at. He began to paint portraits of people in Europe. Not everyone would give Morse money for painting portraits of them and he almost gave up painting.

In October 1832, Samuel Morse sailed back home. One day during his trip, he heard some passengers talking about electricity. Suddenly, Samuel had an idea. Maybe electricity could transmit messages. For the rest of the trip, he worked on an alphabetical system that was later called Morse code. The only symbols that he made up were a dash and a dot. Common letters had short codes and not so common letters had longer codes. This is the same for numbers. For example, the code for s is ... (three dots) and the code for w is . – – (one dot and two dashes).

Source: www.kidsnewsroom.org

## Check your understanding

1  Give one example of how letters were transported before computers, telegraphs, and telephones.

2  What job did Morse decide he wanted to have while at college?

3  Why did Morse's parents allow him to travel to England?

4  Overhearing a conversation about what, gave Morse the idea for his code?

5  What is the Morse code for "s"?

6*  Research how you would write your name in Morse Code.

## Urgent message!

You are living in the nineteenth century and urgently need to communicate with a friend in the next town. You can only send your message once and you need to be certain that it will reach your friend. Which method of communication would you use? Why? Decide this with your partner. Give some reasons as to why you didn't choose the other forms available to you. When may you have chosen these?

# Communication in children

What happens when we do not grow up in an environment that shows us how to communicate? There have been several reports over the years of young teenagers being found who have apparently been brought up by animals and, thus, have not developed their speech as expected. However, they have retained an ability to communicate. Some have inspired fiction and film, for example, *The Jungle Book*, but there are true stories as well. Read about Oxana, who for five years lived with dogs.

## Oxana Malaya

For five years, Oxana Malaya lived with dogs and survived on raw meat and scraps. When she was found she was running around on all fours barking. She bounds along on all fours through long grass, panting towards water with her tongue hanging out. When she reaches the tap she paws at the ground with her forefeet, drinks noisily with her jaws wide and lets the water cascade over her head.

Up to this point, you think the girl could be acting – but the moment she shakes her head and neck free of drops of water, exactly like a dog when it emerges from a swim, you get a sense that this is something beyond imitation. Then, she barks.

The furious sound she makes is not like a human being pretending to be a dog. It is proper barking and it is coming from the mouth of a young woman, dressed in T-shirt and shorts. Oxana Malaya learnt to do this as a young child, when she was brought up by a pack of dogs on a rundown farm in the village of Novaya Blagoveschenka, in the Ukraine.

One night, her parents put her, as a three-year-old, outside and she crawled over to where the dogs were sleeping. No-one came to look for her or even seemed to notice she was gone, so she stayed where there was warmth and food – raw meat and scraps – forgetting what it was to be human, losing what toddler's language

she had and learning to survive as a member of the pack.

Five years later, a neighbour reported a child living with animals. When she was found, Oxana could hardly speak and ran around on all fours barking, copying her carers.

The British child psychologist and expert on feral children, Lyn Fry, went to the Ukraine to visit her. "I expected someone much less human," says Fry, the first non-Ukrainian expert to meet Oxana, "but she did everything I asked of her. Her language is odd. She speaks flatly as though it's an order. There is no cadence or rhythm or music to her speech, no inflection or tone. But she has a sense of humour. She likes to be the centre of attention, to make people laugh. You would never know this was a young woman raised by dogs."

She can count but not add up. She cannot read or spell her name correctly.

Experts agree that unless a child learns to speak by the age of five, the brain misses its window of opportunity to acquire language, a defining characteristic of being human.

Oxana was able to learn to talk again because she had some childish speech before she was abandoned. At an orphanage school, they taught her to walk upright, to eat with her hands and, crucially, to communicate like a human being.

**Source: www.telegraph.co.uk**

## Check your understanding

1  Give two examples of how Oxana behaves that she has learned from her time living with dogs.

2  How old was Oxana when a neighbour reported she was living with some dogs?

3  Give two examples of how her speech is different from normal human speech.

4  What can Oxana do with numbers?

5  By what age must a child learn to speak if there are not to be problems communicating later?

6*  What can Oxana do having been discovered by her neighbour that she could not do when she lived with the dogs?

# How young children and babies communicate

Without the ability to communicate, progress is much slower, not just for the individual, but also for society. So it is important for babies and young children to practise their communication skills regularly, through speaking and through story-telling.

**Track 11.3** Listen to the interview with Julia Donaldson, who has written several children's books and who understands the need for even small children to communicate.

## Check your understanding

1   In which year did Julia start writing books?

2   Does Julia use a pen or a computer if her writing is not going to rhyme?

3   Why did Julia write about a Gruffalo rather than a tiger?

4   Give one adjective Julia uses to describe Axel Schaeffler's drawings.

5   How many books for schools has Julia written?

6*  How do illustrations help us to understand a story?

# Babies communicating

## Building your vocabulary

Match the words and phrases to their definitions:

| | |
|---|---|
| struggle | relax, to rest or sleep |
| confusing | ability to explain the meaning of something |
| settle down | have difficulty with something |
| understanding | unclear |
| remembering | to find something for the first time |
| theory | a possible explanation for something that is unproven |
| hypothesis | able to speak two languages |
| accompanying | ability to recall an event or fact |
| discovering | to go with a person or object |
| bilingual | rules and ideas that relate to something |

# Language focus

## Present tense versus continuous tense

We can change the tone and pace of a piece of writing when we change the verb form we are using. Look at this pair of sentences:

- I have chosen to run in the race tomorrow.
- I am running in that race tomorrow.

Which one seems more immediate and which one seems more formal?

Now compare this pair of sentences:

- I have made my friend a cake for her wedding.
- I am making a cake for my friend's wedding.

Which sentence flows better? Why do you think this is?

With a partner, add the correct form of a verb to these sentences. Which verb forms don't work in the gaps?

1   The woman _____ back to the store along the footpath.

2   The train _____ at 8 a.m. every morning.

3   Once he had retired, he spent his free time _____ a new language.

4   Juan is _____ the ball against the garage. Please ask him to stop.

5   He has a great talent in _____ stories, especially to young children.

Now with your partner try the verb tense game! Your partner shouts out a verb in any form or tense he or she likes, and then you respond with a brief sentence that uses it properly. Your teacher will walk around as you do this and act as a referee.

# Is your baby talking to you?

The newborn stage is an amazing time in the life of your baby, when changes happen right before your eyes as your baby grows, smiles and laughs for the first time. But for new parents, it can also be a time of many challenges as you **struggle** to understand what your baby needs from one moment to the next.

As patient as you are, it can be **confusing** trying to calm a crying baby who won't **settle down**. Wouldn't it be wonderful if there was a simple way to read your baby's mind and understand what exactly he or she needs? Well, read on and you will see that there already is someone who understands what babies are communicating.

Priscilla Dunstan, founder of Dunstan Baby Language, believes she has unlocked the secret to **understanding** newborn babies' cries. Dunstan was able to hear the differences between the sounds of infant cries and unlock the meaning behind them.

"I was able to pick out certain patterns and then, **remembering** what those patterns were later on when he cried again," Dunstan says. "I realised that other babies were saying the same words."

Dunstan tested her baby language **theory** on more than 1,000 infants around the world and her **hypothesis** proved true. There are just a handful of words that babies (age 0–3 months) are saying, and they are telling you exactly what you need to know.

Are you ready to become **bilingual** in baby talk? Here's how. There are four main sounds that babies will make when they need something and they fall into the categories you might expect – tired, sleepy, hungry and need to be burped. Here's a breakdown of the sounds and their meanings:

- Owh      *I'm sleepy*
- Heh      *Change me*
- Eh        *Burp me*
- Neh      *I'm hungry*

It may take some practice to learn how to identify the sounds and their **accompanying** meanings, but parents who've used the system can't praise it enough. They have said that they have found it amazing as they have been **discovering** that babies can actually communicate with us in a way mums can actually understand.

**Source: www.sheknows.com**

# Check your understanding

1  Give a synonym from the passage that means the baby is very young.

2  How did Priscilla Dunstan realize babies were saying the same words?

3  What age range of babies did Priscilla study?

4  Give two of the four main sounds Priscilla identified.

5  What is the reaction of parents who have used the system?

6*  Why is Priscilla Dunstan so popular?

# Communicating without speaking

**Thinking out loud**

Look at the artwork of the girl with the red balloon and decide what you think about the picture and what you think the artist is trying to achieve. Think also for a few minutes about how other pieces of art you know act as means of communication.

## Banksy

The artist responsible for this work is Banksy, a graffiti artist; this artwork is on the side of a bridge in London. Does knowing this change your views of the picture?

Banksy is a graffiti artist from Bristol, UK, whose artwork has appeared throughout London and other locations around the world. Despite this, he carefully manages to keep his real name from the mainstream media.

Banksy, despite not calling himself an artist, has been considered by some as talented. Some believe that his graffiti provides a voice for those living in urban environments; many others disagree, saying that his work is simple vandalism. Banksy does, however, also do paid work for charities as well as getting up to £25,000 for canvases.

Another of Banksy's tricks involves hanging a piece of his own art in famous museums around the world. In May 2005, Bansky's version of a cave painting showing a human hunting while pushing a shopping cart was found hanging in the British Museum [in London]. Banksy has also self-published several books that contain photos of his work in various countries as well as some of his canvas work and exhibitions.

**Source: www.briansewell.com**

## In my town!

There have been several incidents of art graffiti in your town, created by someone working in a similar style to Banksy. Some of the local residents are in favour of the new pictures, seeing them as art. Others think it is wrong to draw on the walls of buildings in the town, however pretty some people think it looks. What are your views? Prepare a short speech to deliver to the class, explaining whether you are for or against graffiti.

# Study tips

## Speaking

### The structure criterion

One of the three ways you will be assessed during your Speaking test is by how accurate your spoken structures are. In addition to the accuracy of your structures, you will also need to demonstrate a wide range of structures in your speaking. But what does this actually mean?

### Accuracy

Here are some common spoken structure errors:

"I saw her at the shop and he said hello."

"Too many people come to this shop last year and we was much too busy to cope."

"Shop is busy now. Man came in yesterday. Bought $1,000 of goods."

With a partner, spot these errors (hint – there are two in the second one). How would you correct the errors?

### Range

Here are some examples of a limited range of structures:

"Yesterday I went swimming. I swam for two hours. I rested then for an hour. I swam again for another hour."

"He said go so I went and then she said he said wrong. I said who is right. He said he was. She said she was."

"I like fish, I like boat too. But most of all I like to sun tanning."

Again, with your partner, see if you can tidy these up and broaden the range of structures. By sorting each of them out so that they make better sense you will be improving the use of structures.

Now think of some times when you make mistakes when you speak. Have a conversation about a topic, any topic you like, and point out each other's structure errors – the times when you feel that what you say doesn't quite work or doesn't sound right.

In the Speaking test, it's better to be accurate with what you do say rather than to try to say too much. So think carefully about what you're saying and perhaps speak slightly more slowly than you normally would. Paying attention to your structures will start you off with the chance to get a good mark for speaking.

## Sample student responses

**Student A**

Here's a strong response to a question about why a smartphone is important:

**Q: Could you survive without your phone?**

"No way. My phone is my life. It does everything for me; what I mean is that it meets my daily needs. All of my friends communicate with one another using social networking sites and I am registered with all of these sites. I've programmed the phone to use different ring tones for the different groups of friends. I forgot my phone the other day. You should have seen how much more work I did though. Hardly surprising I suppose."

**Student B**

And here's a weaker response to the same question:

"Not survive. I need my phone. I need it every day. I need it for my social sites. It has different ring tones you know. I know which friends are saying what. When I leave my phone at home, I work more I think so all is not too bad."

Can you see why the second response is limited in the range of structures?

## Evelyn Glennie

Evelyn was very young when she lost her hearing; this, however, did not stop her communicating. In fact, it led her to a whole new career, and a global audience, which she may otherwise not have had.

 Watch the interview with Evelyn Glennie available at **www.youtube.com/watch?v = BuJk-r8GZF4**

## Check your understanding

1  Why does Evelyn go on stage without any shoes?

2  How many concerts does she perform each year?

3  How many instruments does she have? Where are they from?

4  How old was Evelyn when she started to play the drums?

5  What does she say it is important for every child to be involved in?

6*  Give an example of groups of people you think could be inspired by Evelyn Glennie.

## Sign language

We have already read about people who have been able to communicate while overcoming physical problems. However, they still use words to do so, even if those words have to go through a third party before being communicated to the world.

However, there are people who can freely communicate without using speech at all.

---

Hint: Try to use as few words as you can when responding; ideally, use three words or fewer.

**1a.** What do all sign languages have in common?

**1b.** In what main way does British sign language differ from others?

**2a.** How long does it usually take to qualify?

**2b.** Name one other career that Sonia mentions.

**3a.** How have you made your knowledge about signing available to others?

**3b.** What are you likely to be working on in the next few months?

**4a.** What has inspired you most since doing this job?

**4b.** What would you like to change in the world of sign language if you could?

## Sample student responses

Let's have a look at how three students answered Questions 3a and 3b:

**Student A**

3a) By a DVD

3b) greater access to all people who need sign language

**Student B**

3a) DVD and a book

3b) using the Internet to spread the message

**Student C**

3a) By being qualified

3b) a website project

Which student provides the best responses to Questions 3a and 3b? Is it the same student? Consider the other responses that were quite close. Why would they not be given the marks, though?

(Our questions were: 1. Why does the cyclist need help? and 2. Why is it his lucky day?)

# Check your understanding

Match the first half of each sentence to the second half as you listen to Sonia Hollis:

| | | |
|---|---|---|
| 1 | Sonja is a fully qualified | Sonja felt a bit shy. |
| 2 | Sonja started to learn sign | British Sign Language language Interpreter. |
| 3 | When learning the signs, at first | a set of DVDs. |
| 4 | Sonja feels sign language is | to communicate with a small nursery child. |
| 5 | Sonja has just produced | incredibly important. |

## Building your vocabulary

Match a definition from the list on the right for each of the words and phrases in the list on the left:

| | |
|---|---|
| echolocation | short sounds like taps |
| vocalization | hand signals used to communicate or reinforce words |
| clicks | developed over a period of time |
| evolved | giving words to thoughts |
| gestures | transmit a feeling or thought |
| convey | the way someone passes over a message to others |
| emotional state | a way of locating an object using sound that can be reflected off the object |
| communication system | the way a person is feeling |

# Dolphins

Animals rely on structured communication systems to help transmit information. In fact, all life on this planet is able to communicate, both with other individuals of the same species, and with individuals of different species. The methods used for communication are varied and complicated, and are not limited to vocalisations. Ants, for example, share large amounts of information with other members of the colony through chemical trails and pheromones. Bees are known to communicate complicated information about the location of flower patches by engaging in an intricate "dance" that lets other bees know the distance and direction of tasty nectar-rich flowers.

So, language is a form of communication, but communication can happen in so many different ways – not just through language. So, what about dolphins? Well, like all animals, dolphins have **evolved** a set of behaviours that allow them to communicate. Like humans, they use a variety of kinds of physical contact for communication, for example:

• a gentle nuzzle
• a playful bite
• an aggressive bite
• a smack.

They also use visual signals (sort of like human **gestures**) to **convey** information. For example, the following signals can convey frustration, threat, or anger:

• a bobbing of the head
• a wide open gaping mouth
• an S-shaped swimming position.

Dolphins, like chimpanzees, birds and many other animals, also use **vocalizations** for communication. They produce a whole assortment of sounds that scientists have labelled in any number of ways. Dolphins appear to use these communicative behaviours to express all sorts of things to each other. They can communicate their **emotional state** but also convey information about their age, gender, etc.

Scientists who study communication in dolphins are trying to learn more about the kinds of communication signals dolphins do use, when they use them, in what situations and what these signals might convey for meaning. While dolphins might not have a human language, they do have a **communication system** that is just as fascinating, and just as much fun to study.

Scientists have learned that dolphins are amazing vocal mimics – able to reproduce man-made whistle structures with precise accuracy. Dolphins produce whistles during social situations, when separated from friends, when excited, when happy and when panicked. Different whistles are produced in different situations, and scientists have been attempting to catalogue and categorize whistles from study populations for some time. This is an extremely complicated process, and much has been written about how various species develop and use whistle communication. The whistles and other vocal calls of dolphins have received considerable attention, and scientists have discovered that family groups appear to produce distinct whistles and other calls, and are taught to new members of the group. These calls are so distinct that researchers are able to distinguish different family groups just by listening to their calls.

**Source: www. dolphincommunicationproject.org**

# Check your understanding

1 Give an example of the physical communication dolphins have.

2 Give an example of visual communication dolphins use.

3 Give one other animal apart from dolphins that uses vocalization in order to communicate.

4 What are dolphins communicating with these communicative behaviours? Give one example.

5 Give one example of what scientists are trying to study in dolphins.

6* Which other animals have been studied for the way they communicate?

# Chimpanzees

Dolphins are not the only animals that we think can communicate with us.

Chimpanzees are one of four types of "great ape". The great apes are: chimpanzees, bonobos, gorillas, and orangutans.

Wild chimpanzees only live in Africa. Humans and chimpanzees share 95 to 98 per cent of the same DNA. Biologically, chimpanzees are more closely related to humans than they are to gorillas.

Chimpanzees and other species, including some types of birds, make and use tools. For a long time, scientists thought human beings were the only ones who made tools. Chimpanzees use more tools for more purposes than any other creatures except humans.

Chimpanzees communicate much like humans do – by kissing, embracing, patting on the back, touching hands, tickling. In captivity, chimpanzees can be taught human languages such as ASL (American Sign Language). A chimp named Washoe learnt more than 240 signs.

Chimpanzees in the wild rarely live longer than 50 years. Captive chimps can live more than 60 years. Chimpanzees sometimes hunt and eat small mammals. They also eat fruit, nuts, seeds, leaves and insects. Chimpanzees have a wide variety of tastes and are able to live in a wide variety of habitats, unlike gorillas and orangutans who have narrower diets.

Different chimpanzee groups use tools in different ways. Chimpanzees of the Tai Forest in Cote d'Ivoire crack open nuts with rocks, for example, while the Gombe chimps have never been seen doing this. Chimpanzees walk on all fours and have longer arms than legs. They are called "knuckle walkers" because they use their knuckles for support. Like humans, chimps have opposable thumbs and opposable big toes which allow them to grip things with their feet.

Chimps can be found in about 21 African countries, mostly in central Africa. Most chimps live in rainforest areas on what used to be the equatorial forest belt. Sadly, the rain forests in Africa are being cut down, leaving only patches of forest where the belt once stretched continuously. Another great threat to the continued existence of wild chimpanzees is commercial hunting for meat.

Source: www.janegoodall.org/chimp-facts

 ## Writing a letter of interest

You have seen this advert in your local newspaper. Read it carefully and then send goodcommunicators an email to find out more. You'll need to ask a lot of questions.

## Good communicators needed

Are you interested in animals? Do you enjoy learning about communication?

If you have just answered "yes' to both of these questions, then we need you!

We are looking for researchers to investigate why and how animals communicate.

Email us by using the contact form at goodcommunicators.co.uk

## Check your understanding

1. How much deoxyibonculeic acid (DNA) do humans and chimpanzees share?

2. Give two ways that chimpanzees can communicate in the wild.

3. How many signs did Washoe learn to communicate with?

4. How many countries are chimpanzees found in?

5. Name one factor that is threatening chimpanzees in the wild.

# The Big Issue – alternative ways to communicate
## Jean-Dominique Bauby

Jean-Dominique Bauby was a French journalist and author who had a successful career as the editor of the French version of *ELLE* magazine. Unfortunately, at the age of only 43, Bauby suffered a massive stroke and on waking after it found he could only move his left eyelid, being otherwise virtually paralysed.

Bauby suffered from what is often known as "locked-in syndrome", a state of paralysis where the body cannot be moved but the mind is working perfectly well. Living with such a syndrome can prove extremely difficult, not only on the sufferer, but also on those who live around them and support them.

This did not stop him from communicating, however, and he started to dictate his novel, *The Diving Bell and the Butterfly*, by blinking to his writer until the letter he wanted had been reached; his letters were not in alphabetical order (a, b, c and so forth), but in order of frequency in the French language (e, s, r and so on).

He dictated the novel from his hospital rooms, describing not only how he was feeling, but also the physical description of the room he was in, and the church bells outside, ringing every quarter of an hour. The "diving bell" in the title refers to how Bauby feels, trapped in a body that will not move, as if a heavy weight was stopping him from moving; the "butterfly" refers to his spirit, which is still free to fly to wherever he wishes, be it castles in Spain or discovering imaginary worlds. On the first day of publication, 25,000 copies were sold; Bauby died two days later. A film version of The Diving Bell and the Butterfly was produced in 2007 to great critical acclaim.

## Check your understanding

1   After his stroke, what was the only part of his body that Bauby could move?

2   How did Bauby dictate his novel?

3   How often do the bells ring outside his room?

4   Why does Bauby describe his body as a "diving bell"?

5   Give one example of what Bauby can think of in his mind.

6*  Why is Bauby an inspiration to others?

# Stephen Hawking

Like Bauby, Hawking was born without any apparent physical problem. However, when he was 21, Hawking was diagnosed with motor neurone disease, which has gradually left him dependent on a wheelchair to move and a laptop to speak through. He has, however, been able to communicate to a global audience his views on Space and time, from lectures celebrating the National Aeronautics and Space Administration's (NASA's) fiftieth birthday, to children's books on Space.

Read Dan's letter to Sam, telling him about the day he met Stephen Hawking, before answering the questions.

Dear Sam

I just had to write and tell you that I have had the most amazing day – such days make me so glad I became a journalist – I got to interview Stephen Hawking. Let me tell you a bit about him.

Stephen was born on 8 January 1942, 300 years to the day after the death of Galileo, isn't that an amazing coincidence? He wanted to study Mathematics – rather him than me! – but Mathematics was not available at his university, so he studied Physics instead. After three years, he went on to do some research in Cosmology at Cambridge University. Can you imagine living and studying in Cambridge? What a fantastic way to spend your life!

He told me that he wants to travel into space to encourage public interest in space travel and that if the human race is to have a future, we have to travel into space – wouldn't that be amazing! He communicates using a computer and uses his eyes to choose the words which have been pre-programmed into his computer – it is really interesting to see.

Stephen was diagnosed with ALS, a form of motor neurone disease, shortly after his 21st birthday. It is such an inspiration to me to see someone achieving so much despite all the difficulties he has had to overcome – I shan't be complaining about anything ever again, really.

I asked Stephen about his role in the Paralympic Games and he said he was honoured to open the 2012 Paralympic Games and welcome athletes from the whole world to London. He told me we need to celebrate excellence, friendship and respect – I think this is a great life motto, don't you?

Did you know he has also written a children's book, with his daughter? The only children's book to have been updated because of the discovery of the Higgs-like boson at CERN [European Council for Nuclear Research]!

Well, it was just incredible to have met him – bet you are really jealous that I have – I've lots more to tell you, so give me a call and we'll go to that new café in town later.

Take care

Dan

Source: www.hawking.org.uk/about-stephen.html

## Check your understanding

1 What is special about the day Stephen was born?

2 Why did he study physics at university?

3 How does Stephen Hawking communicate?

4 What did Stephen do during the London Paralympic Games?

5 Who has he written a children's book with?

6* Which of Stephen's achievements interests you the most?

# Comparing and contrasting

You have now read two brief accounts of people who have continued to communicate despite the physical difficulty of doing so. There are some areas where Stephen and Jean are similar, but others where they are very different. Complete the chart to demonstrate these similarities and differences.

| Similarities between Bauby and Hawking | Differences between Bauby and Hawking |
|---|---|
|  |  |
|  |  |

## Asking interesting and open questions

Look at the following questions an interviewer asked someone they were writing a biography about, as well as the responses that were given:

I: *Where were you born?*

R: *In Oldham, which is just outside Manchester, in the north of England.*

I: *Where did you go to school?*

R: *In Oldham, but I left when I was 14.*

I: *What's your favourite town?*

R: *Oldham.*

I: *Do you like football? Who do you support?*

R: *Yes. Oldham Athletic.*

I: *When did you first come to London?*

R: *In 1996.*

Is there anything wrong with this series of questions? How could you improve the questions?

We need to ask questions that are going to result in interesting responses. So, rather than asking short and closed questions, we need to think of questions that will give us more valuable information and longer responses. These could be questions such as:

● Tell me about an event that has had an effect on you and why it had an effect on you.

● What one thing would you change about your life so far?

We also need to be able to respond to the information that the person being interviewed is giving us – so we need to listen carefully to what is being said.

For example, when the interviewee says, " ... but I left school at 14", what should the next question have been? Discuss this with a partner and come up with a better question than the one that was asked.

With your partner, try both approaches – use closed questions to find out about each other and then improve on this by introducing open questions. You will soon be developing interesting and spontaneous conversations.

You have the chance to meet either Bauby or Hawking. Who would you choose to meet and what three or four open questions would you like to ask them?

# Literary connections
## First-person narrative

**Thinking out loud**

What would you do if you discovered that one of your friends was unhappy? How would you try to make him or her happy? Or wouldn't that approach work? Do you feel sometimes that you don't like your friends and have to be careful about what you say? Think about how people interact. Are human beings naturally friendly or naturally self-centred?

## Developing a discussion

What would you do if you found out that your friend's unhappiness was being caused by a non-life-threatening condition? You might research the condition on the Internet, ask your parents or other adults about it, visit a charity that specializes in the condition, or do something else maybe? Compare your thoughts with your partner, and spend 2 to 3 minutes discussing approaches to this situation.

## *World Enough and Time*

*World Enough and Time* is a novel about Anna, a 15-year-old girl, whose experiences growing up have been affected by her rare condition that has left her unable to speak as well as she would like. She approaches life with a dry humour while always wondering if she will ever look like what is thought of as normal.

---

## Building your vocabulary

Look at these words and phrases and check the meaning of any that you are unsure about:

**dressing table    mission    flattering    convince    toddler**

**illusion    indicate    hazy    articulate    reactions**

Now, fill in the gaps in this passage:

From the very beginning, she knew she would enjoy her latest ..................... but she knew it was not going to be easy. She stood up from her ..................... where she had been putting on her make-up, and left her hotel room.

Downstairs, in the restaurant, she walked over to the ambassador and started to say some ..................... things to him, so he would take her into his confidence. She knew she had to ..................... him to sign up to her company's business plan but she was also under no ..................... about how difficult this would be.

Fortunately, she had had a good education and was ..................... when promoting the business. She was just about to ..................... to her colleague that he should join them, to help continue the promotion when everything in the restaurant went ..................... and she had no control over her ..................... She had failed to do what even a ..................... would know – never drink from a glass that someone else has given you.

Back at home, Dad was mowing the lawn and the two cats were helping by getting in the way. He waved cheerfully as we arrived but kept on going, a man on a **mission**. Mum started on the dinner and I sat in front of the television. After a while, I went upstairs and sat at my **dressing table**.

Sometimes I look in the mirror and things don't seem so bad. Maybe when the light is **flattering**, or a shadow falls in just the right place. I can spend hours examining myself, trying to **convince** myself that this better version of my face appears to the world more often than I imagine. That every time I sit face to face with Michael, *this* is what he sees.

Other times, I will catch a stranger staring, or a **toddler** will ask its mummy what's wrong with the big girl over there, and the **illusion** shatters.

I am lucky to live in a big house with parents that love me. I am also lucky to be bright and talented, or so I am told. I am good at most subjects (except PE, but that doesn't count). I can play the piano. I can write well. I can act. I am good at public speaking and can put on a jolly good show of being confident as well as **articulate**.

But I would swap it all to be beautiful.

It would probably surprise most people to know that my surgery is something I look forward to. Hidden inside one of my drawers at home is a calendar, and every day I put a cross through the date, taking me one step closer to the long-awaited event. The calendar currently **indicates** that I have thirty-six days to go.

The plan is to transplant a small section of one of my ribs and somehow pin it into place where my jawbone was meant to be. They will also move some flesh around at the same time, although I am a little **hazy** about that; it sounds like something out of a Science Fiction movie and best not thought about in detail.

When you have spent every waking minute of your life dealing with people's awkward **reactions** to the way you look, surgery that might put a stop to all that seems like a miracle.

Source: *World Enough and Time*
by Emma C. Williams

# Check your understanding

1  What is the first thing Anna does when she gets home?

2  Give an example of something that breaks the illusion she sometimes has.

3  Anna is good at several things. Give two examples.

4  What would Anna most like to be?

5  Give a detail of the surgery that she will have.

6*  Write a tweet to send to Anna to encourage her.

 ## Writing in the first person

Anna approaches her life with optimism and humour, although there are times when things are not always going to plan.

It is a few months later and Anna has had her surgery and is back at school. Write a few paragraphs to continue her story.

Remember these key elements of writing in the first person:

- Bring your reader in close; draw them in to your situation straight away.

- Use a good range of active verbs – not just *be* and *am*.

- Use emotional language; say how you feel.

- Try to plot a journey; there needs to be a path that the reader can follow.

Now compare your writing to a partner's. How similar are the two pieces in style? And what about content? You may be surprised at how similar they are.

# Reflection

In this chapter, you have learned about a wide range of ways that humans and animals communicate with one another, including times when regular communication methods cannot be used so other means of communicating have been developed. Let's have some fun now with a method of communication that has been used during war time – secret codes!

In small groups, you are going to design and develop your own secret code. The aim of this activity is to produce a code that can be deciphered, or understood by other people once they know the rules.

Your code doesn't necessarily have to be written – you could be more adventurous and come up with a visual code.

The best way to go about this is to assign a particular task to each group member and then to meet up again as a group to discuss the way forward:

**Code researcher** – this person finds out about other secret codes and reports back with what has been used before and some ideas of a good code to develop.

**Codebreaker** – this person researches how codes have been broken in the past, and the ways that this has been done; which codes are the easiest to break?

**Message sender** – this person explores what message you want to send and what the purpose of your secret message is.

**The infiltrator** – this person talks to people from the other groups and tries to ascertain what they are up to!

But feel free to come up with other roles if they work better for you.

Now design your secret code and decide as a group how you want to present it. All of the other groups will then spend about five minutes trying to break or "crack" your code. So there should be a winning group each time!

## ☑ My progress

Each chapter includes four study skills. These are skills that will feature in your final examinations. So let's check your progress with these key skills in mind.

| Where am I now? | Very pleased – I think I'm good at this | OK – but I do need more practice | One of my weaker areas – so I need a lot more practice |
|---|---|---|---|
| Using formal register when writing | | | |
| Speaking with accurate and wide-ranging structures | | | |
| Listening for follow-on details and information | | | |
| Identifying themed detail in a written article | | | |

Now pick out one skill that you would like to prioritize for improvement and produce a short action plan to help you become stronger. Use a template similar to the following – that is filled out for you with an example.

## Action plan

Skill I want to improve "listening for follow-on detail and information"

- **planning** – how I will try to improve this skill:
  "listen to some interviews"

- **implementing** – what I will need and what my exact strategy is:
  "access to some news-based interviews and focusing on the second question asked; the follow-up question"

- **monitoring** – how I will know I am improving and what evidence I may keep:
  "I'll be able to spot the follow-up questions more easily, and I will be able to predict what they are"

# 12 Global issues

## In this chapter you will:

- visit China, Paraguay, and Singapore
- read about trade between countries, living a carbon-neutral life, and global diets
- write about your favourite brands and ethical trade
- listen to a company boss, a nuclear power plant worker, and a musician
- talk about how to look after the planet better, how you would rebrand a favourite product, and how we can improve the way we recycle.

## Key study skills

- Using open questions when *speaking*
- Recognizing people's views and opinions when *listening*
- *Reading* and interpreting diagrams and charts
- Practising the use of sub-headings when *writing* notes

# Global trade and advertising

**Thinking out loud**

There are some brands that are familiar in nearly every country around the world. They are a global presence. However, it is not always just their names that are familiar, but also their advertising slogans, or taglines, which are also well-known. If the company is "connecting people" then we will probably think of Nokia; when we are told to "just do it" then we will think of Nike. Language and images are powerful forms of branding for companies. What are your favourite brands? Are they advertised by well-known film stars or sports stars?

## 🗨 Developing a discussion

There are many reasons why we choose a particular brand. Look at some examples below.

- Peer pressure
- Advertising skill
- Price
- Tagline
- Ethics
- Quality

In pairs, ask each other about your favourite brands. Try to choose questions that will encourage interesting answers.

## Study tips

### Using open questions

In conversations, it is best not to use too many questions that could be answered quite simply with "yes" or "no" – these are called **closed questions**. If you ask a question that invites a longer response, it is called an **open question**. Open questions usually lead to more effective dialogue.

Think about the discussion you have just had about your favourite brands – were there lots of yes and no responses? How did you invite the other person to speak at length? A good way to ensure an open question is to begin the question with "Why". Let's practise this, as it will help you when you take your speaking test.

One of the ways that you will be assessed in your speaking test is according to the fluency and development of your conversational skill. So it follows that you will need the right questions and prompts to enable you to demonstrate this. During the test, the teacher will ask a series of open questions to help you respond, but you can also contribute to the discussion by asking a few questions yourself. A two-way conversation is the aim, so that both of you are involved in discussing the topic.

Here's an example of a closed question, an open question, and then a prompt:

**Closed question** – "Have you ever been to India?"

**Open question** – "What do you think you may like about India?"

**Prompt** – "India seems a fascinating place to me. I think everyone should go there at least once ... "

Can you see how open questions and prompts help to develop a conversation?

Now try it yourself. With a partner, start off with a closed question, and between you convert it to an open question. Now develop this into a prompt – a statement that is not actually a question, but that invites a response from the listener. Try a few of these until you are both happy with this new skill.

## Sample student responses

 **Track 12.1** Listen to these three short discussions.

- Which one do you think is the most productive conversation? Which one uses more open questions and prompts?

- Which is the least productive? How would you improve this particular discussion?

- The other discussion is acceptable in parts, but it has some areas where it would be difficult to respond if you were the student. Can you spot these areas?

Here's a hint – if you are taking part in a conversation and you are being asked too many closed questions, do two things:

1 Convert these to open questions – respond with "yes" or "no", but then go on and add more information, detail, and examples.

2 Ask the other person an open question, and maybe they will realize that a lively discussion needs open questions! For example: "No, I haven't been to India – but I think you have, though, what's it like?"

## Ethical beauty

Many national companies, and multinational companies, now make a promise to their customers that the products they are buying have been made in an **ethical** way. Ethical means that the product has been made in a way that is not harmful to the environment, animals, or people, and, in many cases, helps them. Beauty products in particular often promote the fact that they have been made without any animal cruelty or animal testing.

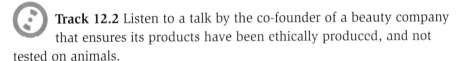 **Track 12.2** Listen to a talk by the co-founder of a beauty company that ensures its products have been ethically produced, and not tested on animals.

## Check your understanding

1 What made the co-founder first start her company?

2 What reasons does she give for being ethical? Give two examples.

3 Who can use her beauty products?

4 Where do some of the company's profits go? Give one example.

5 How can we find out more? Give two examples.

6* Find out the names of two ethical beauty companies.

 ## Writing a review

You have been asked to test a product from the beauty company, and write a review based on your experience of using it. In your review, include the following:

* what attracts you to this company and why it has been successful

* a description of the product and how effective it was

* why you would, or wouldn't, recommend the company and its products to others.

---

## Building your vocabulary

 Watch the following video clip and tick some of the words that the advertisers have used to try to create a positive impression:

**www.youtube.com/watch?v = SJ1lhMHd0YU&list = PL07D55B4A1 B410082&index = 2**

| | | | |
|---|---|---|---|
| ☐ | Premium | ☐ | Organically certified |
| ☐ | Modern | ☐ | Specially blended |
| ☐ | Traceability | ☐ | Pure |
| ☐ | Hand-gathered | ☐ | Best-selling |
| ☐ | Highest quality | ☐ | Fair price |
| ☐ | Cheap | ☐ | Enriching |

In small groups, pick a product that you are going to advertise to the class; it could be a real one or a made-up one.

Use some of the words from the tick list and create a 1-minute advert for your product. Now present your advert to the class.

---

## Image is everything!

Sometimes, and often at great expense, companies decide to change their image. Look at some of the reasons below and, with a partner, try to add to the list:

* Making the company seem more modern

* Changing the name to make it sound catchier

* Using fresh images and/or colours to make the company more appealing

* Adjusting themselves for a new and different market

You are going to research a company that has changed its image. With your partner, research your chosen company. Find out what the original name for the company was and whether they have changed it. Or have they changed the name of any products they sell? Or have they redesigned their company logo? Why have they made changes? What was their aim in looking so closely at their previous image?

Now, present your findings to the class. How many people were surprised to hear of the rebranding of your company?

## Creating your own label

Now, think of your favourite brand – the name, the logo, and the packaging. If it were up to you to rebrand the company, how would you do it?

Choose a product you are going to rebrand for a global market. Decide what features need to be changed – colour, letter font, name of product, and/or packaging material – and what you are going to change them to.

If you can, create the new packaging, either physically or on a computer, so that you can actually show the class what changes you have made in your rebranding.

Do a quick head count. How many people prefer the new branding to the old version?

## Early traders

Before we had the Internet to shop with, and before there were shopping centres, people used to buy the items they needed locally, perhaps from the people who had actually made the goods. It is likely that each person in a local area had a skill to make a specific item, which was then traded for other items.

Ever since we have produced food, we have been able to trade. This in turn led to exchanges that meant a product could be swapped for other goods, and perhaps even a long way away from the place it was made. An example of this is the Silk Road, in China, along which goods were traded.

### Building your vocabulary

First, look at the words below, which you will read in the next article:

**region  caravan  stock valuable  import**

Check their meaning. Have you used any of the words before?

Now put each word into one of the gaps below:

1  He had plenty of ................;
   he just needed more customers.

2  Since we have few natural resources in our country, we have to .................... what we need.

3  The necklace was very beautiful, and ............... too.

4  There was a long ....................
   of camels crossing the desert.

5  The northern ....................
   of the country is also the coldest part.

# The Silk Road

The Silk Road is the most well-known trading route of ancient China. Trade in silk grew under the Han Dynasty (202 BC–AD 220) in the first and second centuries AD.

### Origins
At first, the Chinese traded silk within their country. **Caravans** from China would carry silk to the western edges of the **region**. Often small Central Asian tribes would attack these caravans hoping to capture the traders' valuable **stock**. As a result, the Han Dynasty extended its military defences further into Central Asia from 135–90 BC in order to protect these caravans.

Chan Ch'ien, the first known Chinese traveller to make contact with the Central Asian tribes, later had the idea of expanding the silk trade and so the Silk Road was born.

The route grew with the rise of the Roman Empire because the Chinese gave silk to the Roman-Asian governments as gifts.

### Spanning two continents
The 7,000-mile route spanned China, Central Asia, Northern India, and the Parthian and Roman Empires. It connected the Yellow River Valley to the Mediterranean Sea and passed through places such as the Chinese cities Kansu and Sinkiang and the present-day countries Iran, Iraq and Syria.

North-western Indians who lived near the Ganges River played prominent roles in the China–Mediterranean silk trade because, as early as the third century AD, they knew that silk was a **valuable** product of the Chinese Empire. The trading relationship between the Chinese and the Indians grew stronger with increased Han expansion into Central Asia. The Chinese would trade their silk with the Indians for precious stones and metals such as jade, gold, and silver, and the Indians would trade the silk with the Roman Empire. Silk proved to be an expensive **import** for the Roman Empire since its trade across Indian and Central Asia was heavily controlled by the Parthian Empire.

### Social consequences of the Silk Road
While the Chinese silk trade played a minor role in the Chinese economy, it did increase the number of foreign merchants present in China under the Han Dynasty, exposing both the Chinese and visitors to their country to different cultures and religions. In fact, Buddhism spread from India to China because of trade along the Silk Route, similar to the way Islam spread along trans-Saharan routes in medieval West Africa.

### The Silk Road's decline
The Chinese traded silk for medicines, perfumes and precious stones. As overland trade became increasingly dangerous, and overseas trade became more popular, trade along the Silk Road declined at the end of the fourteenth century.

Source: www.thinkquest.org

# Check your understanding

1 Approximately when was the Silk Road started?

2 Where did people trade on the Silk Road at first?

3 Give the names of two modern-day countries that the Silk Road passed through.

4 Give two examples of items the Indians traded silk for.

5 Give an example of a social change the Silk Road brought.

6* Think of a reason why the Silk Road expanded beyond China.

 # Writing a travelogue

What would it have been like to have been part of a group travelling with your goods along the Silk Road?

Using the photo and the article to help you, write an account of your journey along the Silk Road. Include the following:

- how you felt when you started on the journey

- some events that occurred during the journey that were particularly memorable

- whether you would go on the return journey.

## Key skills

# Responding concisely with appropriate detail

When completing short-answer listening questions, you may be limited to a maximum number of words in your response. This means that you need to be concise when giving information, so it is useful to know exactly which information is being asked for.

Let's analyse the following questions:

1 How many people are there in the world?

Pick the best response from these options below:

a. Seven billion.

b. Seven billion people including adults and children.

c. Seven billion people who all need places to live.

How about this question – What is the most likely response?

2 When was the Ford car company started?

a. Since 1929.

b. In 1929.

c. After 1929.

What kind of detail is this question looking for?

3 Where are Peter and Jane?

a. One of them is at the main square.

b. Discussing what to do with their day.

c. At their hotel.

Note how much information is needed here. Which is likely to be the best response?

4 Give two reasons why Sunny is buying the soap.

a. Pure and organically certified.

b. It is the cheapest soap he has seen and he likes it.

c. It is organically certified, cheap, and pure.

**Track 12.3** Listen to the recordings on the CD. Even though you had not heard what is actually said, how many of the four questions did you get right? Predicting what detail is needed and providing it as concisely as you can are important listening skills.

273

## Study tips

## Recognizing and understanding opinions and attitudes

There will be occasions in your Listening test where you will be asked to match a speaker to his or her opinion, based on comments that each person makes about a particular topic or issue. Let's practise this here.

Before we listen to the recording, form a small group of four or five people and discuss the following opinion for about five minutes:

> *We need to develop the transport industry so that it becomes global. The best way to bring people together around the world is without doubt to make them travel more and visit each others' countries more often.*

How many different views were raised in your group discussion? How many people agreed with the opinion, and how many disagreed? What were some of the other, connected, issues that emerged?

**Track 12.4** Listen to the views that six people present about a proposed new rail link. They each have different opinions but of course may also agree with one another to some extent. However, the key skill here is for you to identify the way in which each person *differs* in his or her views from the others.

Now try to match the speakers to the opinions. Just to make it interesting, we have added an opinion that none of the six people have. Can you tell which one it is?

| | |
|---|---|
| Jane | A Thinks that faster trains means more effective business |
| Mohammed | B Believes that the investment is well worth it |
| Sarah | C Thinks that there is no evidence that the rail link is needed |
| Miguel | D Takes a balanced view |
| Trevor | E Would rather see the airline industry developed |
| James | F Wants to see much quicker train journeys |
| | G Understands the need for the link but is pessimistic |

# Conjuncts and conjunct phrases

Subjects like new rail links, or favourite brands, invite us to give an opinion. When we are explaining why we have a particular opinion, there are certain words we tend to use that signal to the reader (or listener) that an opinion may be forthcoming. These words are called "conjuncts". You may already use words such as:

**Because   Since   As   Also   Therefore   However**

Have a look at these two examples of how we may use linking words:

Since we have learnt about fair trade in school, we have decided to buy products from ethical companies only.

One company we have heard about pays their farmers extra money. Therefore, the farmers are able to look after their families better and send their children to school.

We can increase the range of linking words we use by including linking phrases – these are sometimes called "conjunct phrases":

**Due to          As a result          Ever since**
**Following on from          As a consequence**

Here are two examples of how linking phrases can be used:

Due to the fact that the company has made some ethical choices, all the farmers who work for it have benefited a lot.

Ever since they publicized their ethical trading views, the company's profits have increased each year.

Now, look at the five phrases below. Add an opinion to each one, using one of the conjuncts or conjunct phrases above. You can modify the beginning of the phrase or you can end with an opinion.

1    ... my favourite brand of shoe is ...

2    ... the music shop near the school has closed ...

3    ... my mother always cooks pasta ...

4    ... my best friend has just ...

5    ... I always have to watch ...

Now create five sentences of your own using linking words and phrases – be sure to convey an opinion in each of them. Share your sentences with a partner and try to spot each other's use of conjuncts.

# Global population
## Too many people?

One reason why people have been tempted to destroy some of the natural land around them has been because of a constantly increasing global population. As each decade passes, there are millions more people in the world.

| | |
|---|---|
| **Thinking out loud** | There are more and more people in the world with every passing day. Do you think that this is a good thing, or will we find that one day there are simply too many people in the world for us all to cope? What do you think is the best way to manage population? Maybe we need to build some homes on the moon? |

 ## Writing a letter to the editor

Write a brief "letter to the editor" to a newspaper in response to an article about population control. The article suggested that Earth already has enough people and too many problems as a result of this. Examples given were poverty, lack of food in certain places, wars, too many differences of opinion between different cultures, and spreading disease.

In your letter, respond to these views and provide your own very strong opinion on this matter.

 ## A public meeting

There is going to be an open debate at the local town hall tonight. The local council are proposing to build an additional 2,000 houses in the town and they want to collect the views of the current residents and of people who feel they will be affected by the plans. There will be a panel of experts taking part in the debate.

Each person attending has been asked to submit one question for the panel.

1   Prepare your question.

2   In turn, pose your questions to the class and discuss what the different responses may be.

# The sky's the limit

Around the world more and more cities are having to build upward rather than outward. Read about one hotel that did just that and now offers its guests incredible views while they swim.

## Building your vocabulary

Before you read the article, see if you can pick the correct word from the pair given that will complete each sentence below. When you read the article, you should be able to use these context clues to see whether you were correct.

1   When deciding where to stay on holiday, the quality of the *accommodation/living* is important.

2   When on top of the highest peak, he was able to have a *poor/panoramic* view of the city.

3   From above, the city's *skyline/hemline* is impressive, full of modern buildings.

4   The building of the tallest hotel in the world was incredibly *complex/easy*.

5   The new company headquarters in the city is their *crowning/heading* glory.

Singapore's newest entertainment destination, Marina Bay Sands, offers luxury **accommodation**, shopping, dining, world-class entertainment, and business facilities.

The biggest hotel in Singapore has three 55-storey towers, 2,560 luxury rooms and suites, and 18 different room types. Its 230 luxury suites

come with a waiter; VIP privileged access; and **panoramic** views of the South China Sea and the Singapore **skyline**.

With its sloping towers (angled as steep as 26 degrees) and connecting legs at Level 23 to form a single building, the hotel is one of the most **complex** establishments ever built.

One of the largest art commissions ever completed as part of a building, the hotel will also be home to the Marina Bay Sands Art Path. The Art Path features seven artworks by five world-famous artists.

**Crowning** the three hotel towers of Marina Bay Sands at 200 metres in the sky, the Sands SkyPark stretches longer than the Eiffel tower when laid down. The Sands SkyPark is also home to a 150-metre infinity-edged swimming pool to complete the luxurious experience.

Source: www.yoursingapore.com

# Carbon-neutral

Some people believe an increasing population has had a negative effect on the environment in which they live and so have decided to move away from increasingly busy towns and cities to live a life in more rural areas. In some cases, their lives are completely carbon-neutral. This means that the energy they are consuming has no negative effect on the environment around them.

## Thinking out loud

Imagine you had to survive without technology for a week. What would you miss most? How much would it affect your daily life to not be able to rely on technology?

## Building your vocabulary

Below are some words and phrases from the article that you are going to read next. Find a synonym for each one. The first one has been done for you:

| | |
|---|---|
| symbolizes | represents |
| energy efficiency | |
| sacrifices | |
| responsible | |
| climate change | |
| motivation | |
| sustainable | |
| participated | |

## Vinod – my carbon-neutral life

Asia **symbolizes** the progress that has been achieved in reducing poverty but also highlights **climate change**. It's rightly said that the war on climate change will be won or lost in Asia. The Asian Development Bank (ADB) is uniquely positioned not only to support a more environmentally sustainable development agenda, but also to lead in this.

The great challenge would be to make it carbon-neutral to encourage all development, especially those which include building, to adopt carbon-neutral ideas.

Nearly 1,400 people at the ADB **participated** in the week-long campaign to reduce environmental impact, trying out more sustainable options in transport, food, energy and water use.

I suggest at least three changes for people to make:

- First, we'd like to go *fully paperless*, avoiding printing anything.

- Second, we'd like to contribute to *greater energy efficiency* by turning off lights which are not needed, for example.

- Third, I have always wanted to *go vegetarian*. The No Impact Week program gave me the extra **motivation** to go meatless every other day from now on.

When you think of these steps, as well as the bigger picture of a carbon-neutral world, what is striking is that they do not really involve **sacrifices** or discomfort. Whether it's going paperless, or using less energy, or turning vegetarian, such actions testify to a more **responsible** way of living – and with greater satisfaction and joy.

All of us can be involved in our own distinct ways in the drive for a more a **sustainable** lifestyle and pattern of growth. Taken together, we can make a better life and a better planet.

By Vinod Thomas on Wednesday, 30 January 2013

# Check your understanding

1 How many people took part in the ADB's campaign to reduce our effect on the environment?

2 Give two examples of sustainable options that participants tried.

3 How does Vinod suggest we can be more energy-efficient? Give one example.

4 What inspired Vinod to eat less meat?

5 Give two examples Vinod gives for living in a more responsible way.

6* Why is Asia used to represent the need to tackle climate change?

## Don McCarthy – a carbon-neutral life

It was a trip to the Amazon that really changed the way Don McCarthy viewed the world. He was a ballet dancer until he was injured in a dramatic accident after hitting the stage after diving off a man's shoulders and not being caught properly. During his recovery his therapist invited him to the Amazon where he spent a month, an experience that triggered an enormous change in his lifestyle.

Don fitted London's first grid connected solar panels onto his house. Five years later he installed solar panels to produce hot water. Having a digital display on his wall that monitors his electricity usage has made him increasingly efficient and for the last ten years Don has produced and exported more electricity than he imports.

He uses a large aluminium copper kettle to heat water for cooking and washing dishes. A rain water tank captures water on his roof, which flushes his toilets and comes through a tap for washing food and shaving.

Waste disposal is something Don is particularly passionate about. He avoids using disposable materials. Last year Don's gas bill was £20, his water bill on top of standing charge is £10 a year, he is neutral on electricity and he uses 16 litres of mains water a day, with the rest being rain water. To put this in context the average person in Britain uses over 160 litres of water a day.

An area he is trying to improve on is food, admitting "I'm not the best vegetable grower. You really are at the mercy of the climate." He also doesn't drive or own a car; instead he opts for cycling on his bike, which is also convenient for taking on the train when he has to travel across the country.

As a vegetarian, Don doesn't condone meat-eating and says just cutting back slightly on meat intake can make a huge difference. Meat is responsible for eighteen percent of carbon emissions compared to the aviation industry, which is accountable for three to five percent.

Don believes it's completely possible for people to live the same quality of life using 80 percent less resources than we currently do. And it's not just about making big dramatic changes either. While most people throw out the whole toothbrush when it's worn out Don just disposes the head and keeps the same handle for years. He says, "We're in a major emergency mode for the safety of our planet and this applies to people in London as much as in Africa. It's really crucial we all do something about this, in the home, in the work place and as a wider community."

**Source: www.weekenderlife.co.uk**

# Key skills

## Comparing and contrasting

When we *compare* two ideas, we are looking at the ways in which they are either the same or very similar.

To compare two ideas, we may use words like:

**both   each   neither   similarly   likewise   also**

When we *contrast* two ideas, we are focusing on the ways in which they differ.

To contrast two ideas, we may use words and phrases like:

**but      while      on the other hand
contrary to this      in contrast      however**

Let's compare and contrast two ideas related to energy sources:

- Solar energy is a form of energy that uses heat and light coming from the sun. It is a sustainable form of energy that has no apparent negative impact on the environment. Solar energy can be used for many things including heating water and powering air conditioning systems. Increasingly, people are installing solar panels on their roofs to provide their houses with a free form of energy.

- Nuclear energy is a form of energy that is created when the nucleus of an atom is split. Nuclear power can only be generated in nuclear power plants, which have large cooling towers giving off water vapour into the atmosphere.

Nuclear energy needs to be contained within the power plant because if a leakage occurs the results can be disastrous for the environment.

Now, look at the statements below and for each one decide whether the two ideas are being *compared* or *contrasted*:

1   Solar energy is natural energy from the Sun, while nuclear energy splits atoms and uses the resulting energy in a man-made environment.

2   When both forms of energy are working as they should, neither has a negative effect on the environment.

3   Individual homeowners are able to create a private source of solar energy by putting solar panels on their roofs. It is not possible, however, for individuals to create a private source of nuclear power safely.

4   There would probably be only a small threat to the environment if there were an explosion at a factory that relied on solar panels for energy. In contrast, an explosion at a nuclear power plant could be catastrophic.

Which words helped you decide whether they were comparing or contrasting sentences?

What ideas did Vinod and Don have that are the same? And how did their ideas differ? Compare and contrast their ideas by filling in a diagram similar to this one:

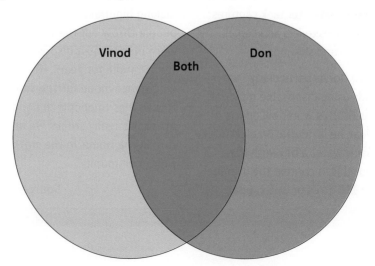

# Study tips

## Questions using diagrams or charts

It is likely that you will be asked to obtain information from a diagram or a chart that is included in an informative article. The diagram provides additional details – usually in the form of data – and the question will invite you to interpret the diagram to extract a particular piece of information. Don't worry, your mathematics skills are not being tested here! The skill being tested is that of retrieving facts and details.

Let's have a look at an example of this so that you can see what we mean. Remember – the diagrams have details that you *cannot find anywhere else in the article*. Take a look at the bar chart that is based on the extract about Don McCarthy and his carbon-neutral life, and then answer the question.

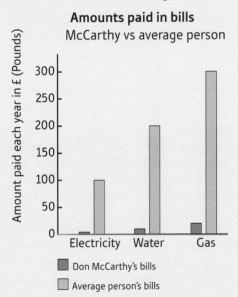

**Amounts paid in bills**
McCarthy vs average person

**According to the chart, how much does an average person spend on gas each year?**

It is best to start by ignoring all of the details in the diagram that do not relate to the question, just as you do when scanning a text.

First, you need to look at the bars of the chart and decide which one refers to an "average person". One of the key words in the question is "gas" so you need to find that first. Then look at the figures on the left-hand side. The amount that corresponds to gas is "300". In your answer you need to make sure that you make it clear what the number "300" refers to, because just "300" on its own has no meaning. Look at the information at the side and select the words that you need. You do not need all of them … the important detail is "pounds" or "£".

Your answer can then be written as "300 pounds" or "£300".

In pairs, see if you can find some other bar charts or diagrams, perhaps in your maths books, and write a question that begins with: "According to the diagram …" Now pass the diagram and question to another pair and see if they can answer the question.

## Sample student responses

Look at the responses to these two questions below and decide which is the best response, which is close but lacks precision, and which contains inappropriate information.

Q1. Which bill is the most expensive for Don McCarthy, and how much is it per year?

    Student A – *Gas and £20*

    Student B – *Gas and 20*

    Student C – *Gas and 20 $*

Q2. Which utility service would Don regard as his least significant concern?

    Student A – *Electricity*

    Student B – *Electricity, and then water, and then gas*

    Student C – *$10 worth of electricity*

## Meat-free diets

One of the suggestions both Vinod and Don make is to eat less meat. One person who would agree with that idea is the singer Paul McCartney. Perhaps most famous for being one of The Beatles band in the 1960s, today he campaigns for people not to eat meat on Mondays, which he calls "Meat free Monday".

 Have a look at Paul trying to build up some support for his cause.

http://www.youtube.com/watch?v = XQ2PH5pG9fs

 ## Writing a protest song

Can you, as Paul suggests, write a better song than his to support Meat Free Monday? Have a go! But make your song a protest song – and you are protesting against eating meat. You don't have to write the music, just the lyrics.

---

### Help our beautiful planet

According to the Food and Agriculture Organization of the United Nations (FAO), the livestock sector is currently "one of the top two or three most significant contributors to the most serious environmental problems, from local to global". The FAO estimates that livestock production is responsible for 14.5 per cent of global greenhouse gas emissions, while other organisations have estimated it could be as much as 51 per cent. World scientists on the UN Intergovernmental Panel on Climate Change (IPCC) agree that we need to reduce the amount of greenhouse gases in the atmosphere by 80 per cent by 2050 in order to avoid catastrophic climate change.

### Be healthy and happy

Many of the world's leading health organizations now encourage a reduction in the amount of meat people consume. The World Cancer Research Fund recommends we "choose mostly plant foods, limit red meat and avoid processed meat".

In 2010, a study found that eating meat no more than three times a week could prevent 31,000 deaths from heart disease, 9,000 deaths from cancer and 5,000 deaths from stroke, as well as save £1.2 billion in costs each year.

### Save the pennies

According to Office for National Statistics figures, the average UK family spends £13.10 a week on meat and fish, with £3.70 and £3 being spent on fresh vegetables and fresh fruit respectively. The cost of meat has risen 10 per cent, yet most of the basics of a meat-free diet are comparatively cheaper: plant proteins such as dried beans or lentils typically cost less than the equivalent amount of animal protein. In fact, most of the world's people eat a mostly meat-free diet made up of inexpensive foods such as beans, rice and corn. Eat less meat + more vegetables = save money!

Source: www.meatfreemondays.com

---

# Check your understanding

Fill in the gaps below using information from the text:

1 The ............................... sector is currently in the top three contributors to local and global problems.

2 We should reduce greenhouse gases by ............................... per cent.

3 One piece of advice the World Cancer Research Fund recommends is ............................... .

4 £ ............................... would be saved in costs each year by eating meat no more than three times a week.

5 The cost of meat has risen by ............................... per cent.

6* Apart from avoiding climate change, what else can we save when avoiding meat?

## Facts about global hunger

Of course, some of the world's population do not have access to as much food as they would like. So what can be done about this? Here are some facts about global hunger:

- Hunger is the world's No. 1 health risk. It kills more people every year than AIDS, malaria and tuberculosis combined.

- **870 million people** in the world do not have enough to eat. This number has fallen by 130 million since 1990, but progress slowed after 2008.
  **(Source: State of Food Insecurity in the World, FAO, 2012)**

- The majority of hungry people **(98 per cent) live in developing countries**, where almost 15 per cent of the population is undernourished.
  **(Source: State of Food Insecurity in the World, FAO, 2012)**

- Asia and the Pacific have the **largest share of the world's hungry** people (some 563 million) but this is decreasing.
  **(Source: State of Food Insecurity in the World, FAO, 2012)**

- Undernutrition contributes to **2.6 million deaths of children** under five each year – one third of the global total.
  **(Source: Levels and Trends in Child Mortality, UNICEF, 2011)**

- One out of six children – roughly 100 million – in developing countries is **underweight**.
  **(Source: Global health Observatory, WHO, 2011)**

- 66 million primary school-age **children attend classes hungry** across the developing world, with 23 million in Africa alone.
  **(Source: Two Minutes to Learn About School Meals, WFP, 2012)**

- WFP calculates that **US$3.2 billion** is needed per year to reach all 66 million hungry school-age children.
  **(Source: Two Minutes to Learn About School Meals, WFP, 2012)**

## Check your understanding

1 In the world, there are ................. million people who do not have enough to eat.

2 ............................ million children in developing countries are underweight.

3 In Asia and the Pacific, there are ............................ million hungry people.

4 In developing countries, the proportion of underweight children is ............................ .

5 About ............................ billion US dollars need to be spent to reach all school-age hungry children.

6* ............................ is the world's biggest health risk.

# Key skills

## The use of precision in reported speech

When reporting on what someone has said, you should not always rely on the verb "said". For example:

- The World Health Organization **has said** that one in six children in developing countries is underweight.

Could be written more effectively as:

- The World Health Organization **has declared** that one in six children in developing countries is underweight.

The second quote gives an emphasis of authority that the first lacks.

And consider these two versions relating to the views of the World Wildlife Fund for Nature (WWF) members:

- Members of WWF **have said that they think it is important** that we care for the environment.

- Members of WWF **have re-emphasized that they think it is important** that we care for the environment.

The act of re-emphasizing suggests a seriousness that the first statement does not have.

Finally, look at these sentences:

- He **said** it was important for the country to use more wind power.

- He **insisted** it was important for the country to use more wind power.

Why do you think that the second version is better than the first?

Rewrite the following sentences, replacing "said" in the reported speech with more appropriate verbs:

- She *said* it was important that the community had more fresh water.

- The local council *said* it was doing all it could to improve conditions in the town.

- Although not a fan of nuclear power, he *said* he understood how important it was.

With a partner, write five more sentences using "said" to convey reported speech. Pass these on to another pair and ask them to change the word "said" for a better version. When you get your sentences back, discuss how they have changed, and how that represents improvement!

# The global energy problem

We are using more energy on the planet now than at any time in the past and yet we know that the natural resources we are using are not finite – that is, they will not last forever. In fact, some of them will be running out in the next 100 years or so.

## Renewable energy

Nowadays, we are turning more and more to renewable resources to give us energy. Look at the list below. Which ones have you heard of?

What do you think of each of these forms of energy? A suggested response to the first one is given.

Share your views with the rest of the people in your class. How much similarity is there? Are there are any opposing views, or very different views?

| Form of power | My view |
| --- | --- |
| Solar power | I think it should be cheap, but what about countries that don't see much sunshine? |
| Wind power | |
| Biomass – energy from plants | |
| Nuclear power | |
| Hydro power – energy from the sea, rivers, and lakes | |
| Geothermal energy – energy stored under the surface of Earth | |

 **Track 12.5** Listen to James, who works in a nuclear power plant, telling us about the advantages of nuclear power.

## Check your understanding

1   How long has James been working at the nuclear power plant?

2   What was the reaction of his friends when he started his job?

3   What are the benefits of nuclear power? Give two examples.

4   What other job did James nearly do?

5   How does James feel about his job now?

6*  What one thing would you like to know about nuclear power?

## Modern jobs – a role play

Working in a nuclear power plant is one of the modern jobs available to us that have been created in the past few decades. Can you think of any other modern jobs that weren't around 50 years ago?

Which modern job do you think would be the strangest to people living a long time ago? Pick a job and explain what it is to your partner, who has arrived in a time travel machine from a century ago. Your partner will ask you questions about your job.

Now, reverse roles and pick another job.

# Connections

## Pollution

It would be fair to say that, taking the world as a whole, pollution is on the increase. People's keenness to expand and to modernize is probably one of the causes of this, so it is a challenge for us to slow down the rate of pollution but to still try to make technological progress.

Smog hanging over cities is the most familiar and obvious form of air pollution. But there are different kinds of pollution that contribute to global warming. Generally any substance that people introduce into the atmosphere that has damaging effects on living things and the environment is considered air pollution.

Carbon dioxide, a greenhouse gas, is the main pollutant that is warming Earth. Though living things emit carbon dioxide when they breathe, carbon dioxide is widely considered to be a pollutant when associated with cars, planes, power plants, and other human activities that involve the burning of fossil fuels such as gasoline and natural gas.

Other greenhouse gases include methane—which comes from such sources as swamps and gas emitted by livestock—and chlorofluorocarbons (CFCs), which were used in refrigerants and aerosol propellants until they were banned because of their negative effect on Earth's ozone layer.

Another pollutant associated with climate change is sulfur dioxide, a component of smog. Sulfur dioxide and closely related chemicals are known primarily as a cause of acid rain. Volcanoes used to be the main source of atmospheric sulfur dioxide; today people are.

Most people agree that to curb global warming, a variety of measures need to be taken. On a personal level, driving and flying less, recycling, and conservation reduces a person's "carbon footprint" – the amount of carbon dioxide a person is responsible for putting into the atmosphere.

On a larger scale, governments are taking measures to limit emissions of carbon dioxide and other greenhouse gases. One way is through the Kyoto Protocol, an agreement between countries that they will cut back on carbon dioxide emissions. Another method is to put taxes on carbon emissions or higher taxes on gasoline, so that people and companies will have greater incentives to conserve energy and pollute less.

**Source: www. nationalgeographic.co.uk**

## Check your understanding

1 Which gas is the main pollutant of Earth?

2 Give two examples of fossil fuels mentioned in the text.

3 Give a natural source of sulphur dioxide.

4 People can help reduce global warming; give two examples of what they can do.

5 Give two examples of what governments can do to help reduce global warming.

6* What will make people pollute less?

# Water

In some parts of the world there can be, at times, too much water. And of course, in other parts there can often be too little.

One charity, WaterAid, helps people in countries across the globe to gain access to regular supplies of clean water, which also helps to minimize disease.

 Watch the video clip of what WaterAid does and why their role is important.

www.youtube.com/watch?v = _oeWR6uZ87s&feature = youtu.be

## Bottled water or tap water?

If your family is like many in the United States, unloading the week's groceries includes hauling a case or two of bottled water into your home. On your way to a soccer game or activity, it's easy to grab a cold one right out of the fridge, right?

But all those plastic bottles use a lot of fossil fuels and pollute the environment. In fact, Americans buy more bottled water than any other nation in the world, adding 29 billion water bottles a year to the problem. In order to make all these bottles, manufacturers use 17 million barrels of crude oil. That's enough oil to keep a million cars going for twelve months.

Imagine a water bottle filled a quarter of the way up with oil. That's about how much oil was needed to produce the bottle.

So why don't more people drink water straight from the kitchen faucet? Some people drink bottled water because they think it is better for them than water out of the tap, but that's not true. In the United States, local governments make sure water from the faucet is safe. There is also growing concern that chemicals in the bottles themselves may leach into the water.

People love the convenience of bottled water. But maybe if they realized the problems it causes, they would try drinking from a glass at home or carrying water in a refillable steel container instead of plastic.

Plastic bottle recycling can help – instead of going out with the trash, plastic bottles can be turned into items like carpeting or cozy fleece clothing.

Unfortunately, for every six water bottles we use, only one makes it to the recycling bin. The rest are sent to landfills. Or, even worse, they end up as trash on the land and in rivers, lakes, and the ocean. Plastic bottles take many hundreds of years to disintegrate.

Water is good for you, so keep drinking it. But think about how often you use water bottles, and see if you can make a change.

And yes, you can make a difference. Remember this: Recycling one plastic bottle can save enough energy to power a 60-watt light bulb for six hours.

Catherine Clark, www.nationalgeographic.co.uk

## Check your understanding

Add a word from the text into each of the gaps below to complete the sentence.

1  Americans buy more than ........................... bottles of water per year.

2  We need natural ........................... to make plastic bottles, and using them is harming the environment.

3  Only ........................... of the bottles that are made end up being recycled.

4  One example of where water bottles that are not recycled can end up is ...........................

5  A recycled water bottle can provide enough energy to power a 60-watt light bulb for ...........................

6*  Why do people use bottled water?

##  Present a talk

You have been asked to give a short talk of about two minutes responding to the question: "Do people take water for granted?" Do some research – perhaps the work of WaterAid will be useful background information for you – and come up with a plan. Some useful areas you should probably cover include:

Intro – what we depend on water for

Body – (i) ways that people take it for granted

        (ii) ways that people over-use water

        (iii) ways that we could preserve water

Conclusion – well, that's up to you, but make sure you end with a strong message!

# Recycling

**Thinking out loud**

You may not use bottled water, and you may avoid buying things that have lots of packaging, but you probably have some rubbish! What do you do with it? Throw it away? Is there anything you throw away that you think could be used by someone else? Is there another way, apart from recycling, that you can think of that will reduce the amount of rubbish around?

## Everything has a use!

In pairs, make a list of what you have thrown away in the past few weeks. Use your imaginations and come up with another use of some of the items you discarded. The first one is done for you.

| What I have thrown away | What else could this have been used for? |
| --- | --- |
| Tin cans | Paint them, and use as skittles for a bowling game |
| An egg box | |
| | |

Share your list and your alternative uses with other pairs. Which items keep coming up? What is the most useful "useless" item? That is – which item seems to be the most recyclable?

## The Landfillharmonic

Landfill Harmonic is a unique orchestra in South America made up entirely of instruments made from scrap heap rubbish, the creation of Favio Chávez, a landfill worker and musician from Cateura, Paraguay.

Cateura exists virtually on top of a landfill site where residents make their livings recycling and selling other people's rubbish. Situated along the banks of the Paraguay River, 1,500 tons of waste is dumped in the area each day.

But despite the critical levels of pollution and the threat to their health, residents of Cateura manage to find the most positive of uses for the rubbish. Inspired to do something to help the inpoverished families, Chávez began using the trash in the landfill to create instruments for the children.

"One day it occurred to me to teach music to the children of the recyclers and use my personal instruments," explains 36-year-old Chávez, who worked as an ecological technician at the landfill. "But it got to the point that there were too many students and not enough supply. So that's when I decided to experiment and try to actually create a few."

Now watch how the instruments have been made, as well as enjoying how they are played:

**www.youtube.com/watch?v = fXynrsrTKbI**

# The Big Issue: cyber bullying

**Thinking out loud**

We are going to find out about a problem that people may be faced with wherever they live in the world. Can you think of any such issues – similar problems that may affect people who live in very different places and cultures? Think about problems you have faced – are they universal?

## Cyber bullying and how to stop it

Bullying of any kind is, of course, not acceptable but in the modern age, cyber bullying can be a problem as the bully is at a distance to the victim, and can continue to bully them whatever the time, day or night.

Cyber bullying is when a person or group uses the internet, mobile phones, online games or any other kind of digital technology to threaten, tease or upset someone else.

Cyber bullying is a form of bullying but because it happens online or on mobile phones it can happen 24 hours a day, seven days a week. If you are being bullied at school you can usually get away from the bullies when you are at home, but with cyber bullying it can feel like there is no escape. Cyber bullying can be done anonymously. For example, they might set up fake accounts and hide their IP [Internet Protocol] address or block their mobile number. When bullying happens at school it is usually one person or a small group of people, but cyber bullying can be really scary as it could involve a lot more people – you might feel that people are ganging up on you.

Cyber bullying is very serious. It can make you feel scared, upset, and embarrassed. You might feel like it will never end.

No one has the right to make you feel this way. We want you to know there are things you can do to make it stop. You shouldn't have to deal with bullying alone, so think about talking to someone you trust like a parent, carer or teacher. They can help you report the bullying and be there to listen to you. Having someone to talk things through with is really important – it can make you feel less alone and more confident to deal with the situation.

It is a good idea to keep a copy of any abusive texts, emails, comments or messages that you receive and record the date and time they were sent. With cyber bullying there is always a trail and keeping records can be very useful when it comes to reporting the bullying.

You should not reply to any messages you receive because it can encourage the bullies and end up upsetting you more. In addition, you must never give out any personal details on the internet – your real name, address, age or phone number. Even if you tell someone which school you go to it can help them find out more about you. If you are being bullied on a social network you could think about whether you want to delete your profile or make it temporarily inactive. You can block email address or chat users if you are being bullied by email or instant messenger. You can even bar a particular number from contacting another phone on some handsets, so it is a good idea to check your phone user guide to see if yours can.

Source: www.childline.org.uk

289

## Study tips

## Writing

## Note making

The ability to make concise and brief notes is a useful skill to practise and develop for many of your school subjects, and indeed for life beyond school.

When you are given a note-making task, it is a good idea to use subheadings. This will help you to scan the text for the precise detail that you need to include.

With a partner, scan the cyber-bullying article and see if you can come up with some subheadings – main areas that seem to feature and that have specific supporting details or specific information. Compare your subheadings to those suggested by other students.

Now read the article on cyber bullying more thoroughly and make notes under these subheadings:

How cyber bullying is different to other types of bullying (give two details)

*
*

Advice on how to stop cyber bullying (give three details)

*
*
*

When you have found the right information, write it in note form, keeping your answers as short as possible. Here's a hint – you should always write each different piece of information (each note) on a separate line.

## Sample student responses

Here's how three students completed this task. Which do you think is the clearest response? And how could the other two responses have been improved?

**Student A**

How cyber bullying is different to other types of bullying (two details)

* bullying at school is usually one person
* it can make you feel scared

Advice on how to stop cyber bullying (three details)

* keep a copy of any abusive texts
* keep a copy of abusive emails
* record the date they were sent and don't give out any personal details

**Student B**

How cyber bullying is different to other types of bullying (two details)

* cyber bullying is when a person or group uses the Internet or any other kind of digital technology
* cyber bullying can be anonymous

Advice on how to stop cyber bullying (three details)

* you shouldn't have to deal with bullying alone
* keep a copy of abusive texts, emails, comments, and messages
* you don't reply to messages

**Student C**

How cyber bullying is different to other types of bullying (two details)

* bully is at a distance to the victim
* can be anonymous

Advice on how to stop cyber bullying (three details)

* keep a copy of abusive texts
* don't reply to messages
* delete your profile

# Reflection

In this chapter, we have seen several examples of people putting others before themselves and putting general environmental needs before their own. Is being less selfish perhaps becoming more fashionable in the twenty-first century? If we are going to survive and prosper, how important is it that we lead our lives thinking of other people rather than ourselves?

In small groups, discuss how you feel when natural disasters occur. What action do you take, if any? If you do something, how do you feel about those who do not? And if you do not do anything, say why not.

Your group is going to plan a festival to raise money for those who have lost their homes, jobs, and food supplies because of a natural disaster.

First, you need to discuss the following as a group:

- which cause you are going to support and why

- what you will call your fundraising event

- what the main events in your festival are going to be.

Next, give each person in the group a particular role. Here are some that may feature, but you can add other roles if you like:

- Mascot designer – you will design the mascot for the festival and give it a name

- Campaign manager – you will tell people about the event and promote it

- Activity planner – you will decide on the order of events on the day

- Money raiser – you will plan a few fun-filled, money-raising activities to be held on the day

- Web designer – you will decide on the website design and colours for the festival – it has to be eye-catching so people will click on the site and buy tickets.

Now enjoy your festival!

## ☑ My progress

Each chapter includes four Study Skills. These are skills that will feature in your final examinations. So let's check your progress with these key skills in mind.

| Where am I now? | Very pleased – I think I'm good at this | OK – but I do need more practice | One of my weaker areas – so I need a lot more practice |
|---|---|---|---|
| Using open questions when taking part in discussions | | | |
| Recognizing people's views and opinions when listening to them talk about a topic or issue | | | |
| Interpreting charts or diagrams to extract pieces of information from the data given | | | |
| Recognizing and using subheadings when making notes | | | |

Now pick out one skill that you would like to prioritize for improvement and produce a short action plan to help you become stronger. Use a template similar to the following – that is filled out for you with an example.

## Action plan

Skill I want to improve: Recognizing and using subheadings when making notes.

- **planning** – how I will try to improve this skill:
  Break down longer articles into shorter segments using subheadings.

- **implementing** – what I will need and what my exact strategy is:
  Gather some information articles from newspapers, magazines, the Internet, and add three or four subheadings where a new theme seems to emerge.

- **monitoring** – how I will know I am improving and what evidence I may keep:
  Try to make notes using my new subheadings; maybe ask someone to read the article with the subheadings and see if they comment on them.

# Index

Andrew Evans: excerpts from his Twitter feed @WheresAndrew when he visited Tanzania, from www.digitalnomad.nationalgeographic.com, reprinted by permission of the author.

Four Paws: excerpt from 'About Dancing Bears', 14 August 2012, from www.four-paws.org.uk, copyright FOUR PAWS, reprinted by permission.

William Golding: excerpt 'Cry of the Hunters' from Lord of the Flies, copyright 1954, renewed © 1982 by William Gerald Golding, reprinted by permission of G. P. Putnam's Sons, a division of Penguin Group (USA) LLC.

Elizabeth Grice: 'Cry of an enfant sauvage', 17 July 2006, © Liz Grice / The Daily Telegraph, reprinted by permission.

Halsbury Work Experience Abroad: case study 1 by Helena Jones and case study 3 by Rachel Walsh, from www.workexperienceabroad.co.uk, reprinted by permission.

Mark Hughes: 'Felix Baumgartner 'breaks speed of sound', 15 October 2012, The Telegraph, © Mark Hughes / Telegraph.co.uk, reprinted by permission.

Eddie Izzard: excerpt from Eddie's Blog www.eddieizzard.com, reprinted by permission.

The Jane Goodall Institute: 'Chimp facts' from www.janegoodall.org, reprinted by permission.

Landfill Harmonic: article reprinted by permission (www.landfillharmonicmovie.com).

Hari Kunzru: 'When Hari Kunzru met Michael Moorcock', 4 February 2011, The Guardian, reprinted by permission of Curtis Brown Group Ltd, London on behalf of Hari Kunzru, copyright © Hari Kunzru 2011 (interview recorded with actors, permission granted by Hari Kunzru and Michael Moorcock).

Andrew Lane: excerpt from Black Ice, copyright © 2011 by Andrew Lane, published by Macmillan Children's Books, London, UK, reprinted by permission.

Harper Lee: excerpt from To Kill a Mockingbird, published by William Heinemann, reprinted by permission of The Random House Group Limited.

Emily van Lierop: text adapted from 'Ukeplayle – Hobby 23' from PursuitOfHobbyness (http://www.pursuitofhobbyness.com/), reprinted by permission.

Lonely Planet: 'Montevideo', from www.lonelyplanet.com, © 2013 Lonely Planet, reprinted by permission.

Marina Bay Sands: information and image reprinted by permission.

Michael Moorcock: excerpt from Doctor Who: The Coming of the Terraphiles, published by BBC Books, reprinted by permission of The Random House Group Limited.

Michael Morpurgo: excerpt from War Horse, published by Egmont, copyright © 1982 Michael Morpurgo, reprinted by permission.

Fabrice Muamba: excerpt from I'm Still Standing, published by Trinity Mirror Sport Media, 2012, copyright © Fabrice Muamba, reprinted by permission of Trinity Mirror Sport Media.

National Geographic: 'Pollution', from http://environment.nationalgeographic.co.uk, reprinted by permission.

Network for Africa: excerpts from 'Rose's story: a day in the life', from www.network4africa.org, reprinted by permission.

NSPCC: 'Online bullying', www.childline.org.uk, reprinted by permission.

Sarah O'Meara: 'What were we doing a century ago? Meet the 100-year-old you', 24 August 2012, The Huffington Post, © 2012 AOL Inc., all rights reserved, reprinted by permission and protected by the copyright Laws of the United States, the printing, copying, redistribution, or retransmission of this Content without express written permission is prohibited.

Pocket Cultures: excerpt from 'Kiss, hug or shake hands' from http://pocketcultures.com/2010/07/14/kiss-hug-or-shake-hands/, reprinted under the terms of the Creative Commons Attribution 3.0 Unported Licence (http://creativecommons.org/licenses/by/3.0/)

Ceinwen Rataj: interview adapted from 'On the road with the Royal Flying Doctors' by Ceinwen Rataj, 31 October 2012, https://open.abc.net.au, reprinted and recorded with an actor by permission of Ceinwen Rataj.

Jerrell Ross Richer: 'Village Life', 6 February 2013, from www.goshen.edu, reprinted by permission.

Royal Pigeon Racing Association: 'Homing pigeons – how do they do it?' from www.rpra.org, reprinted by permission.

Susanna Rustin: interview adapted from 'What is life like after 100?', 29 June 2012, The Guardian, copyright Guardian News & Media Ltd 2012, reprinted by permission.

Lemony Snicket: excerpt from Who Could That Be at this Hour?, reprinted by permission of the Charlotte Sheedy Literary Agency.

Graham Snowdon: 'A working life: the puppeteer', 23 September 2011, The Guardian, copyright Guardian News and Media Ltd 2011, reprinted by permission.

Sounds and Colours: 'South American Carnival Guide' from www.soundsandcolours.com, reprinted by permission.

The Strong: 'Video Game History Timeline' from www.icheg.org, reprinted by permission of The Strong, Rochester, New York, www.museumofplay.org.

The Tampa Bay Times: from 'Egypt: daily life' from http://www2.sptimes.com/Egypt/EgyptCredit.4.2.html, reprinted by permission.

Vinod Thomas: 'Living a Carbon Neutral Lifestyle', from Asian Development Bank,

http://blogs.adb.org/blog/living-carbon-neutral-lifestyle, reprinted by permission.

Topmarks: 'Chinese New Year Customs' from www.topmarks.co.uk, reprinted by permission.

Stephanie Watson: excerpts from '10 careers for people who love to travel', from www.howstuffworks.com, reprinted by permission of Discovery Access.

H.G. Wells: excerpts from The Time Machine, reprinted by permission of United Agents on behalf of: The Literary Executors of the Estate of H.G. Wells.

WHYY, Inc: interview adapted from 'Lemony Snicket dons a trench coat', 10 December 2012, www.npr.org, reprinted and recorded with an actor by permission of WHYY, Inc., (Fresh Air is produced by WHYY, Inc. and distributed by NPR) and Daniel Handler.

'Wieliczka' Salt Mine: excerpts from 'Healthy sleep', from www.wieliczka-saltmine.com, reprinted by permission.

Patti Wigington: 'Caring for the dead', © 2013 Patti Wigington (http://paganwiccan.about.com/), reprinted by permission of About Inc., which can be found online at www.about.com, all rights reserved.

Wikipedia: 'The Golden Age' uses material from the Wikipedia article http://en.wikipedia.org/wiki/Golden_Age 'Golden Age', which is released under the http://creativecommons.org/licenses/by-sa/3.0, Creative Commons Attribution Share Alike Licence 3.0.

Wildfitness: excerpts from 'Wild Moving' and 'Wild Eating' reprinted by permission of Tara Wood - founder of Wildfitness.

Wild Florida: 'Ecotourism: an alternative educational experience', 27 December 2012, from www.wildfloridaairboats.com, reprinted by permission.

Emma C Williams: excerpt from World Enough and Time, published by Matador 2012, reprinted by permission of the author.

World Book, Inc: adapted excerpt from 'Ant: The Ant Colony', New Standard Encyclopedia (digital edition, as licensed to Discovery.com) © 2006, reprinted by permission of World Book, Inc., www.worldbook.com, no part of this excerpt may be reproduced in whole or in part in any form without the prior written consent of the rights holder.

WWF: excerpt from Save Tigers Now, www.savetigersnow.com, reprinted by permission.

Alex Zanardi: interview based on material from various interviews, recorded with an actor and reproduced by permission of Alex Zanardi.

Any third party use of this material, outside of this publication, is prohibited. Interested parties should apply to the copyright holders indicated in each case.

Although we have made every effort to trace and contact all copyright holders before publication this has not been possible in all cases. If notified, the publisher will rectify any errors or omissions at the earliest opportunity.

Links to third party websites are provided by Oxford in good faith and for information only. Oxford disclaims any responsibility for the materials contained in any third party website referenced in this work.